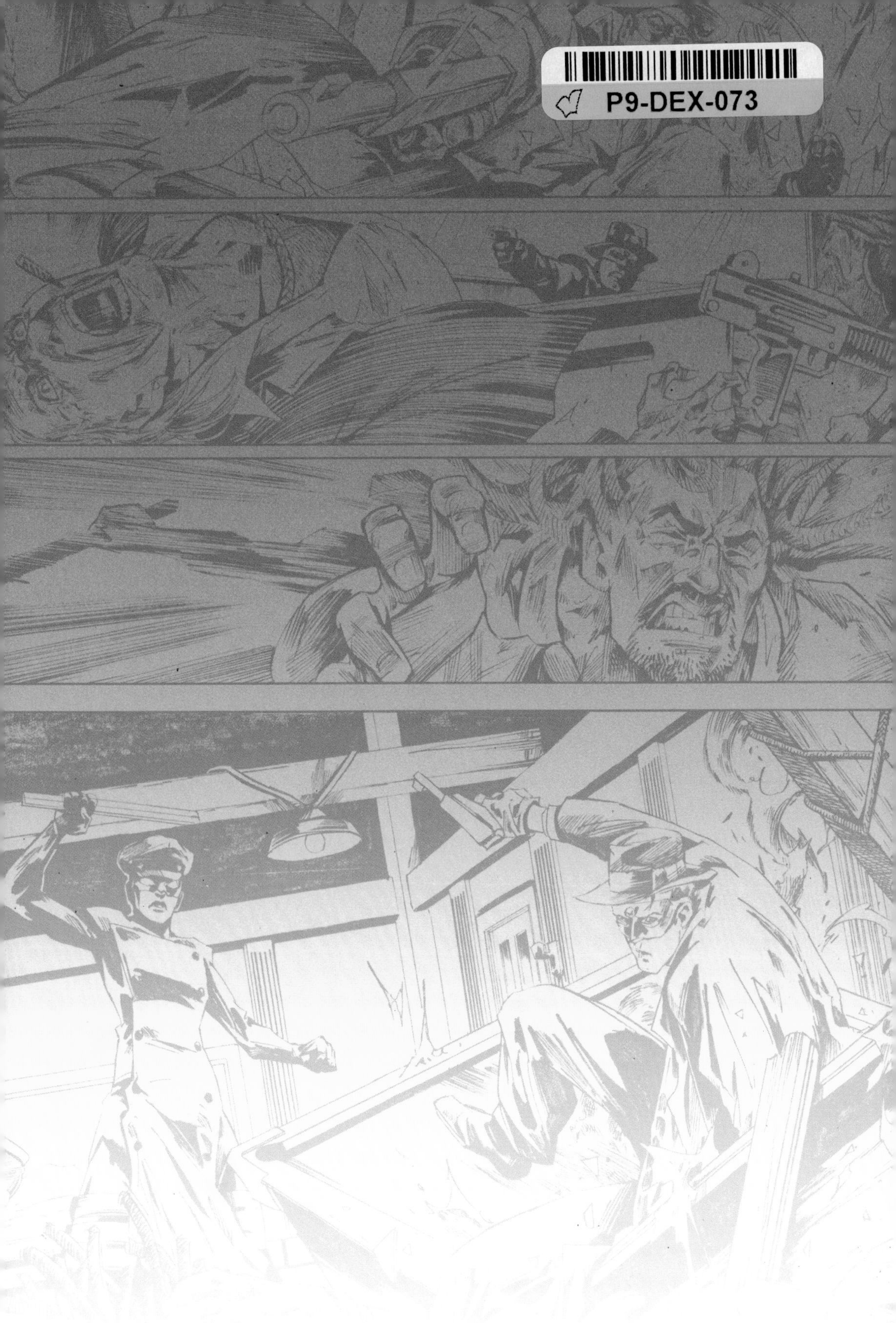

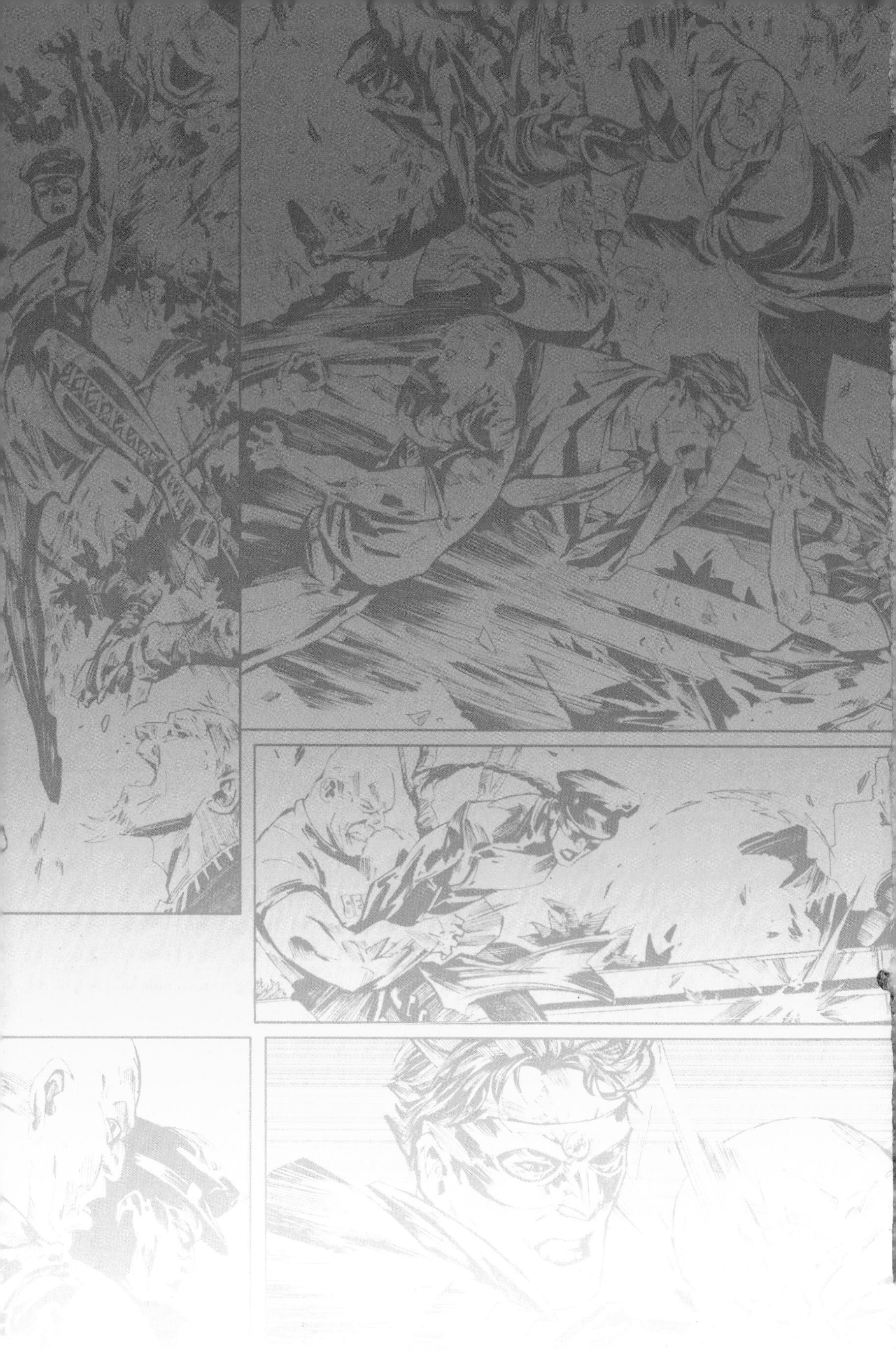

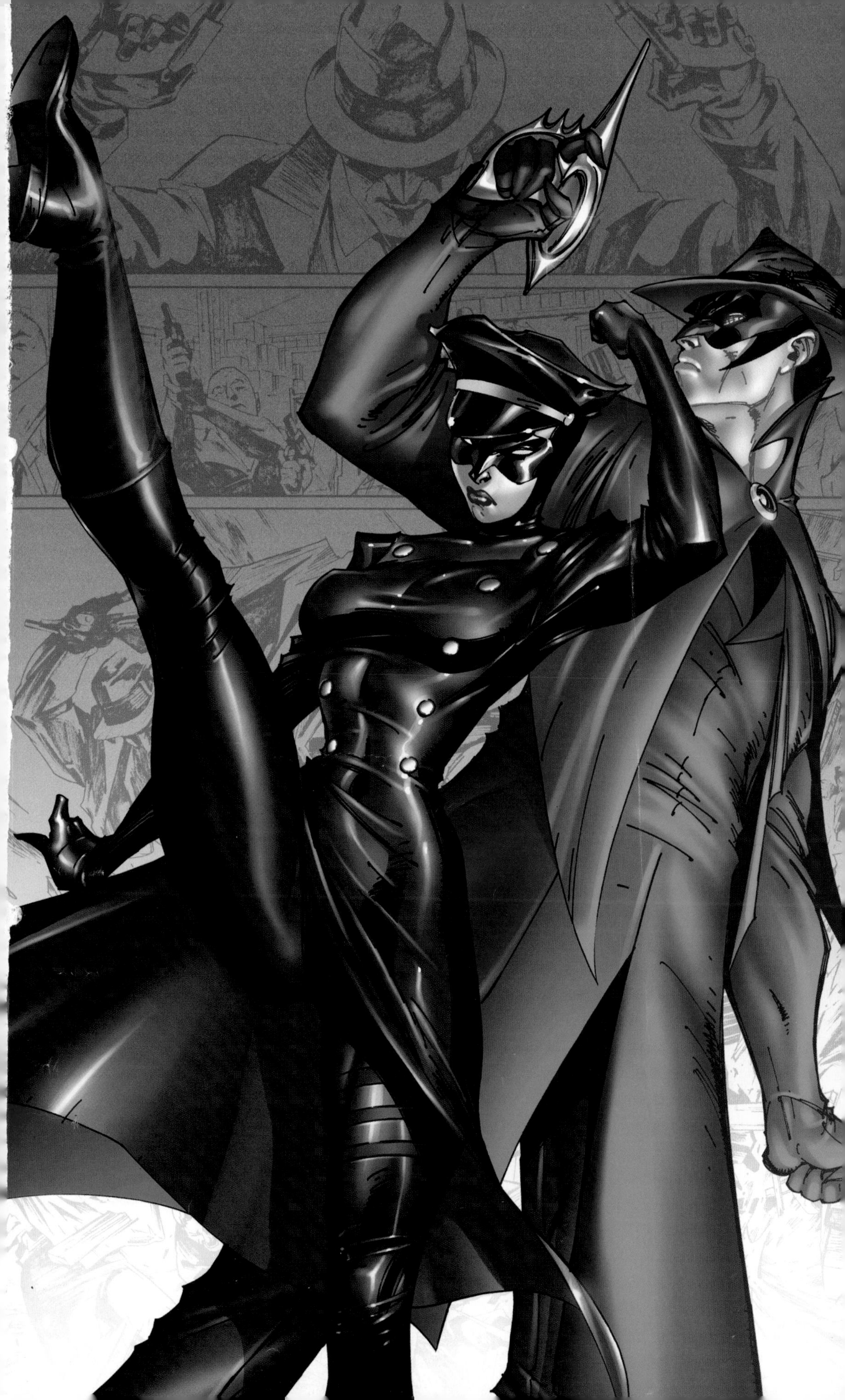

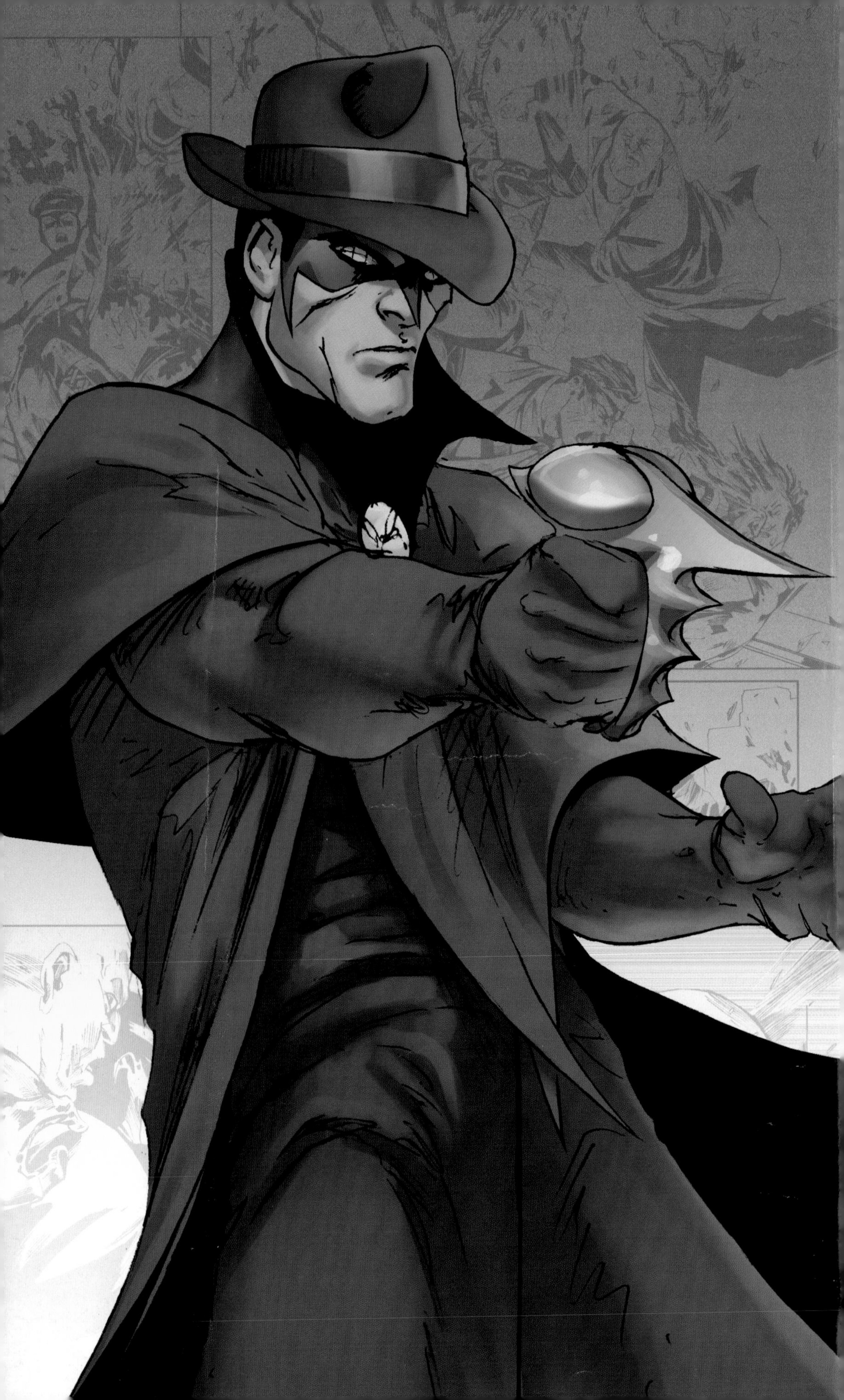

GREEN HORNET

VOLUME ONE: SINS OF THE FATHER

scripts by **KEVIN SMITH**

breakdowns by **PHIL HESTER**   art by **JONATHAN LAU**

colors by **IVAN NUNES** w/ **BRUNO HANG & ADRIANO LUCAS**

letters by **SIMON BOWLAND & TROY PETERI**

collection covers by **ALEX ROSS**

collection design by **JASON ULLMEYER**

special thanks to **DAVID GRACE** at Green Hornet Inc.

First Printing   10 9 8 7 6 5 4 3 2 1
Hardcover ISBN-10: 1-60690-142-7   ISBN-13:978-1-60690-142-7
Signed Limited Edition Hardcover ISBN-10: 1-60690-178-8   ISBN-13: 978-1-60690-178-6
Softcover ISBN-10: 1-60690-191-5   ISBN-13: 978-1-60690-191-5

DYNAMITE®
ENTERTAINMENT

WWW.DYNAMITEENTERTAINMENT.COM

NICK BARRUCCI   •   PRESIDENT
JUAN COLLADO   •   CHIEF OPERATING OFFICER
JOSEPH RYBANDT •   EDITOR
JOSH JOHNSON   •   CREATIVE DIRECTOR

Years ago, I pussed-out of making a GREEN HORNET movie.

Miramax hired me to write *and* direct a motion picture based on the radio-era vigilante, but when I was done writing the script, I had to be honest with myself: I didn't have the directing chops to pull off the flick. I asked Harvey Weinstein to be let out of the directing side of the deal and he obliged. The flick never wound up happening. The script – owned by Disney – languished in a drawer.

Cut to the present: Michel Gondry is NOT a gutless directorial pansy, so he happily took a gig directing Seth Rogen in a script Seth penned for a *different* GREEN HORNET flick. Essentially, this confirmed that the script I'd written was never gonna see the light of day - and as I wasn't confident in what I'd written (or my ability to direct it), I was okay with nobody ever knowing what my HORNET flick might've been.

Then, I get an email from Nick Barrucci. I'd known Nick for years as the head of Dynamic Forces – the company that made comics-related merch and sold creator-signed books. You could always tell DF obviously loved the medium; and if you didn't, you would've when they announced they were getting into comics *publishing* as well.

And it was comics-publishing about which Nick was calling. He told me he'd just secured the rights to publish HORNET comics, and was hoping I'd wanna do a few issues. I told him I had no luck with the Hornet, and wasn't inclined to head back down the path. He apologized for taking my time, but right before we hung up, Nick asked "What about the script for the movie you wrote?"

It was a novel idea: take the script that was never gonna become a real, live flick, and splash it in four colors across the comics page, where it belonged. I sent Nick the script, and he wrote back kind things about the Father/Son feel of it and how fun it played. I hadn't read the script in years, so I assumed he was just being polite, and was actually crossing out the script title on the cover and writing "GREEN TOILET" instead.

We got in touch with Disney (they owned my HORNET, via Miramax) and asked if we could turn the dead script into a living, breathing comic book. Graciously, Disney said we could – so long as I didn't get paid for it *again*. It was a fair (and smart) request: I'd already been paid to write the script years back – no reason I should get to double-dip (but as such, this GREEN HORNET run may have the distinction of being the most expensive comic book script ever written).

Nick asked how involved I could be, but I was working on COP OUT at the time, so I let him know I'd be minimal help (as I wasn't on COP OUT either). So in the pre-production days of the book, my involvement went only so far as having written the original screenplay and approving some hires and/or layouts. Nick brought in my Brother-in-All-Green-Themed-Comic-Book-Characters, Phil Hester, who handled the breakdowns - taking my script and shaping it into 22 page comic book issues (God bless Phil for staying epidermis-close to the source material). From Phil's hands, it went to Jonathan Lau, who took Hester's stick-figure layouts and went to WORK.

And I guess it was when I saw Lau's pencils for issue one that I *really* got involved. Jonathan had expertly captured the tone and feel that I'd had in my head as a writer, but was never gonna be nearly talented enough as a director to translate to film. It was enthralling, watching the story unfold, as "directed" by someone else who had an actual eye for visuals…

and a little bittersweet as well: with every set of pencils, I felt like "Wow – this *would've* worked as a movie…"

And starting from issue one, I'd get in last-licks – which was mostly cleaning up dopey, out-dated dialogue from the six year old script. Joe Rybandt at Dynamite kept me honest, as far as a timeline, to ensure that the book stayed on a monthly schedule (it's made all the difference for me as a reader of the book). And, Jesus: those COVERS! Suddenly, in a very unlikely pairing, Alex Ross and I were on a book together. In fact, it was Alex who redesigned the Hornet, Kato, and the Black Beauty, as well as provided those jizz-worthy splashes before you even open each issue.

But Nick really deserves the most credit, as well as my sincere thanks. It's not often in life our failures can be redeemed and turned into successes: snatching victory from the jaws of defeat, as it were. The HORNET had long been a sore spot for me… until the Dynamite series that Nick engineered. Now, whenever I think of the HORNET, I think about all the love the book's gotten on Twitter, or the strong sales as folks still turned out for the 80 year old crime-fighter. Nick took my blooper and made that shit *super*. Taking a page from THIS book, he was Old Man Kato to my brash, hot-headed Britt Jr.

Which would make Hester Clutch Kato – the mechanic who builds the wonderful toys. And Jonathan would be Mulan Kato – sexy and Asian.

Let's roll, Kato.

Um…

That was NOT meant to be a pass at Lau.

Unless he's interested…

Kevin Smith
Backdoor HORNET writer
July 17, 2010

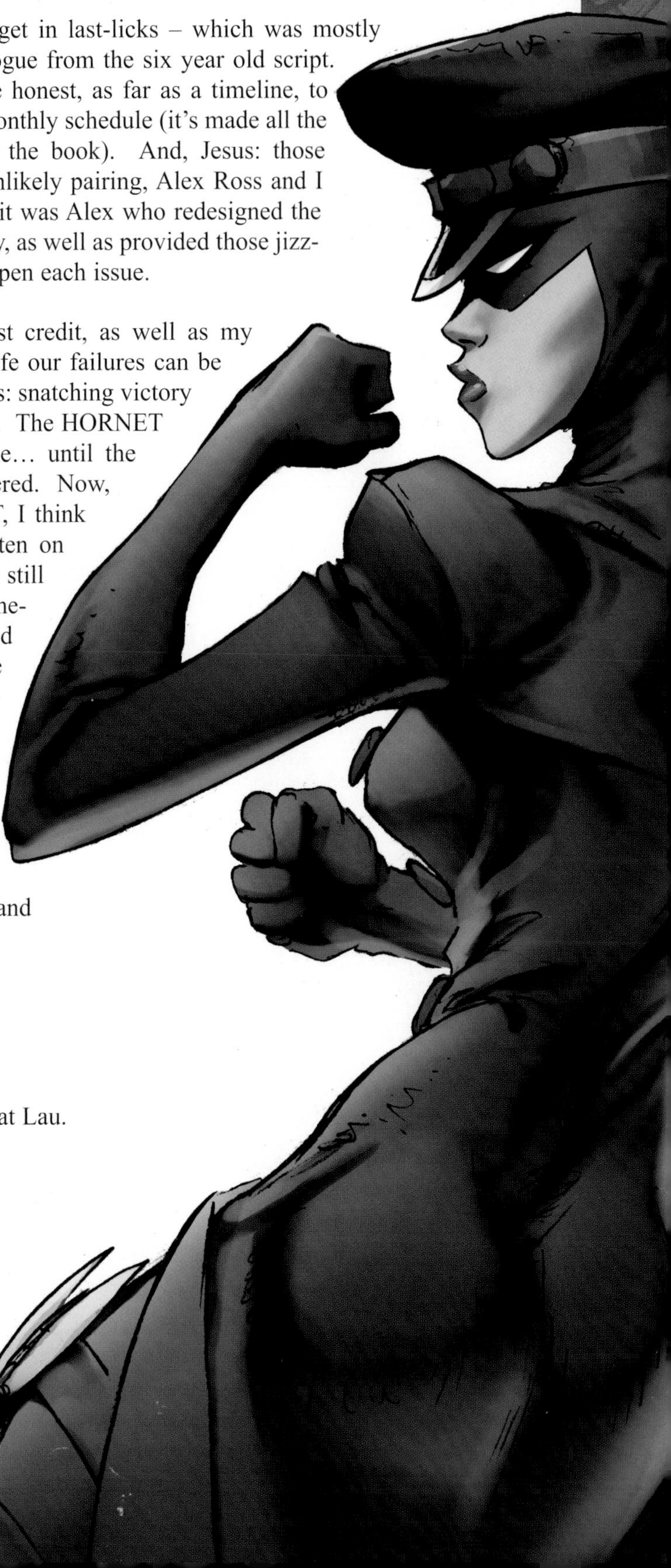

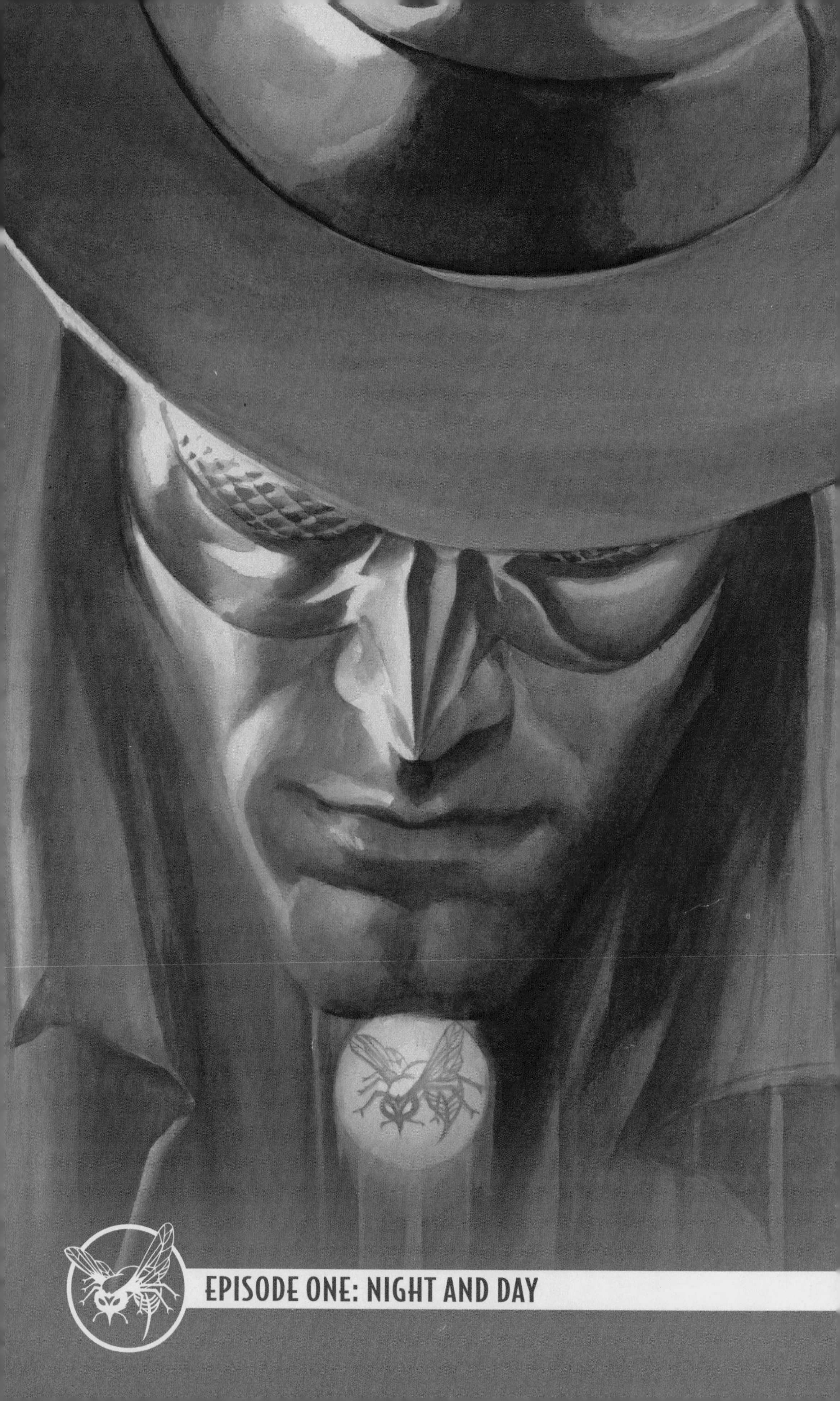

EPISODE ONE: NIGHT AND DAY

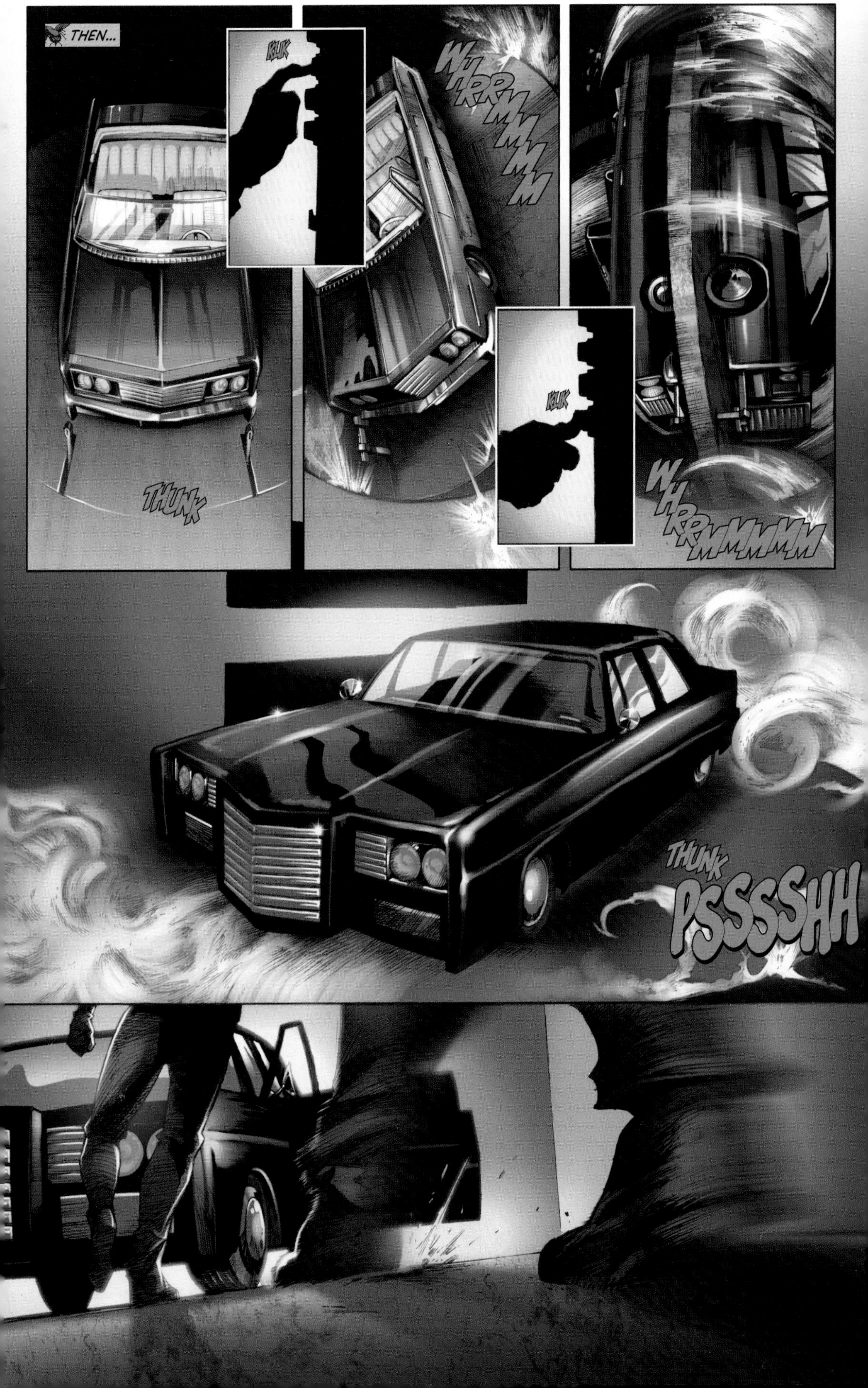

THEN...
KLIK
THUNK
WHRRMMMMM
KLIK
WHRRMMMMMM
THUNK
PSSSSHH

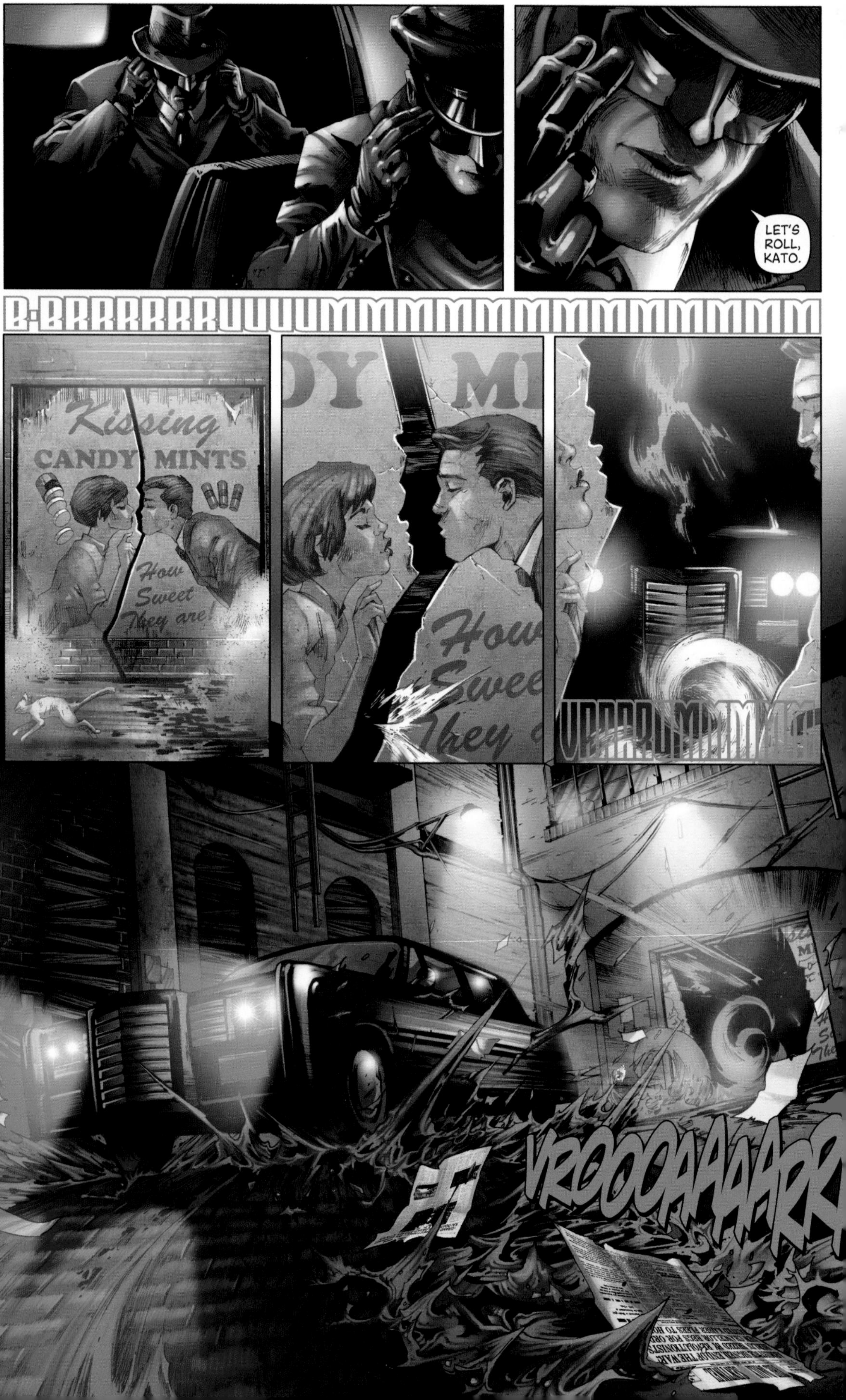
LET'S ROLL, KATO.
B-BRRRRRRRUUUUMMMMMMMMMMMMMM
Kissing
CANDY MINTS
How Sweet They are!
VRRRRUMMMMMM
VROOOAAAARR

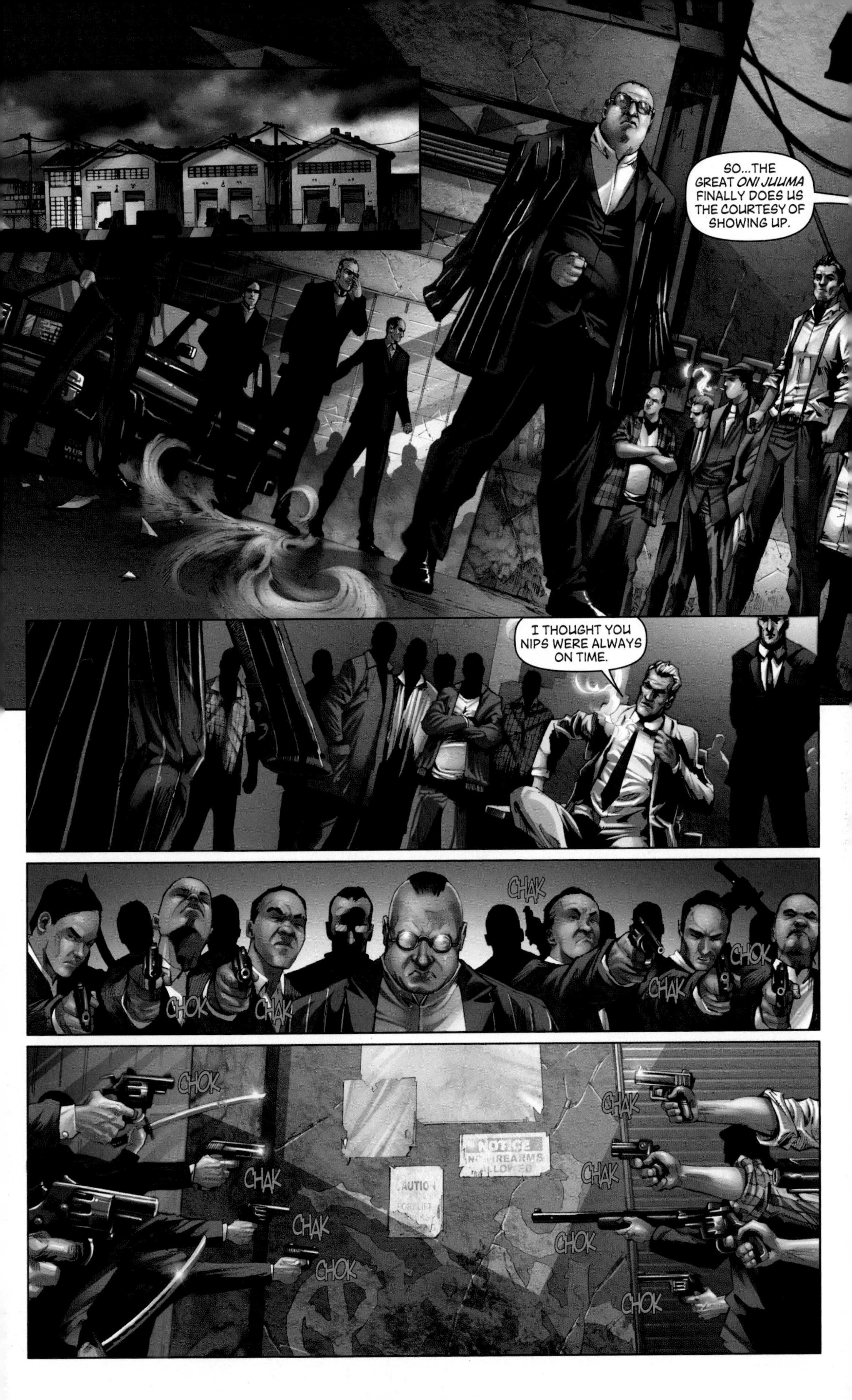
SO...THE GREAT ONI JUUMA FINALLY DOES US THE COURTESY OF SHOWING UP.
I THOUGHT YOU NIPS WERE ALWAYS ON TIME.
CHAK
CHOK
CHAK
CHAK
CHOK
CHOK
CHAK
CHAK
CHAK
NOTICE
CHAK
CHOK
CHOK
CHOK

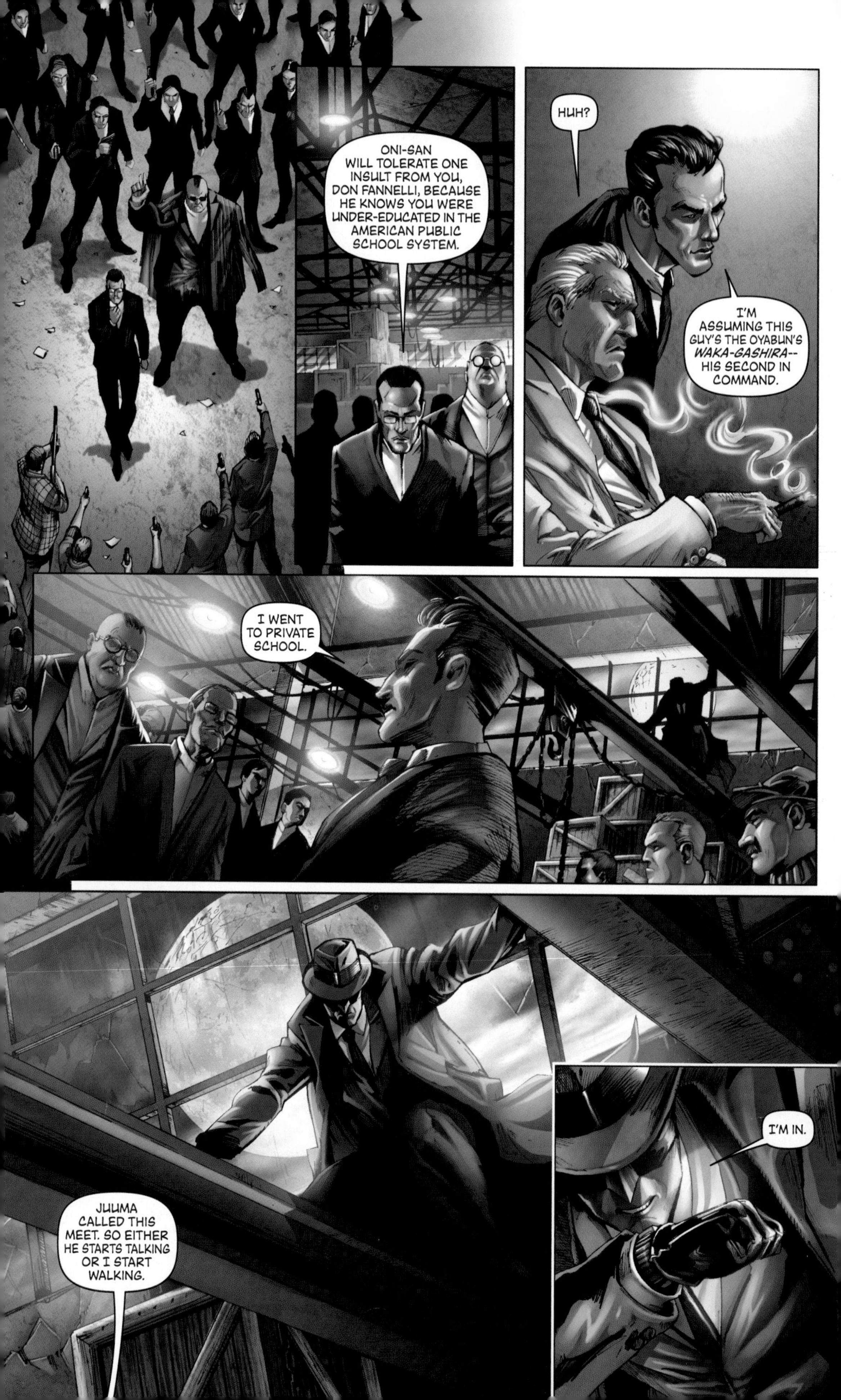
ONI-SAN WILL TOLERATE ONE INSULT FROM YOU, DON FANNELLI, BECAUSE HE KNOWS YOU WERE UNDER-EDUCATED IN THE AMERICAN PUBLIC SCHOOL SYSTEM.
HUH?
I'M ASSUMING THIS GUY'S THE OYABUN'S *WAKA-GASHIRA*-- HIS SECOND IN COMMAND.
I WENT TO PRIVATE SCHOOL.
I'M IN.
JUUMA CALLED THIS MEET. SO EITHER HE STARTS TALKING OR I START WALKING.

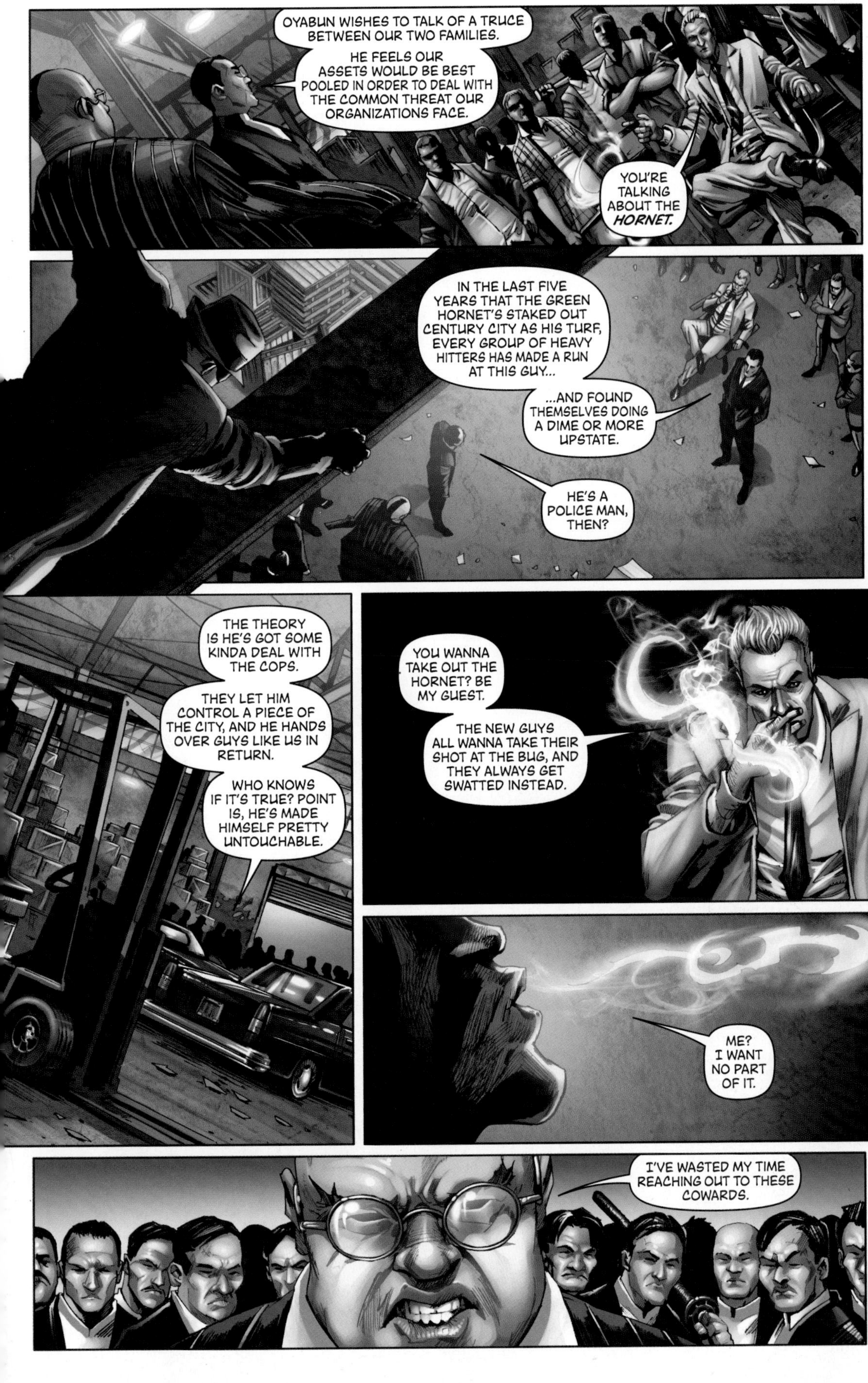
OYABUN WISHES TO TALK OF A TRUCE BETWEEN OUR TWO FAMILIES.
HE FEELS OUR ASSETS WOULD BE BEST POOLED IN ORDER TO DEAL WITH THE COMMON THREAT OUR ORGANIZATIONS FACE.
YOU'RE TALKING ABOUT THE *HORNET.*
IN THE LAST FIVE YEARS THAT THE GREEN HORNET'S STAKED OUT CENTURY CITY AS HIS TURF, EVERY GROUP OF HEAVY HITTERS HAS MADE A RUN AT THIS GUY...
...AND FOUND THEMSELVES DOING A DIME OR MORE UPSTATE.
HE'S A POLICE MAN, THEN?
THE THEORY IS HE'S GOT SOME KINDA DEAL WITH THE COPS.
THEY LET HIM CONTROL A PIECE OF THE CITY, AND HE HANDS OVER GUYS LIKE US IN RETURN.
WHO KNOWS IF IT'S TRUE? POINT IS, HE'S MADE HIMSELF PRETTY UNTOUCHABLE.
YOU WANNA TAKE OUT THE HORNET? BE MY GUEST.
THE NEW GUYS ALL WANNA TAKE THEIR SHOT AT THE BUG, AND THEY ALWAYS GET SWATTED INSTEAD.
ME? I WANT NO PART OF IT.
I'VE WASTED MY TIME REACHING OUT TO THESE COWARDS.

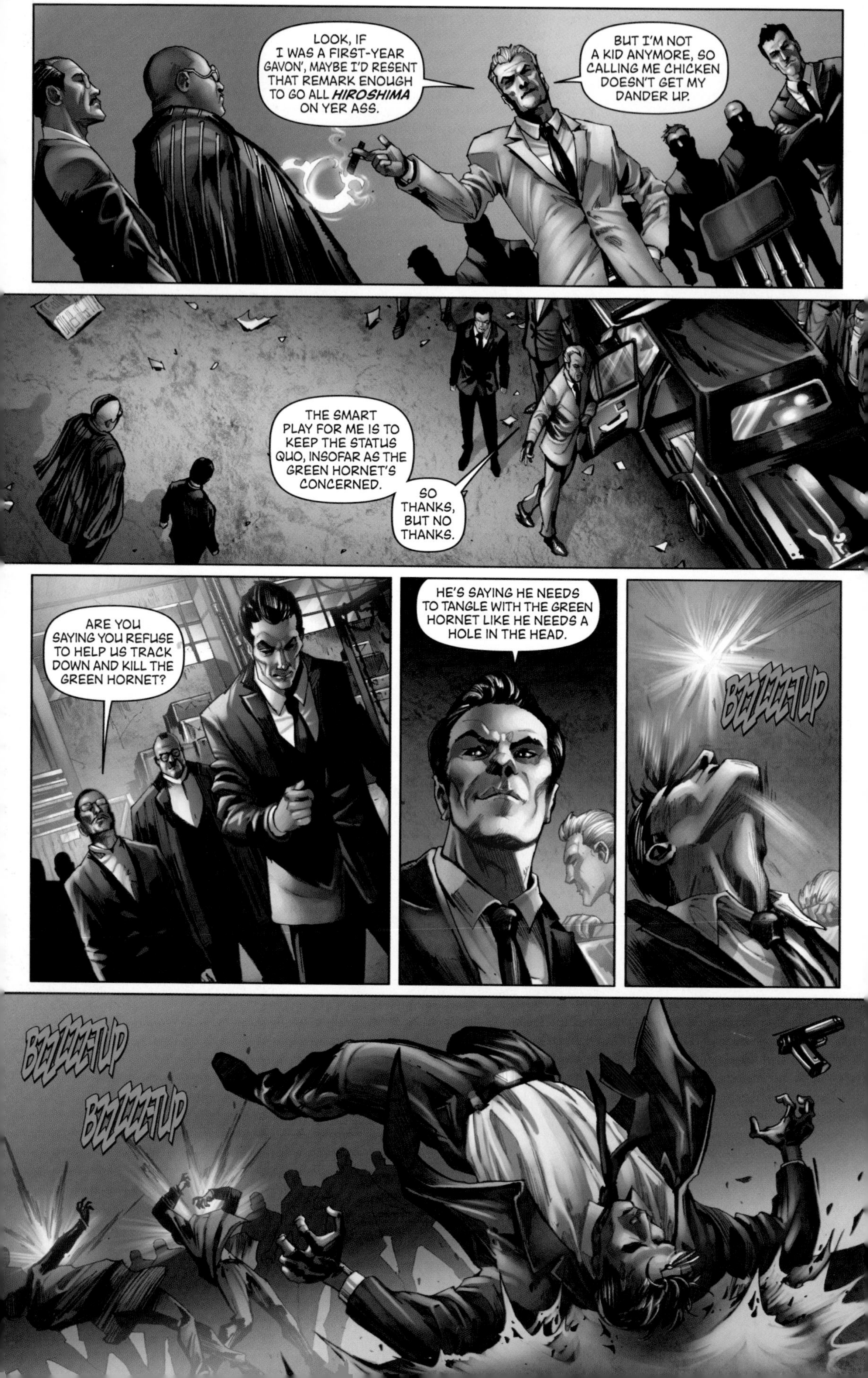
LOOK, IF I WAS A FIRST-YEAR GAVON', MAYBE I'D RESENT THAT REMARK ENOUGH TO GO ALL *HIROSHIMA* ON YER ASS.
BUT I'M NOT A KID ANYMORE, SO CALLING ME CHICKEN DOESN'T GET MY DANDER UP.
THE SMART PLAY FOR ME IS TO KEEP THE STATUS QUO, INSOFAR AS THE GREEN HORNET'S CONCERNED.
SO THANKS, BUT NO THANKS.
ARE YOU SAYING YOU REFUSE TO HELP US TRACK DOWN AND KILL THE GREEN HORNET?
HE'S SAYING HE NEEDS TO TANGLE WITH THE GREEN HORNET LIKE HE NEEDS A HOLE IN THE HEAD.
BZZZZTUP
BZZZZTUP
BZZZZTUP

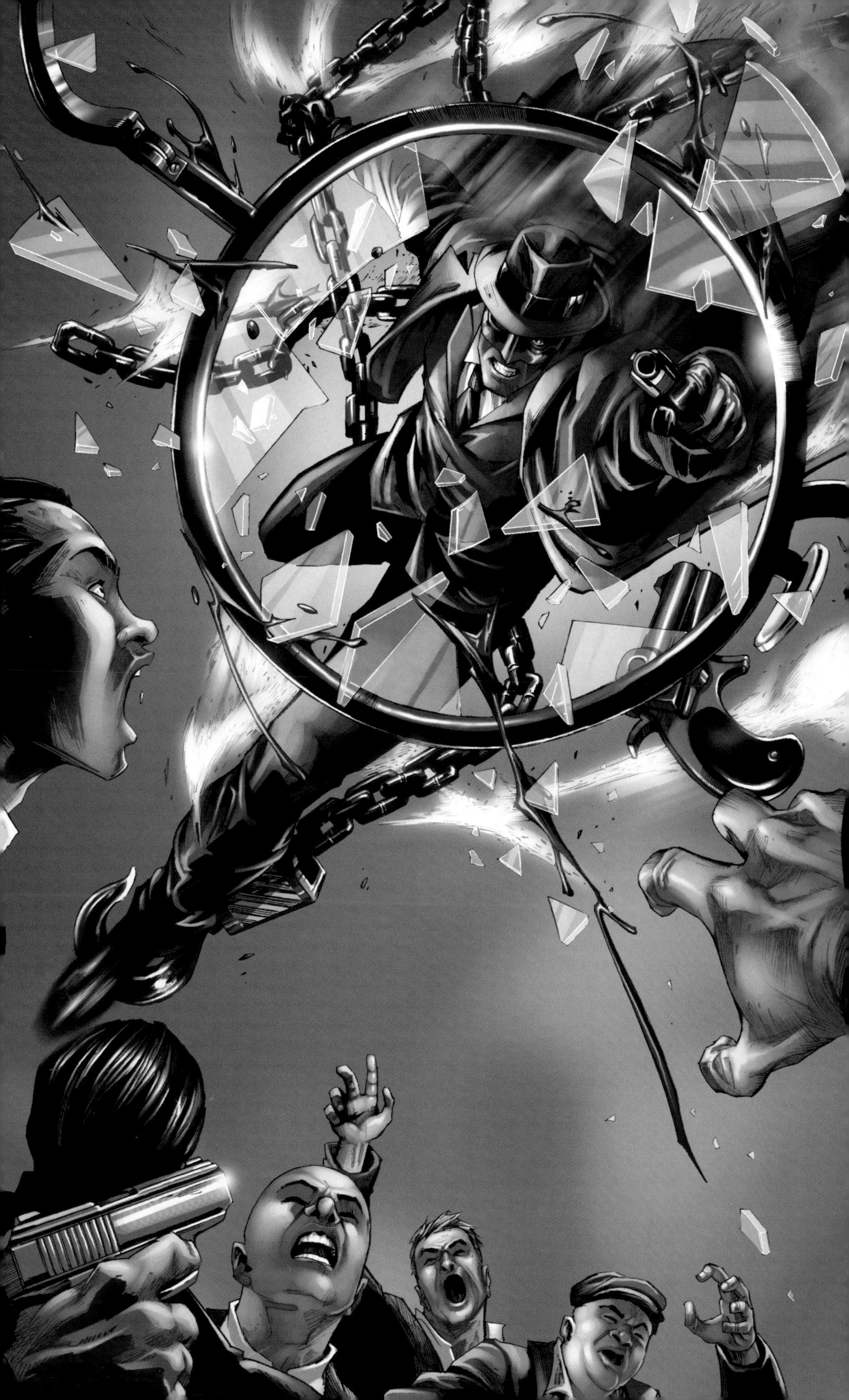

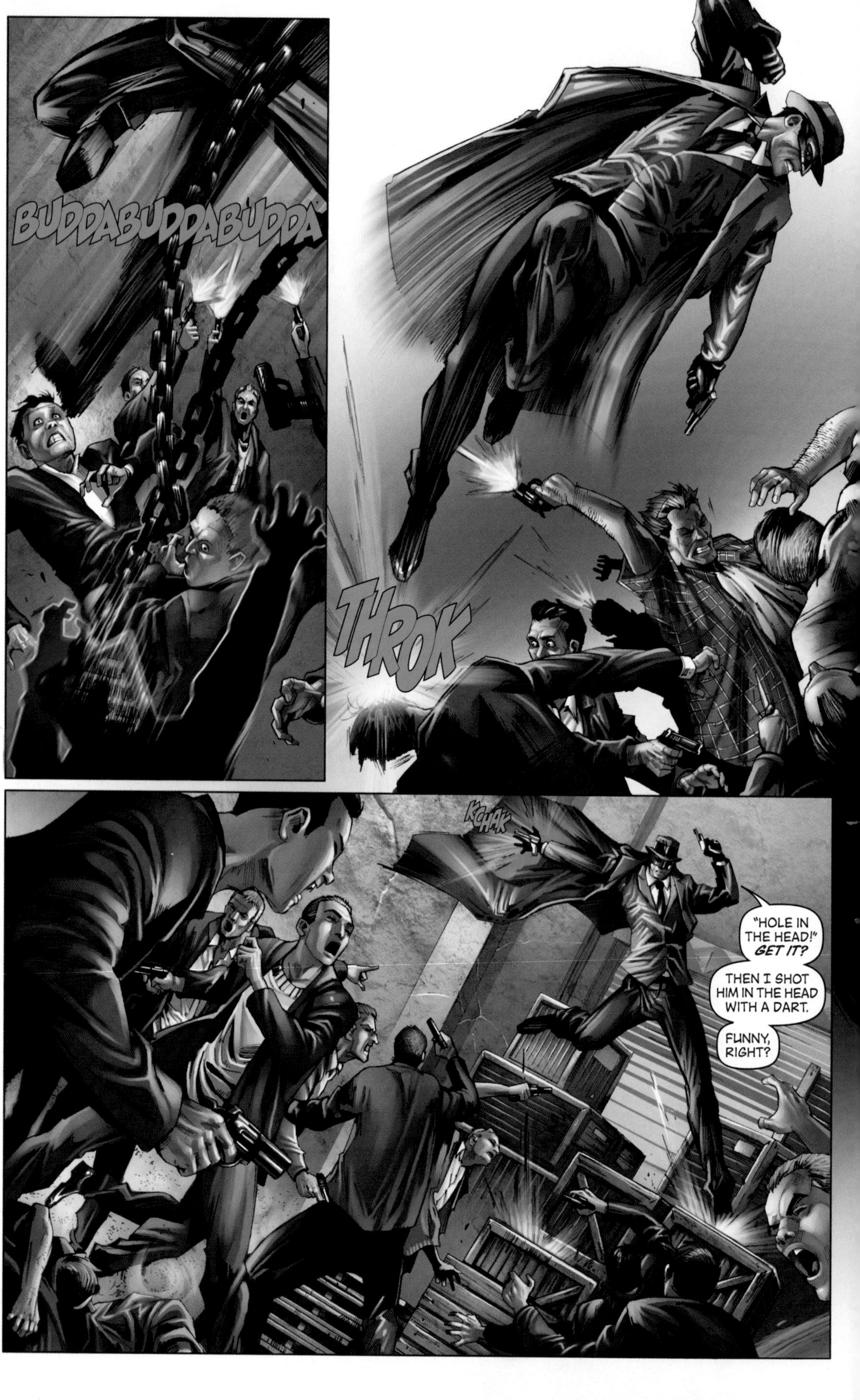
BUDDABUDDABUDDA
THROK
KCHAK
"HOLE IN THE HEAD!" GET IT?
THEN I SHOT HIM IN THE HEAD WITH A DART.
FUNNY, RIGHT?

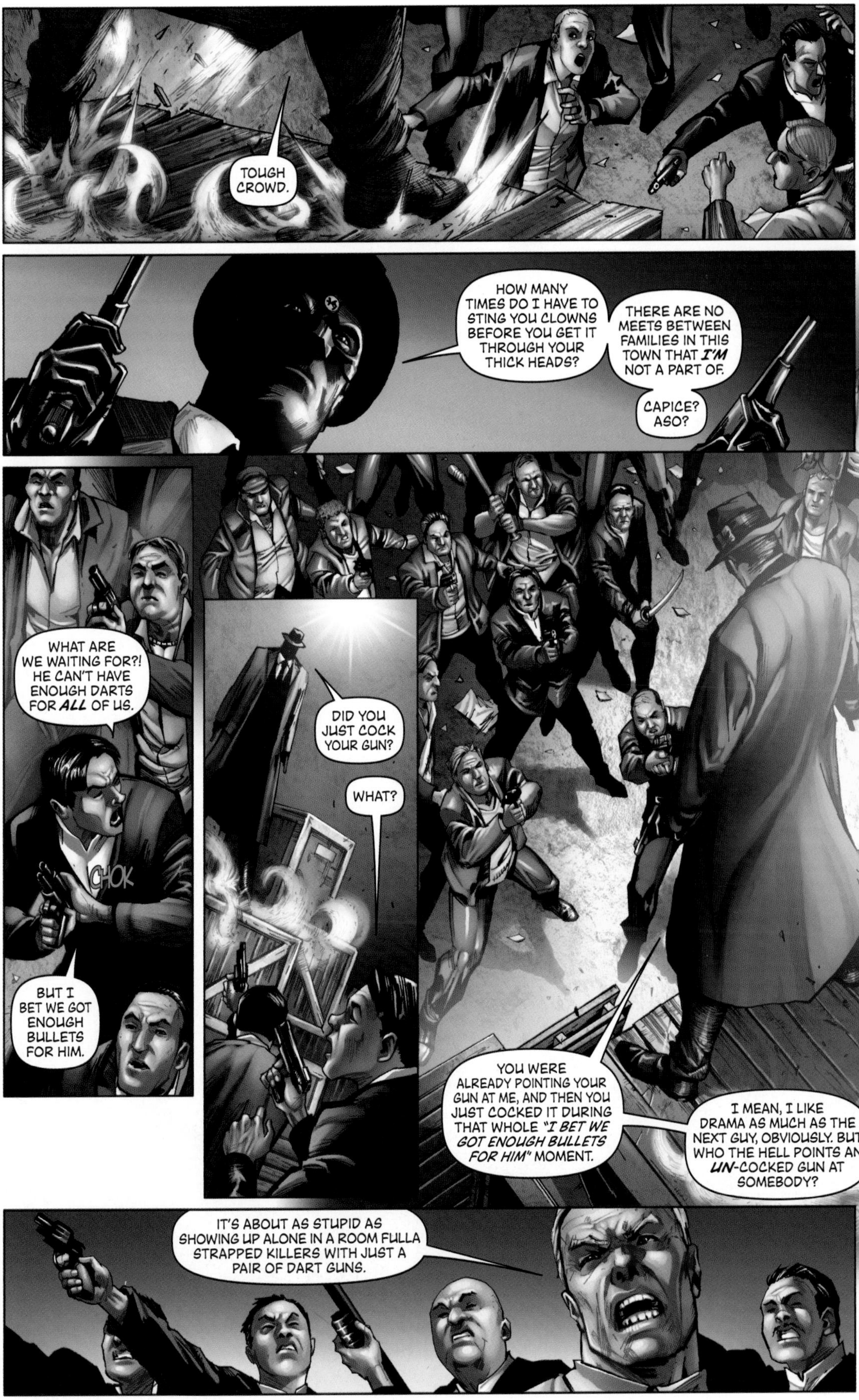
TOUGH CROWD.
HOW MANY TIMES DO I HAVE TO STING YOU CLOWNS BEFORE YOU GET IT THROUGH YOUR THICK HEADS?
THERE ARE NO MEETS BETWEEN FAMILIES IN THIS TOWN THAT *I'M* NOT A PART OF.
CAPICE? ASO?
WHAT ARE WE WAITING FOR?! HE CAN'T HAVE ENOUGH DARTS FOR *ALL* OF US.
CHOK
BUT I BET WE GOT ENOUGH BULLETS FOR HIM.
DID YOU JUST COCK YOUR GUN?
WHAT?
YOU WERE ALREADY POINTING YOUR GUN AT ME, AND THEN YOU JUST COCKED IT DURING THAT WHOLE *"I BET WE GOT ENOUGH BULLETS FOR HIM"* MOMENT.
I MEAN, I LIKE DRAMA AS MUCH AS THE NEXT GUY, OBVIOUSLY. BUT WHO THE HELL POINTS AN *UN*-COCKED GUN AT SOMEBODY?
IT'S ABOUT AS STUPID AS SHOWING UP ALONE IN A ROOM FULLA STRAPPED KILLERS WITH JUST A PAIR OF DART GUNS.

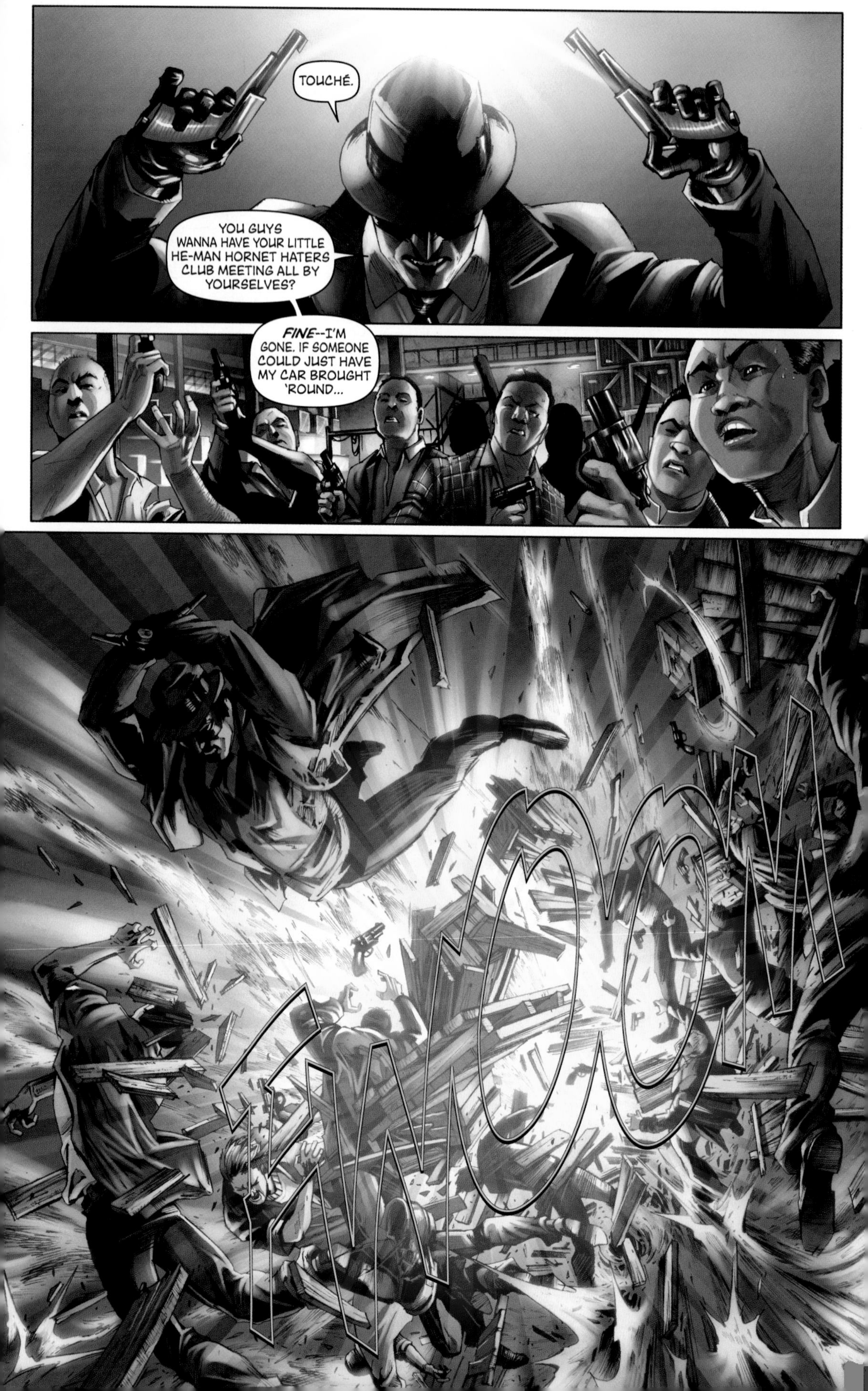
TOUCHÉ.
YOU GUYS WANNA HAVE YOUR LITTLE HE-MAN HORNET HATERS CLUB MEETING ALL BY YOURSELVES?
FINE--I'M GONE. IF SOMEONE COULD JUST HAVE MY CAR BROUGHT 'ROUND...

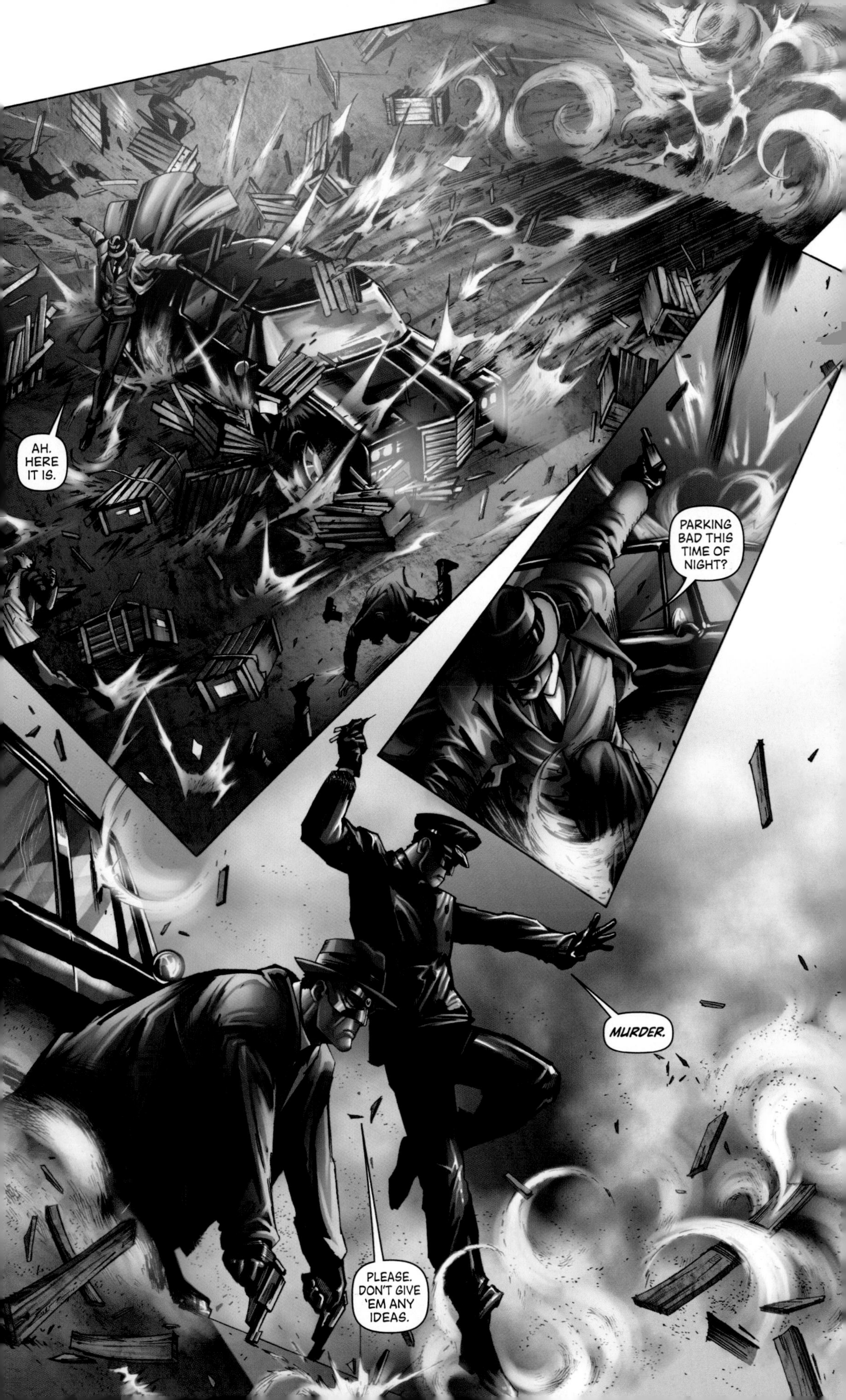
AH. HERE IT IS.
PARKING BAD THIS TIME OF NIGHT?
MURDER.
PLEASE. DON'T GIVE 'EM ANY IDEAS.

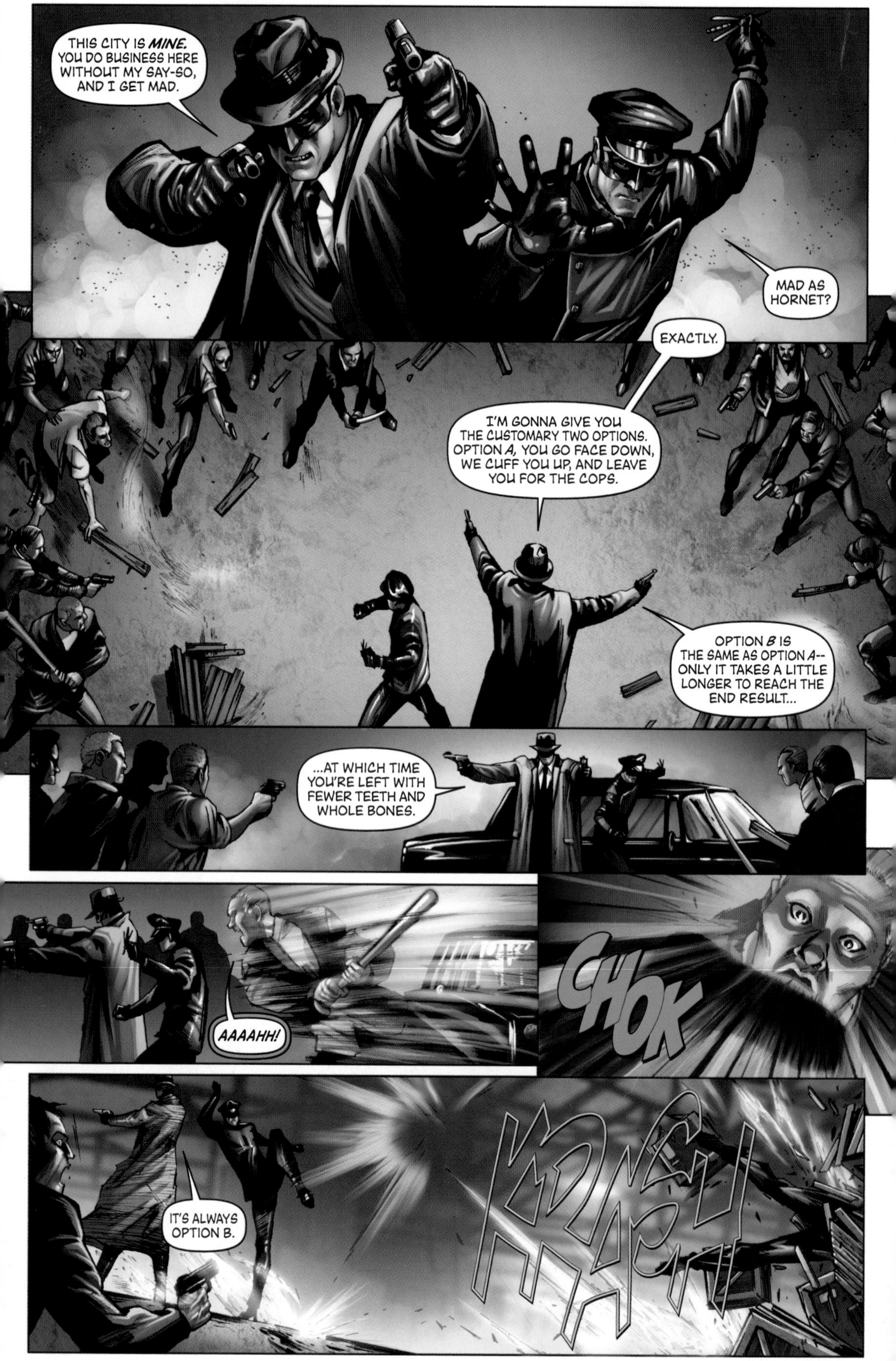
THIS CITY IS MINE. YOU DO BUSINESS HERE WITHOUT MY SAY-SO, AND I GET MAD.
MAD AS HORNET?
EXACTLY.
I'M GONNA GIVE YOU THE CUSTOMARY TWO OPTIONS. OPTION A, YOU GO FACE DOWN, WE CUFF YOU UP, AND LEAVE YOU FOR THE COPS.
OPTION B IS THE SAME AS OPTION A-- ONLY IT TAKES A LITTLE LONGER TO REACH THE END RESULT...
...AT WHICH TIME YOU'RE LEFT WITH FEWER TEETH AND WHOLE BONES.
AAAAHH!
CHOK
IT'S ALWAYS OPTION B.

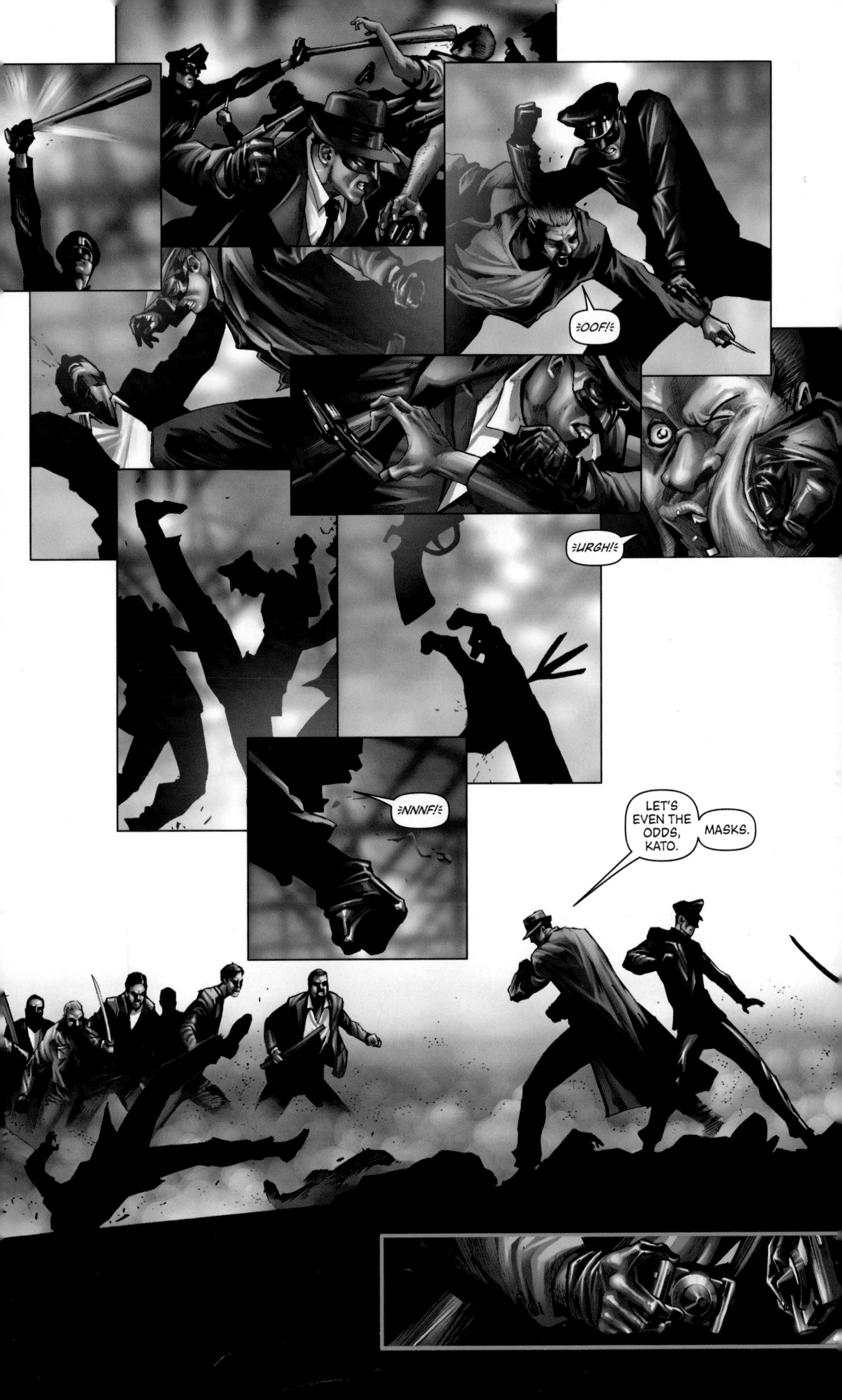
OOF!
URGH!
NNNF!
LET'S EVEN THE ODDS, KATO.
MASKS.

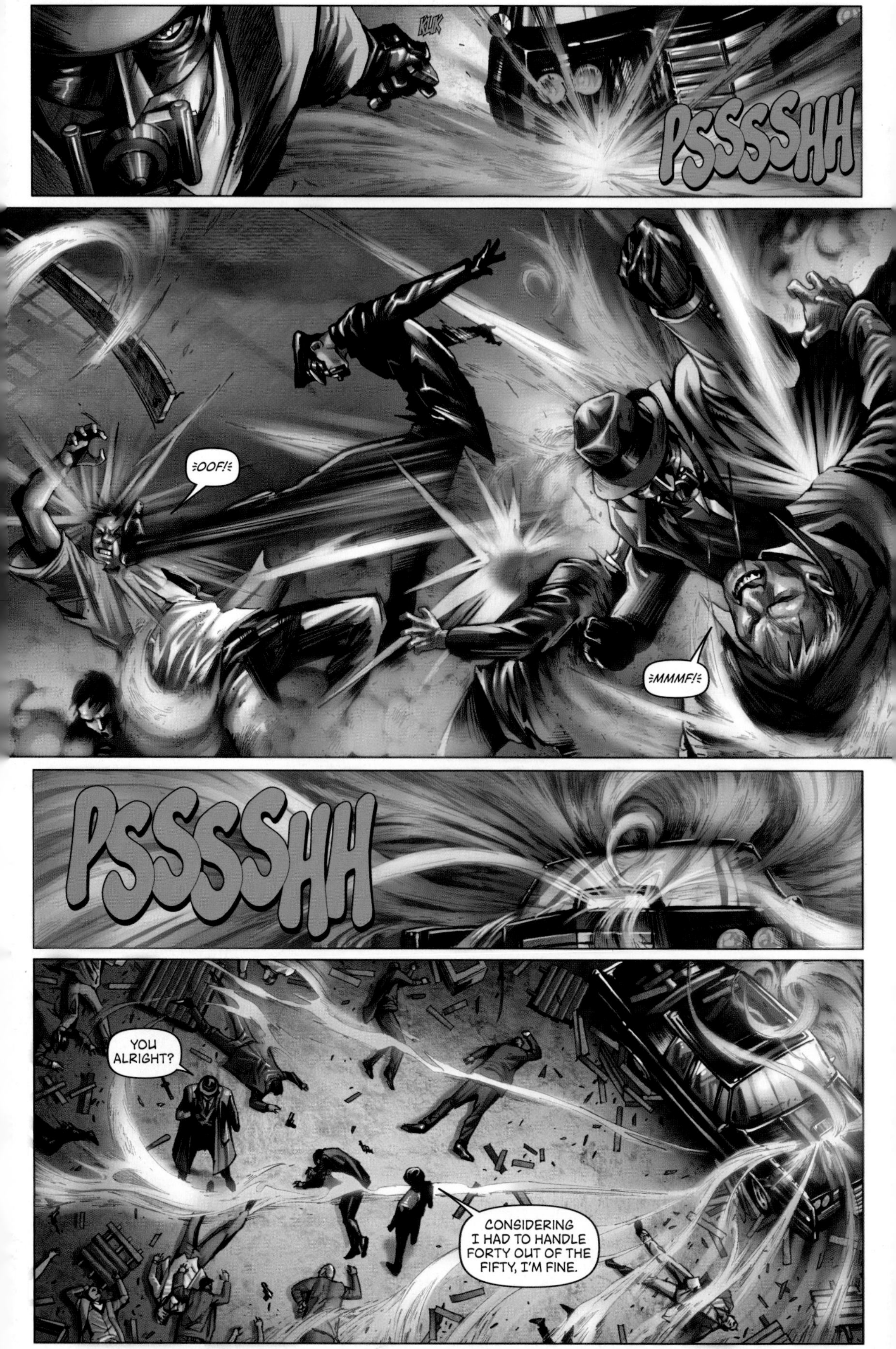
KLIK
PSSSSHH
OOF!
MMMF!
PSSSSHH
YOU ALRIGHT?
CONSIDERING I HAD TO HANDLE FORTY OUT OF THE FIFTY, I'M FINE.

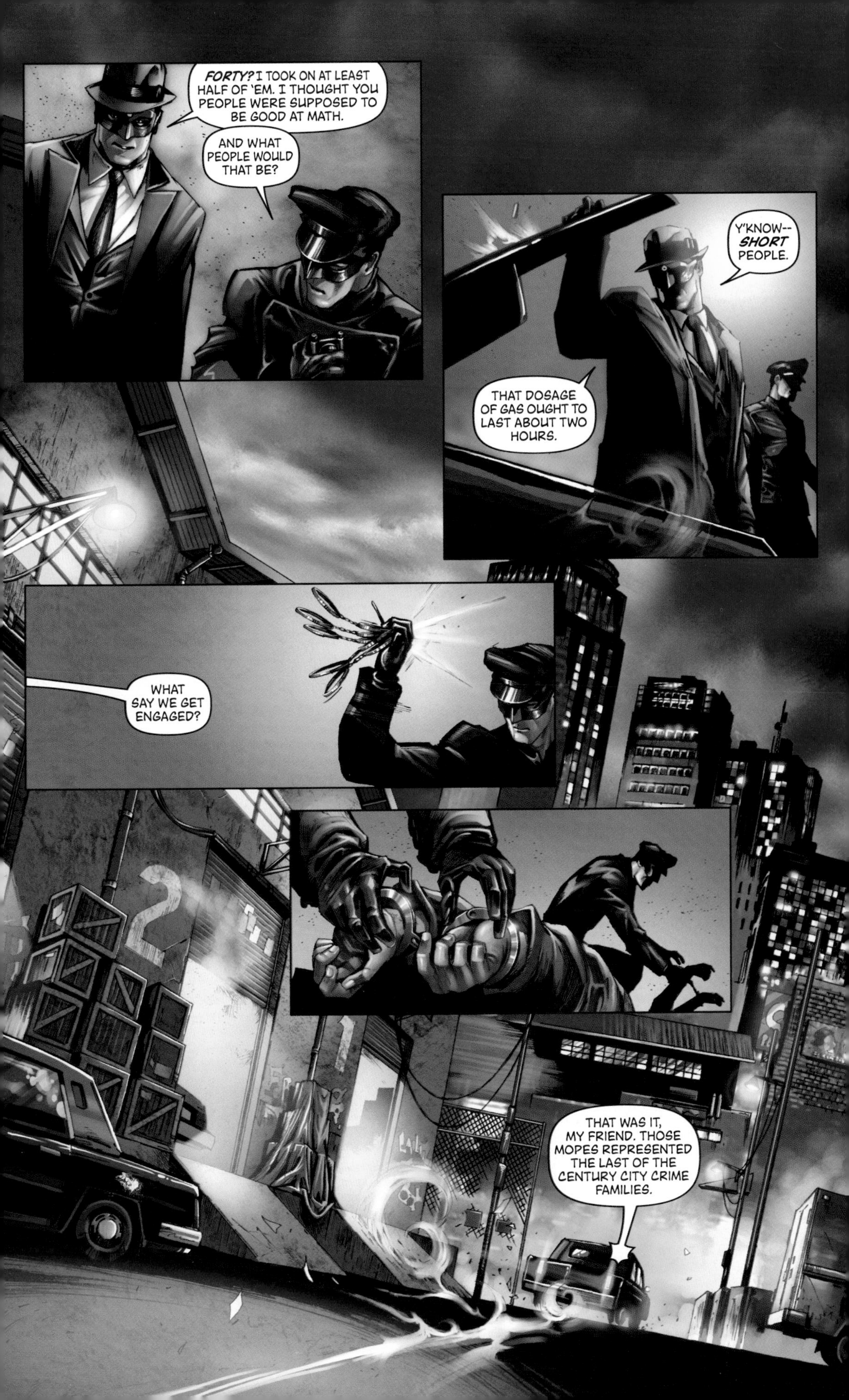
FORTY? I TOOK ON AT LEAST HALF OF 'EM. I THOUGHT YOU PEOPLE WERE SUPPOSED TO BE GOOD AT MATH.
AND WHAT PEOPLE WOULD THAT BE?
Y'KNOW-- SHORT PEOPLE.
THAT DOSAGE OF GAS OUGHT TO LAST ABOUT TWO HOURS.
WHAT SAY WE GET ENGAGED?
THAT WAS IT, MY FRIEND. THOSE MOPES REPRESENTED THE LAST OF THE CENTURY CITY CRIME FAMILIES.

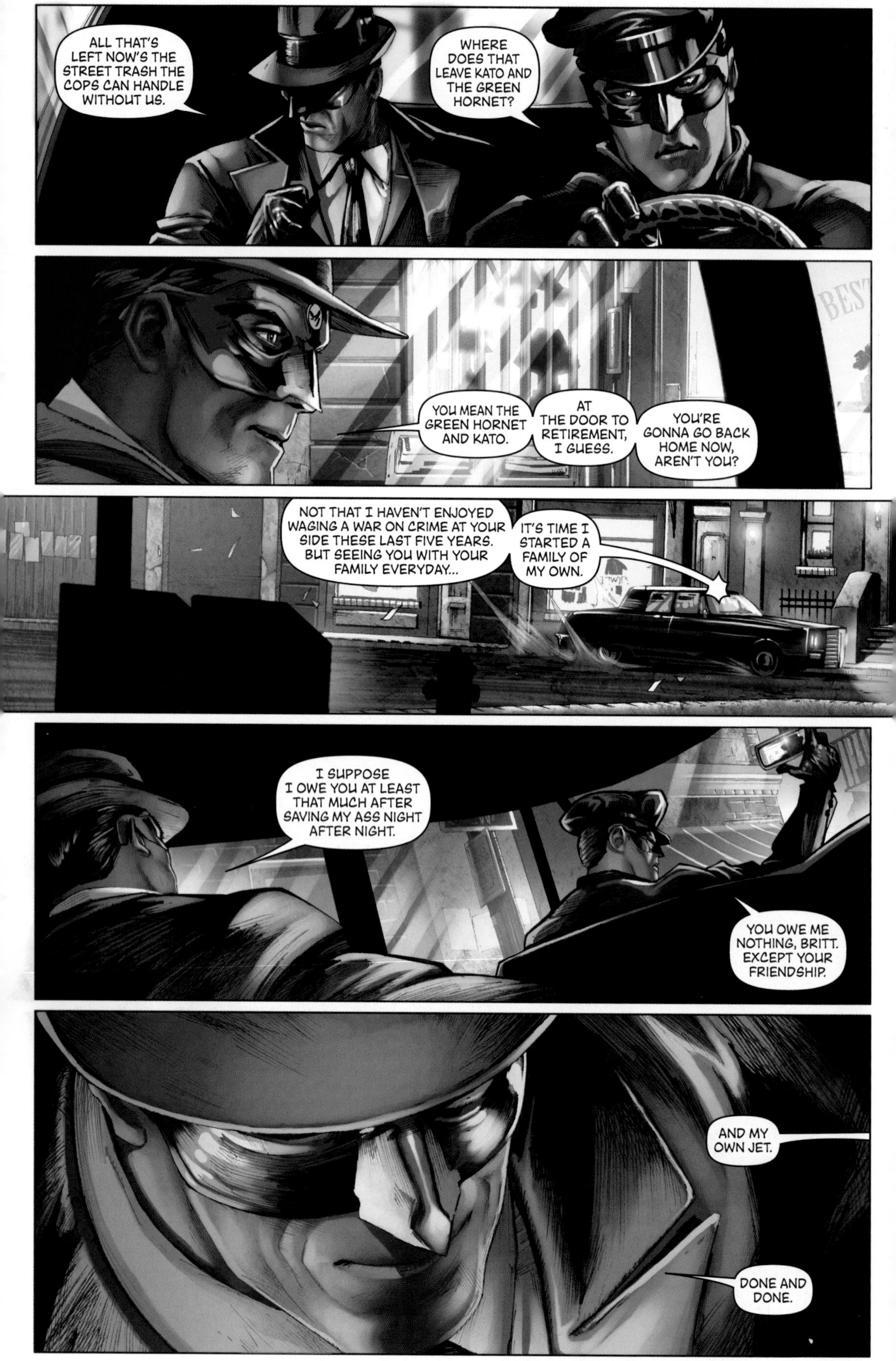
ALL THAT'S LEFT NOW'S THE STREET TRASH THE COPS CAN HANDLE WITHOUT US.
WHERE DOES THAT LEAVE KATO AND THE GREEN HORNET?
YOU MEAN THE GREEN HORNET AND KATO.
AT THE DOOR TO RETIREMENT, I GUESS.
YOU'RE GONNA GO BACK HOME NOW, AREN'T YOU?
NOT THAT I HAVEN'T ENJOYED WAGING A WAR ON CRIME AT YOUR SIDE THESE LAST FIVE YEARS. BUT SEEING YOU WITH YOUR FAMILY EVERYDAY...
IT'S TIME I STARTED A FAMILY OF MY OWN.
I SUPPOSE I OWE YOU AT LEAST THAT MUCH AFTER SAVING MY ASS NIGHT AFTER NIGHT.
YOU OWE ME NOTHING, BRITT. EXCEPT YOUR FRIENDSHIP.
AND MY OWN JET.
DONE AND DONE.

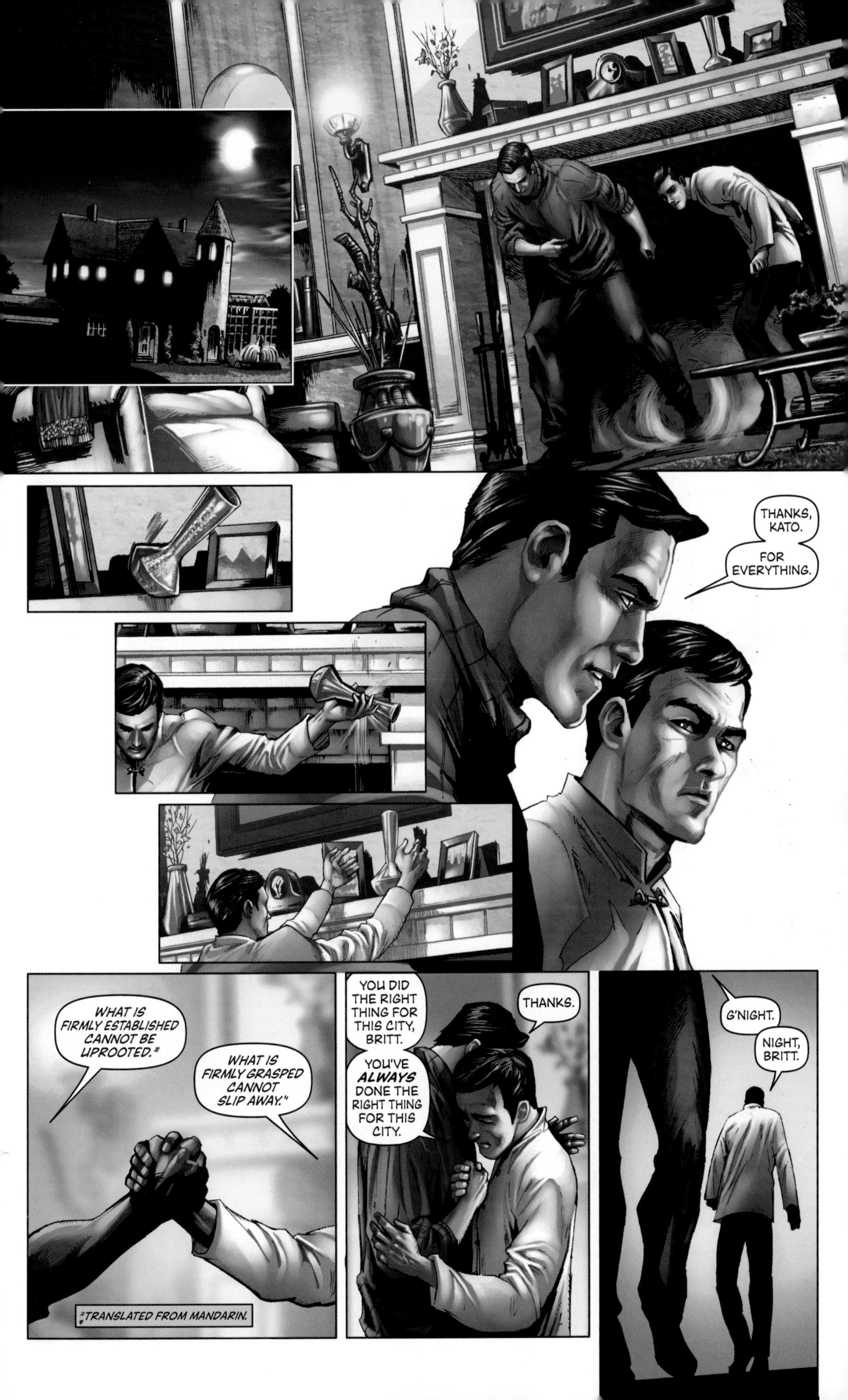
THANKS, KATO.
FOR EVERYTHING.
WHAT IS FIRMLY ESTABLISHED CANNOT BE UPROOTED.*
WHAT IS FIRMLY GRASPED CANNOT SLIP AWAY."
*TRANSLATED FROM MANDARIN.
YOU DID THE RIGHT THING FOR THIS CITY, BRITT.
THANKS.
YOU'VE ALWAYS DONE THE RIGHT THING FOR THIS CITY.
G'NIGHT.
NIGHT, BRITT.

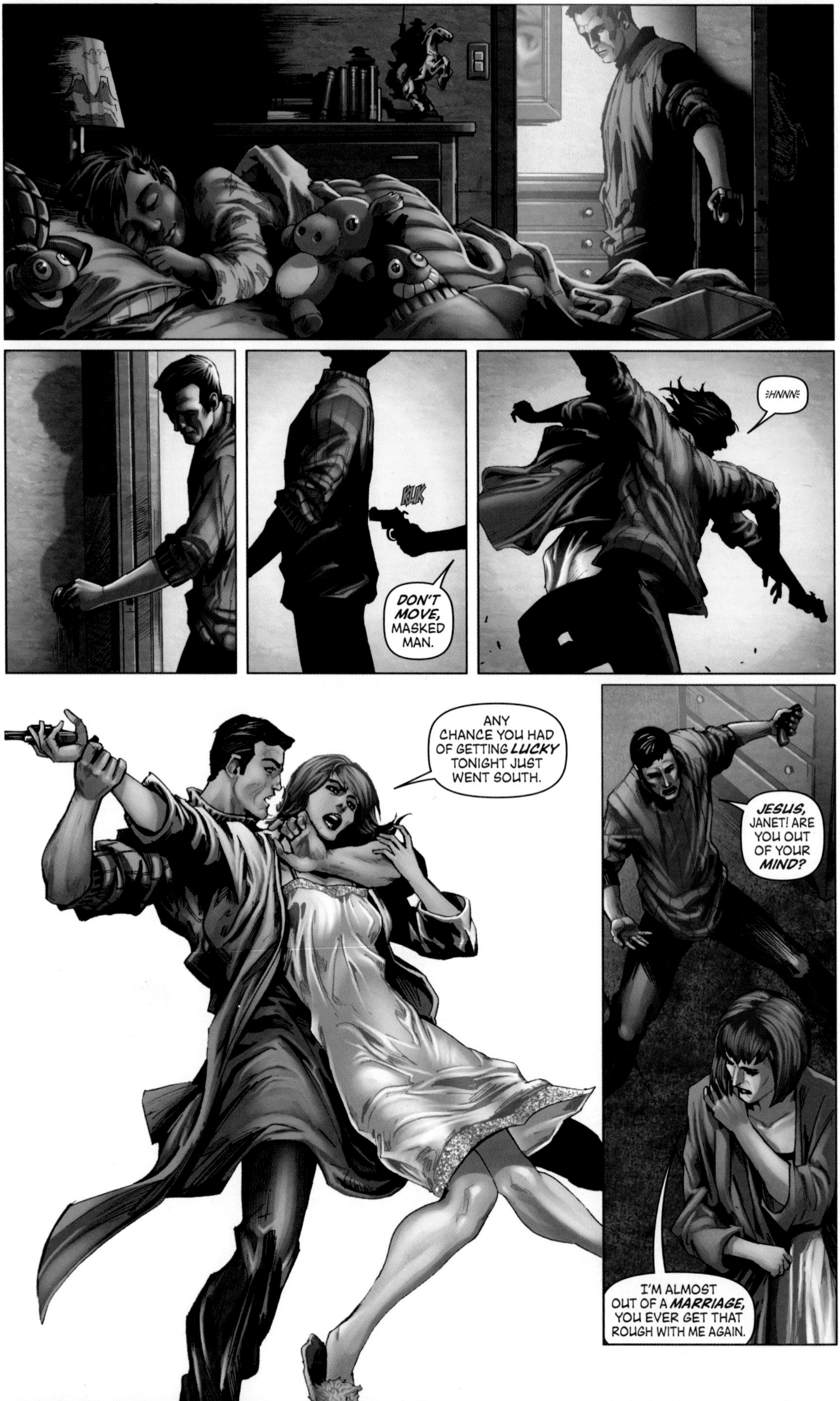
KLIK
DON'T MOVE, MASKED MAN.
HNNN
ANY CHANCE YOU HAD OF GETTING LUCKY TONIGHT JUST WENT SOUTH.
JESUS, JANET! ARE YOU OUT OF YOUR MIND?
I'M ALMOST OUT OF A MARRIAGE, YOU EVER GET THAT ROUGH WITH ME AGAIN.

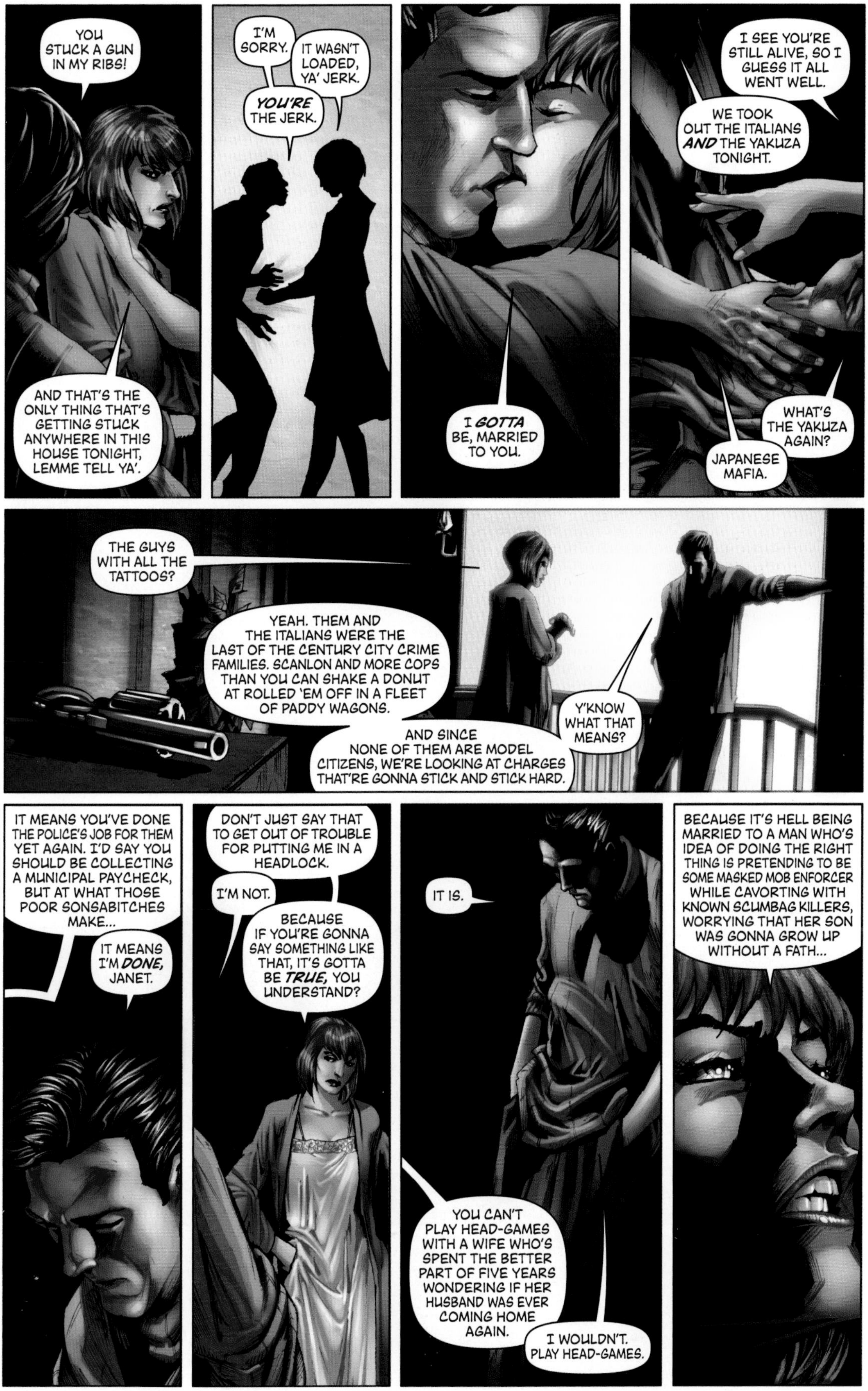
YOU STUCK A GUN IN MY RIBS!
AND THAT'S THE ONLY THING THAT'S GETTING STUCK ANYWHERE IN THIS HOUSE TONIGHT, LEMME TELL YA'.
I'M SORRY.
IT WASN'T LOADED, YA' JERK.
YOU'RE THE JERK.
I *GOTTA* BE, MARRIED TO YOU.
I SEE YOU'RE STILL ALIVE, SO I GUESS IT ALL WENT WELL.
WE TOOK OUT THE ITALIANS *AND* THE YAKUZA TONIGHT.
WHAT'S THE YAKUZA AGAIN?
JAPANESE MAFIA.
THE GUYS WITH ALL THE TATTOOS?
YEAH. THEM AND THE ITALIANS WERE THE LAST OF THE CENTURY CITY CRIME FAMILIES. SCANLON AND MORE COPS THAN YOU CAN SHAKE A DONUT AT ROLLED 'EM OFF IN A FLEET OF PADDY WAGONS.
AND SINCE NONE OF THEM ARE MODEL CITIZENS, WE'RE LOOKING AT CHARGES THAT'RE GONNA STICK AND STICK HARD.
Y'KNOW WHAT THAT MEANS?
IT MEANS YOU'VE DONE THE POLICE'S JOB FOR THEM YET AGAIN. I'D SAY YOU SHOULD BE COLLECTING A MUNICIPAL PAYCHECK, BUT AT WHAT THOSE POOR SONSABITCHES MAKE...
IT MEANS I'M *DONE,* JANET.
DON'T JUST SAY THAT TO GET OUT OF TROUBLE FOR PUTTING ME IN A HEADLOCK.
I'M NOT.
BECAUSE IF YOU'RE GONNA SAY SOMETHING LIKE THAT, IT'S GOTTA BE *TRUE,* YOU UNDERSTAND?
IT IS.
YOU CAN'T PLAY HEAD-GAMES WITH A WIFE WHO'S SPENT THE BETTER PART OF FIVE YEARS WONDERING IF HER HUSBAND WAS EVER COMING HOME AGAIN.
I WOULDN'T. PLAY HEAD-GAMES.
BECAUSE IT'S HELL BEING MARRIED TO A MAN WHO'S IDEA OF DOING THE RIGHT THING IS PRETENDING TO BE SOME MASKED MOB ENFORCER WHILE CAVORTING WITH KNOWN SCUMBAG KILLERS, WORRYING THAT HER SON WAS GONNA GROW UP WITHOUT A FATH...

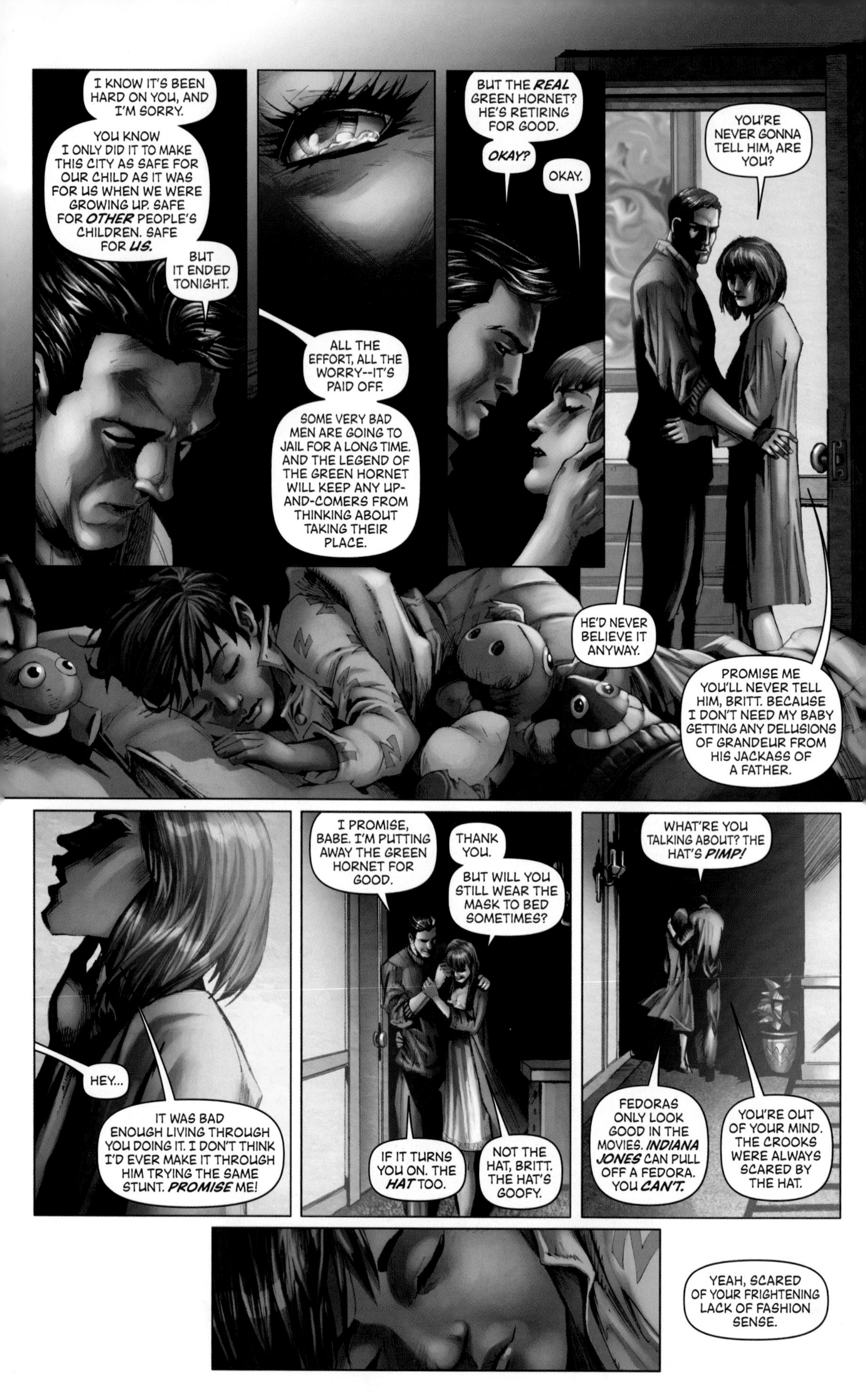

I KNOW IT'S BEEN HARD ON YOU, AND I'M SORRY.
YOU KNOW I ONLY DID IT TO MAKE THIS CITY AS SAFE FOR OUR CHILD AS IT WAS FOR US WHEN WE WERE GROWING UP. SAFE FOR *OTHER* PEOPLE'S CHILDREN. SAFE FOR *US.*
BUT IT ENDED TONIGHT.
ALL THE EFFORT, ALL THE WORRY--IT'S PAID OFF.
SOME VERY BAD MEN ARE GOING TO JAIL FOR A LONG TIME. AND THE LEGEND OF THE GREEN HORNET WILL KEEP ANY UP-AND-COMERS FROM THINKING ABOUT TAKING THEIR PLACE.
BUT THE *REAL* GREEN HORNET? HE'S RETIRING FOR GOOD.
OKAY?
OKAY.
YOU'RE NEVER GONNA TELL HIM, ARE YOU?
HE'D NEVER BELIEVE IT ANYWAY.
PROMISE ME YOU'LL NEVER TELL HIM, BRITT. BECAUSE I DON'T NEED MY BABY GETTING ANY DELUSIONS OF GRANDEUR FROM HIS JACKASS OF A FATHER.
HEY...
IT WAS BAD ENOUGH LIVING THROUGH YOU DOING IT. I DON'T THINK I'D EVER MAKE IT THROUGH HIM TRYING THE SAME STUNT. *PROMISE* ME!
I PROMISE, BABE. I'M PUTTING AWAY THE GREEN HORNET FOR GOOD.
THANK YOU.
BUT WILL YOU STILL WEAR THE MASK TO BED SOMETIMES?
IF IT TURNS YOU ON. THE *HAT* TOO.
NOT THE HAT, BRITT. THE HAT'S GOOFY.
WHAT'RE YOU TALKING ABOUT? THE HAT'S *PIMP!*
FEDORAS ONLY LOOK GOOD IN THE MOVIES. *INDIANA JONES* CAN PULL OFF A FEDORA. YOU *CAN'T.*
YOU'RE OUT OF YOUR MIND. THE CROOKS WERE ALWAYS SCARED BY THE HAT.
YEAH, SCARED OF YOUR FRIGHTENING LACK OF FASHION SENSE.

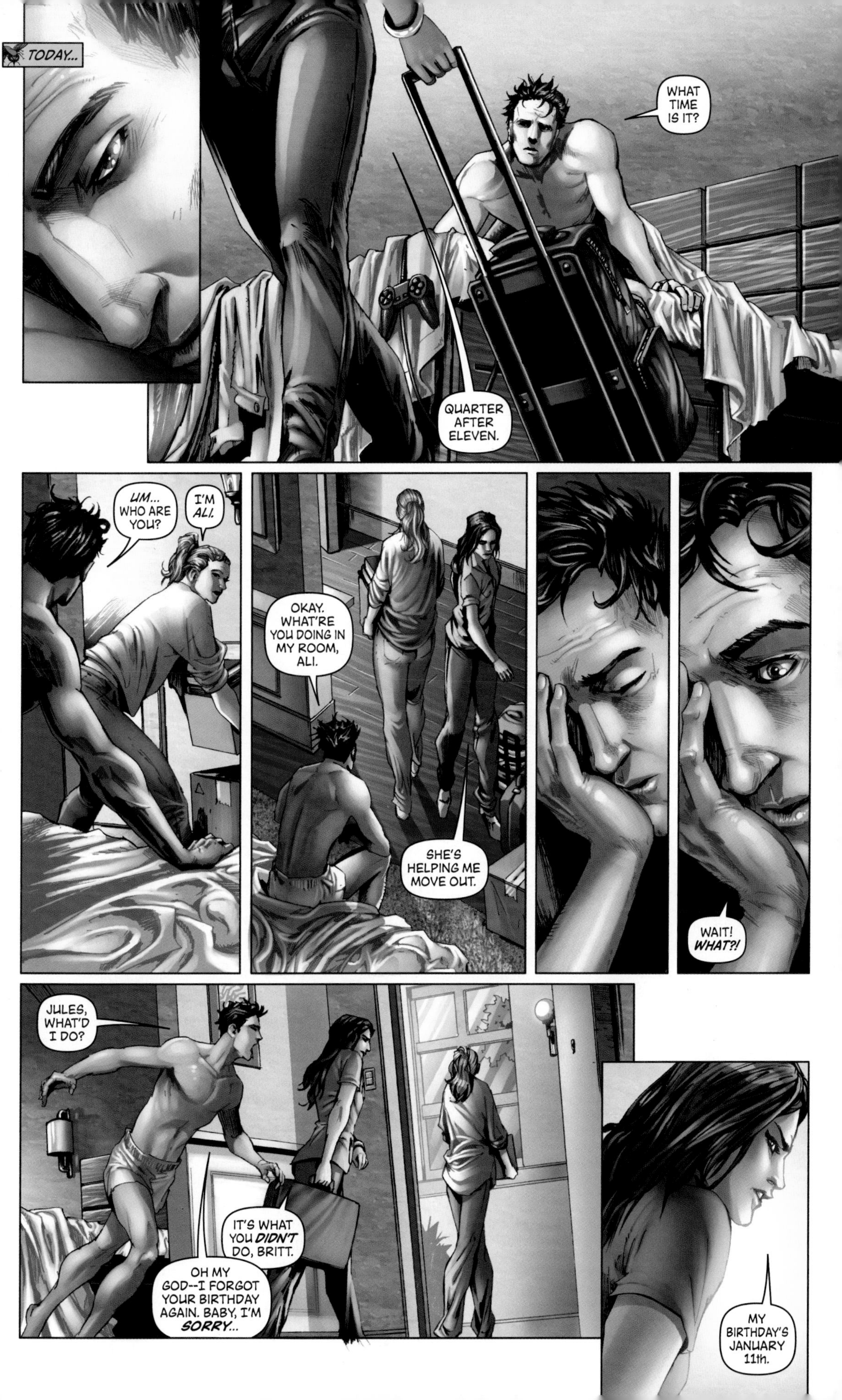
TODAY...
WHAT TIME IS IT?
QUARTER AFTER ELEVEN.
UM... WHO ARE YOU?
I'M ALI.
OKAY. WHAT'RE YOU DOING IN MY ROOM, ALI.
SHE'S HELPING ME MOVE OUT.
WAIT! WHAT?!
JULES, WHAT'D I DO?
IT'S WHAT YOU DIDN'T DO, BRITT.
OH MY GOD--I FORGOT YOUR BIRTHDAY AGAIN. BABY, I'M SORRY...
MY BIRTHDAY'S JANUARY 11th.

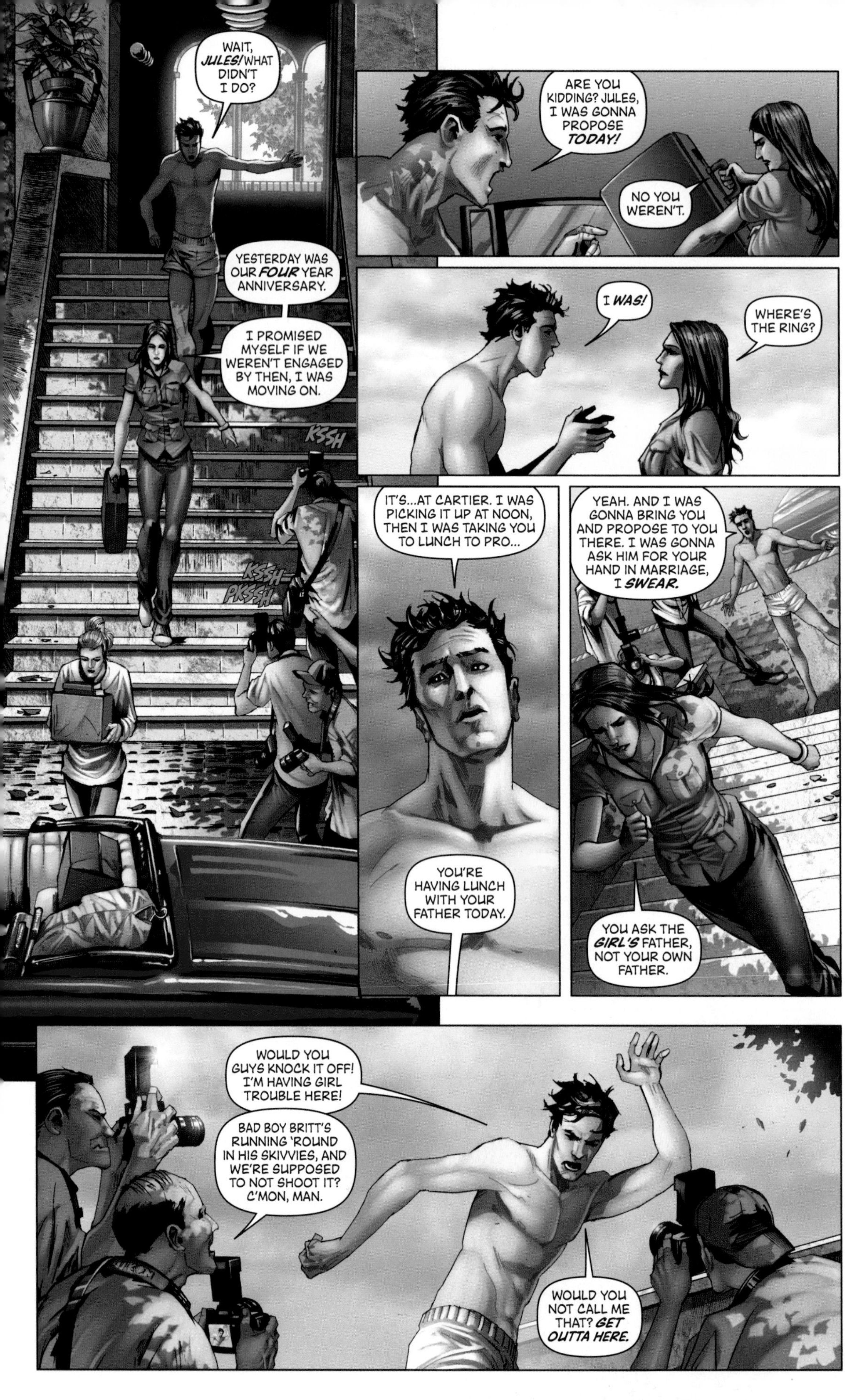
WAIT, JULES! WHAT DIDN'T I DO?
YESTERDAY WAS OUR FOUR YEAR ANNIVERSARY.
I PROMISED MYSELF IF WE WEREN'T ENGAGED BY THEN, I WAS MOVING ON.
KSSH
KSSH-PKSSH
ARE YOU KIDDING? JULES, I WAS GONNA PROPOSE TODAY!
NO YOU WEREN'T.
I WAS!
WHERE'S THE RING?
IT'S...AT CARTIER. I WAS PICKING IT UP AT NOON, THEN I WAS TAKING YOU TO LUNCH TO PRO...
YOU'RE HAVING LUNCH WITH YOUR FATHER TODAY.
YEAH. AND I WAS GONNA BRING YOU AND PROPOSE TO YOU THERE. I WAS GONNA ASK HIM FOR YOUR HAND IN MARRIAGE, I SWEAR.
YOU ASK THE GIRL'S FATHER, NOT YOUR OWN FATHER.
WOULD YOU GUYS KNOCK IT OFF! I'M HAVING GIRL TROUBLE HERE!
BAD BOY BRITT'S RUNNING 'ROUND IN HIS SKIVVIES, AND WE'RE SUPPOSED TO NOT SHOOT IT? C'MON, MAN.
WOULD YOU NOT CALL ME THAT? GET OUTTA HERE.

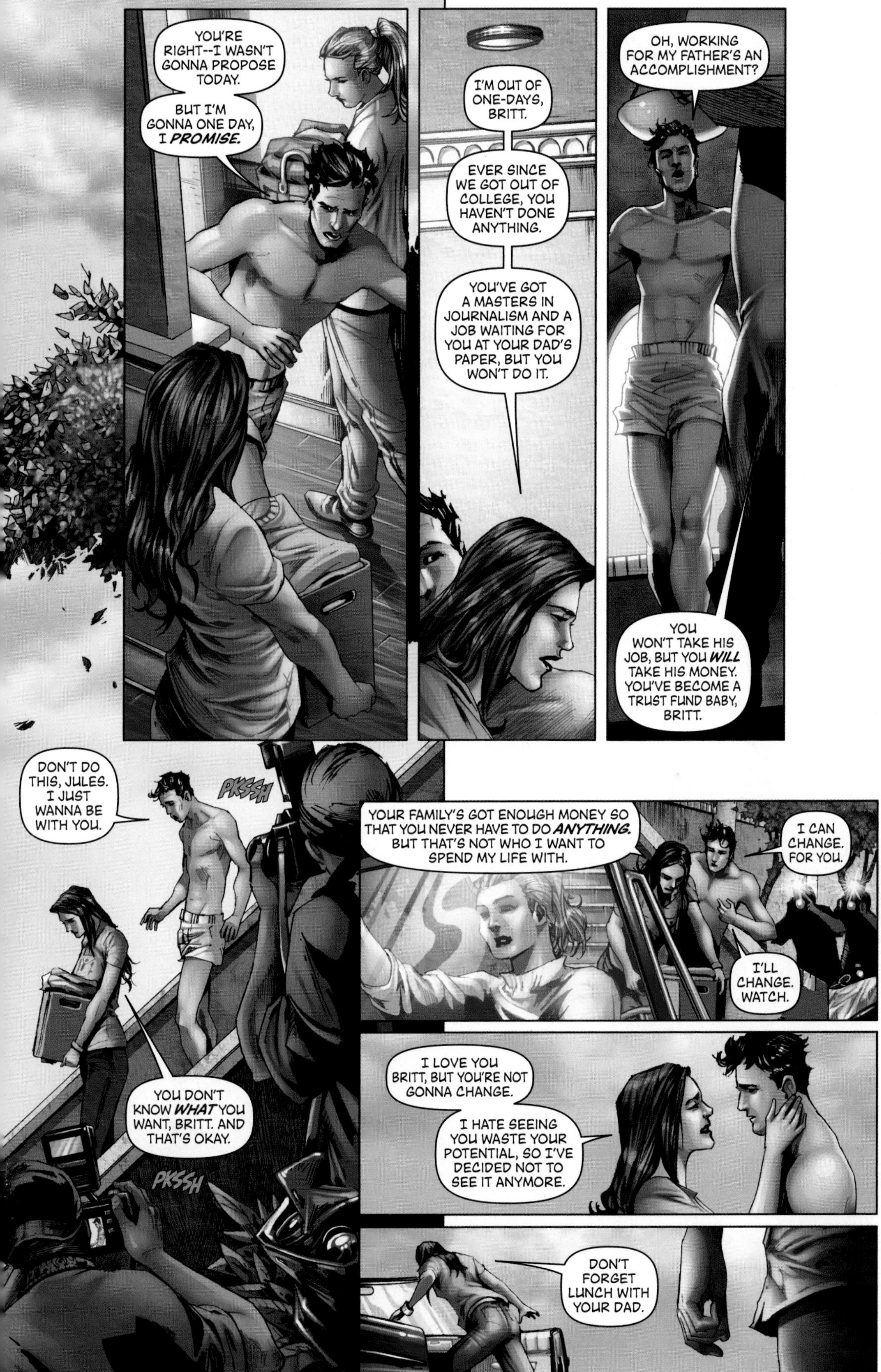
YOU'RE RIGHT--I WASN'T GONNA PROPOSE TODAY.
BUT I'M GONNA ONE DAY, I *PROMISE.*
I'M OUT OF ONE-DAYS, BRITT.
EVER SINCE WE GOT OUT OF COLLEGE, YOU HAVEN'T DONE ANYTHING.
YOU'VE GOT A MASTERS IN JOURNALISM AND A JOB WAITING FOR YOU AT YOUR DAD'S PAPER, BUT YOU WON'T DO IT.
OH, WORKING FOR MY FATHER'S AN ACCOMPLISHMENT?
YOU WON'T TAKE HIS JOB, BUT YOU *WILL* TAKE HIS MONEY. YOU'VE BECOME A TRUST FUND BABY, BRITT.
DON'T DO THIS, JULES. I JUST WANNA BE WITH YOU.
PKSSH
YOU DON'T KNOW *WHAT* YOU WANT, BRITT. AND THAT'S OKAY.
PKSSH
YOUR FAMILY'S GOT ENOUGH MONEY SO THAT YOU NEVER HAVE TO DO *ANYTHING.* BUT THAT'S NOT WHO I WANT TO SPEND MY LIFE WITH.
I CAN CHANGE. FOR YOU.
I'LL CHANGE. WATCH.
I LOVE YOU BRITT, BUT YOU'RE NOT GONNA CHANGE.
I HATE SEEING YOU WASTE YOUR POTENTIAL, SO I'VE DECIDED NOT TO SEE IT ANYMORE.
DON'T FORGET LUNCH WITH YOUR DAD.

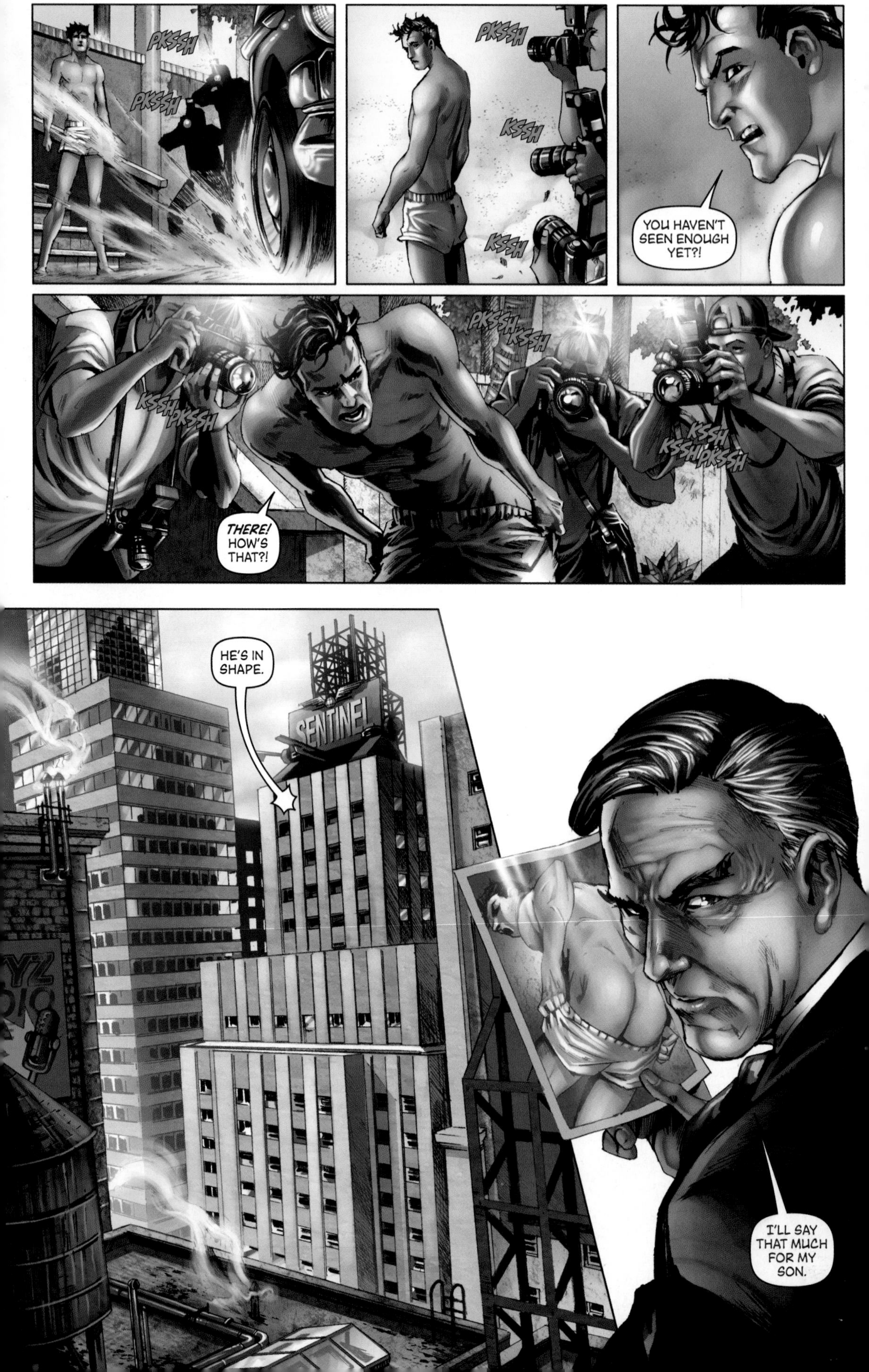
PKSSH
PKSSH
PKSSH
KSSH
KSSH
YOU HAVEN'T SEEN ENOUGH YET?!
KSSH PKSSH
PKSSH KSSH
KSSH KSSH PKSSH
THERE! HOW'S THAT?!
HE'S IN SHAPE.
SENTINEL
I'LL SAY THAT MUCH FOR MY SON.

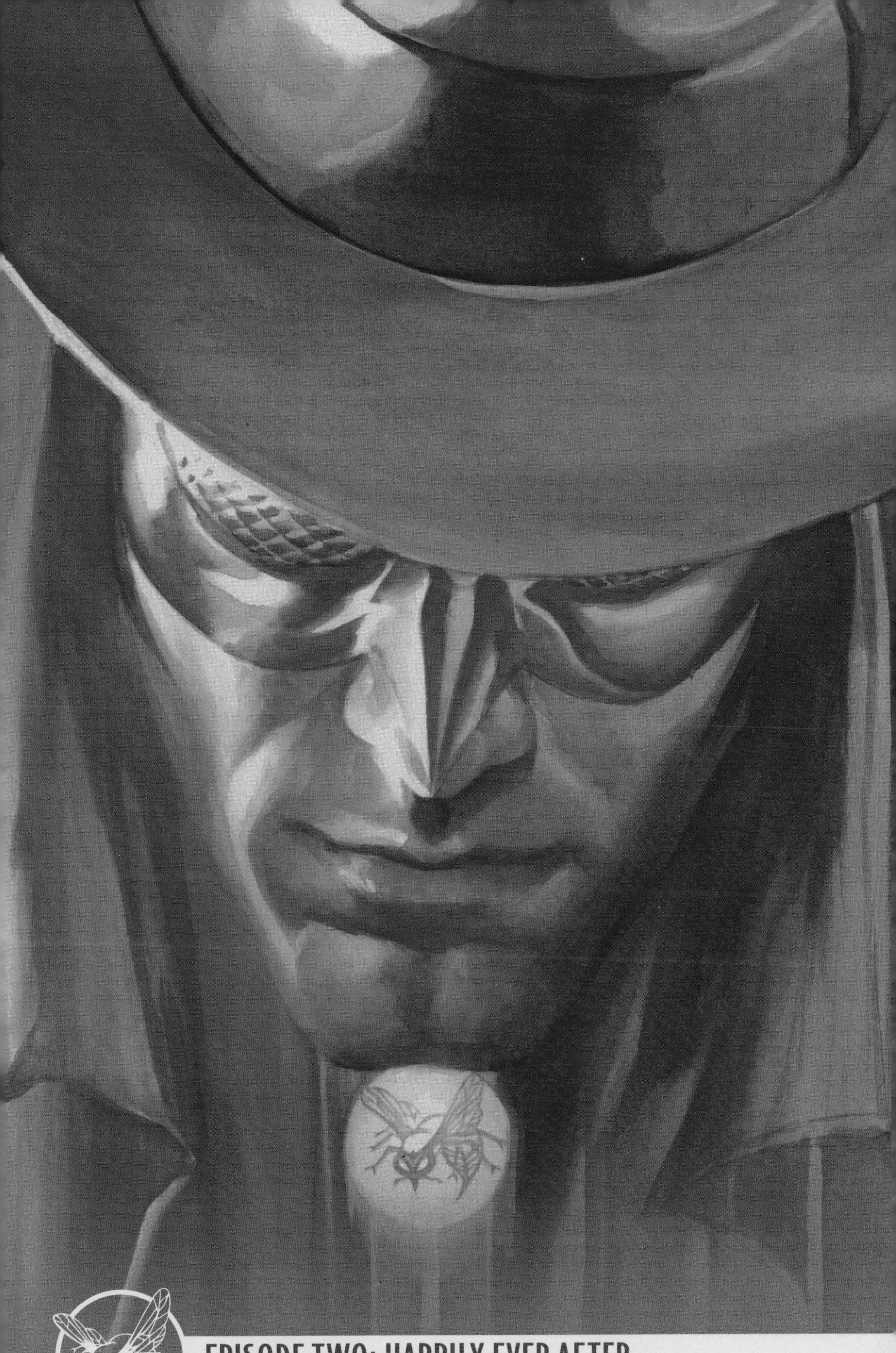

EPISODE TWO: HAPPILY EVER AFTER

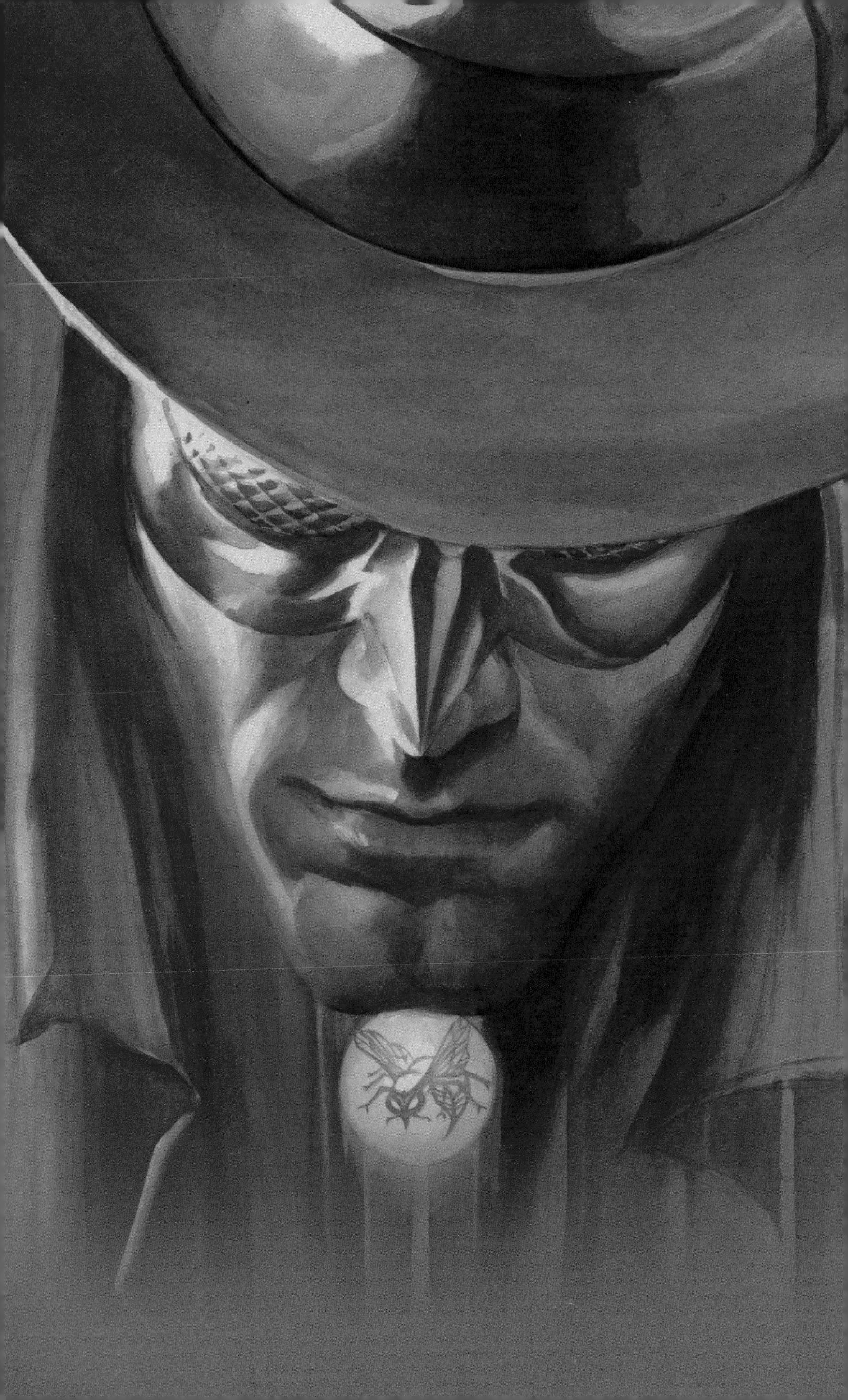

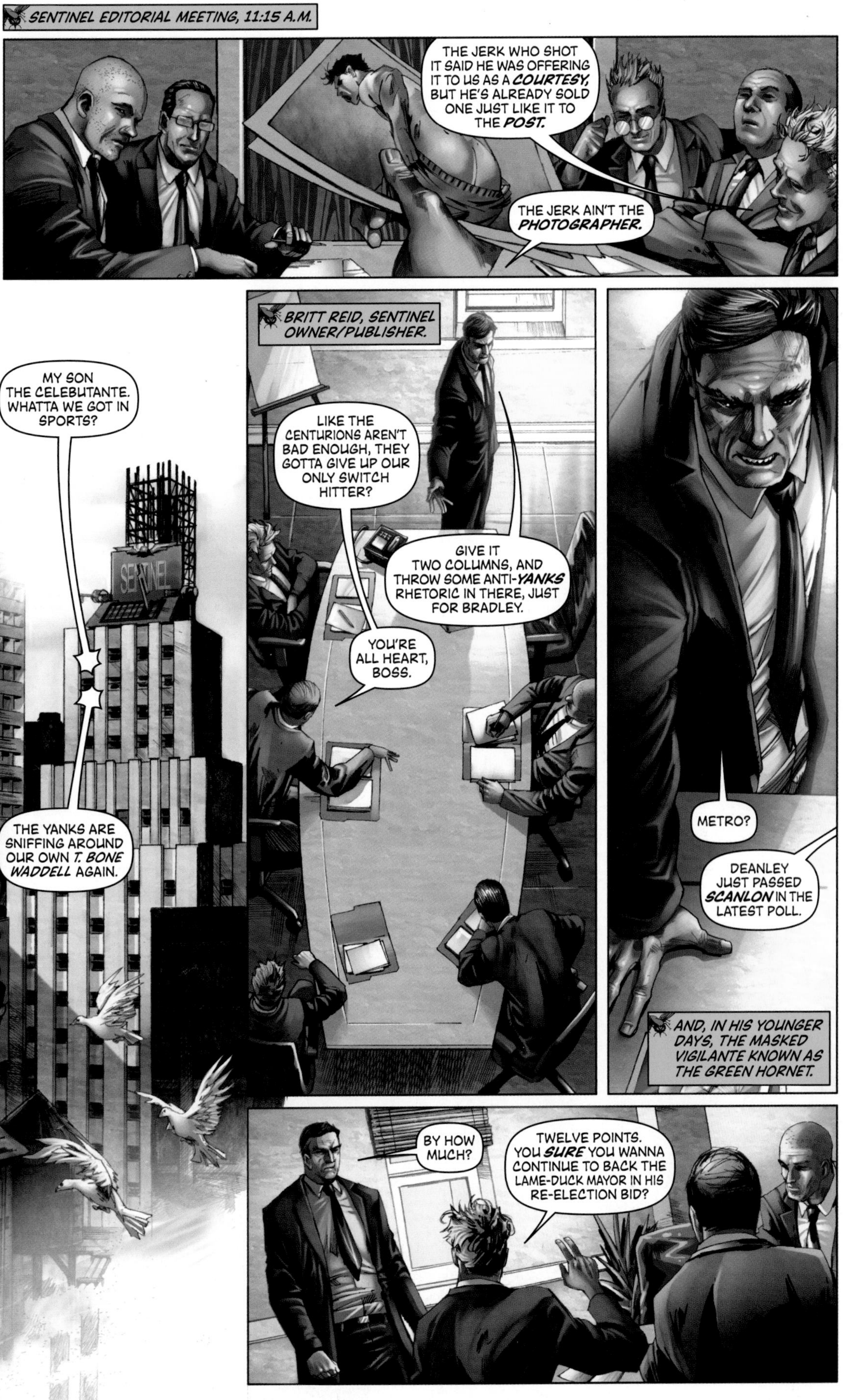
SENTINEL EDITORIAL MEETING, 11:15 A.M.
THE JERK WHO SHOT IT SAID HE WAS OFFERING IT TO US AS A *COURTESY,* BUT HE'S ALREADY SOLD ONE JUST LIKE IT TO THE *POST.*
THE JERK AIN'T THE *PHOTOGRAPHER.*
MY SON THE CELEBUTANTE. WHATTA WE GOT IN SPORTS?
THE YANKS ARE SNIFFING AROUND OUR OWN *T. BONE WADDELL* AGAIN.
SENTINEL
BRITT REID, SENTINEL OWNER/PUBLISHER.
LIKE THE CENTURIONS AREN'T BAD ENOUGH, THEY GOTTA GIVE UP OUR ONLY SWITCH HITTER?
GIVE IT TWO COLUMNS, AND THROW SOME ANTI-*YANKS* RHETORIC IN THERE, JUST FOR BRADLEY.
YOU'RE ALL HEART, BOSS.
METRO?
DEANLEY JUST PASSED *SCANLON* IN THE LATEST POLL.
AND, IN HIS YOUNGER DAYS, THE MASKED VIGILANTE KNOWN AS THE GREEN HORNET.
BY HOW MUCH?
TWELVE POINTS. YOU *SURE* YOU WANNA CONTINUE TO BACK THE LAME-DUCK MAYOR IN HIS RE-ELECTION BID?

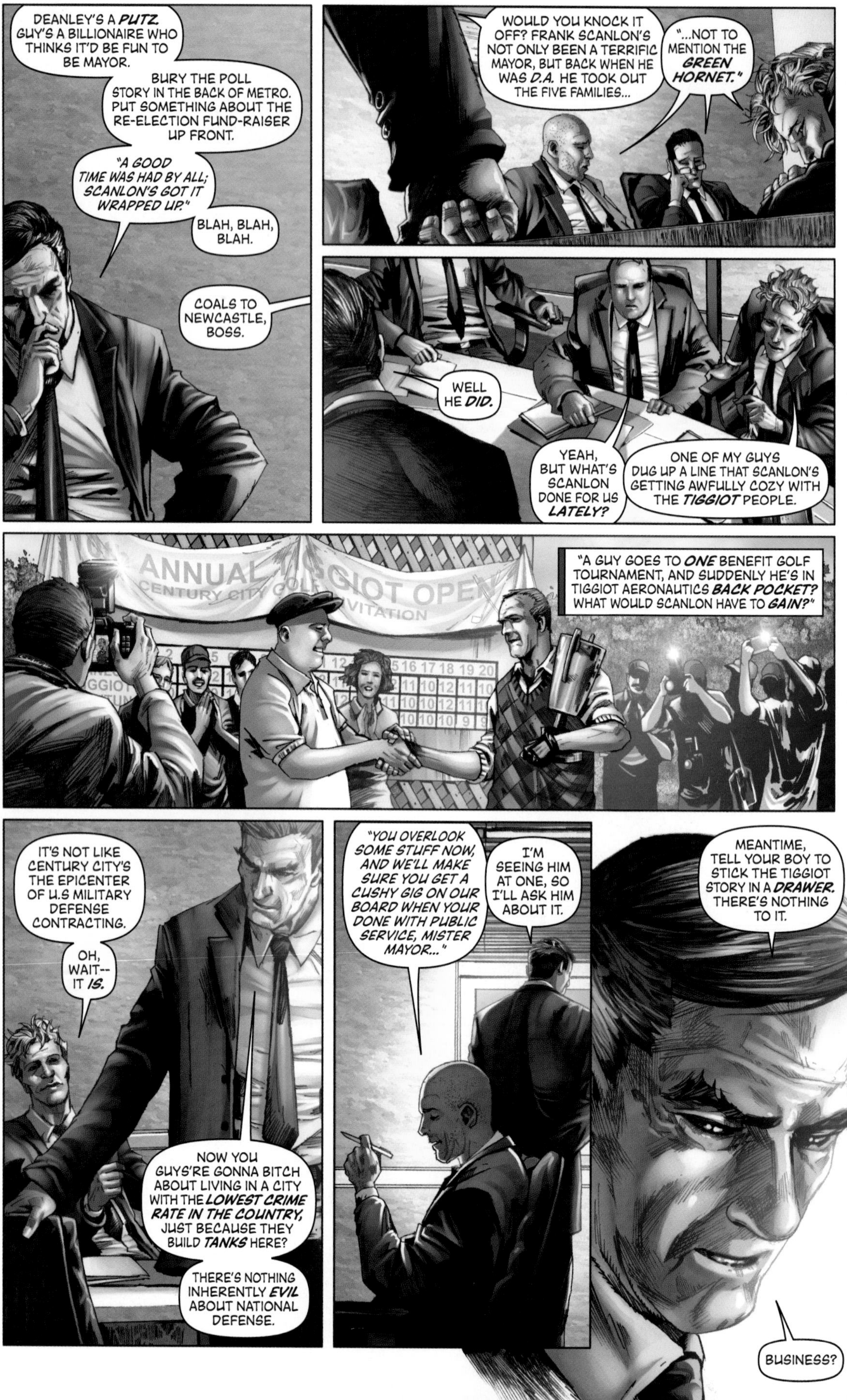

DEANLEY'S A PUTZ. GUY'S A BILLIONAIRE WHO THINKS IT'D BE FUN TO BE MAYOR.
BURY THE POLL STORY IN THE BACK OF METRO. PUT SOMETHING ABOUT THE RE-ELECTION FUND-RAISER UP FRONT.
"A GOOD TIME WAS HAD BY ALL; SCANLON'S GOT IT WRAPPED UP."
BLAH, BLAH, BLAH.
COALS TO NEWCASTLE, BOSS.
WOULD YOU KNOCK IT OFF? FRANK SCANLON'S NOT ONLY BEEN A TERRIFIC MAYOR, BUT BACK WHEN HE WAS D.A. HE TOOK OUT THE FIVE FAMILIES...
"...NOT TO MENTION THE GREEN HORNET."
WELL HE DID.
YEAH, BUT WHAT'S SCANLON DONE FOR US LATELY?
ONE OF MY GUYS DUG UP A LINE THAT SCANLON'S GETTING AWFULLY COZY WITH THE TIGGIOT PEOPLE.
"A GUY GOES TO ONE BENEFIT GOLF TOURNAMENT, AND SUDDENLY HE'S IN TIGGIOT AERONAUTICS BACK POCKET? WHAT WOULD SCANLON HAVE TO GAIN?"
ANNUAL TIGGIOT OPEN
CENTURY CITY GOLF INVITATION
IT'S NOT LIKE CENTURY CITY'S THE EPICENTER OF U.S MILITARY DEFENSE CONTRACTING.
OH, WAIT-- IT IS.
NOW YOU GUYS'RE GONNA BITCH ABOUT LIVING IN A CITY WITH THE LOWEST CRIME RATE IN THE COUNTRY, JUST BECAUSE THEY BUILD TANKS HERE?
THERE'S NOTHING INHERENTLY EVIL ABOUT NATIONAL DEFENSE.
"YOU OVERLOOK SOME STUFF NOW, AND WE'LL MAKE SURE YOU GET A CUSHY GIG ON OUR BOARD WHEN YOUR DONE WITH PUBLIC SERVICE, MISTER MAYOR..."
I'M SEEING HIM AT ONE, SO I'LL ASK HIM ABOUT IT.
MEANTIME, TELL YOUR BOY TO STICK THE TIGGIOT STORY IN A DRAWER. THERE'S NOTHING TO IT.
BUSINESS?

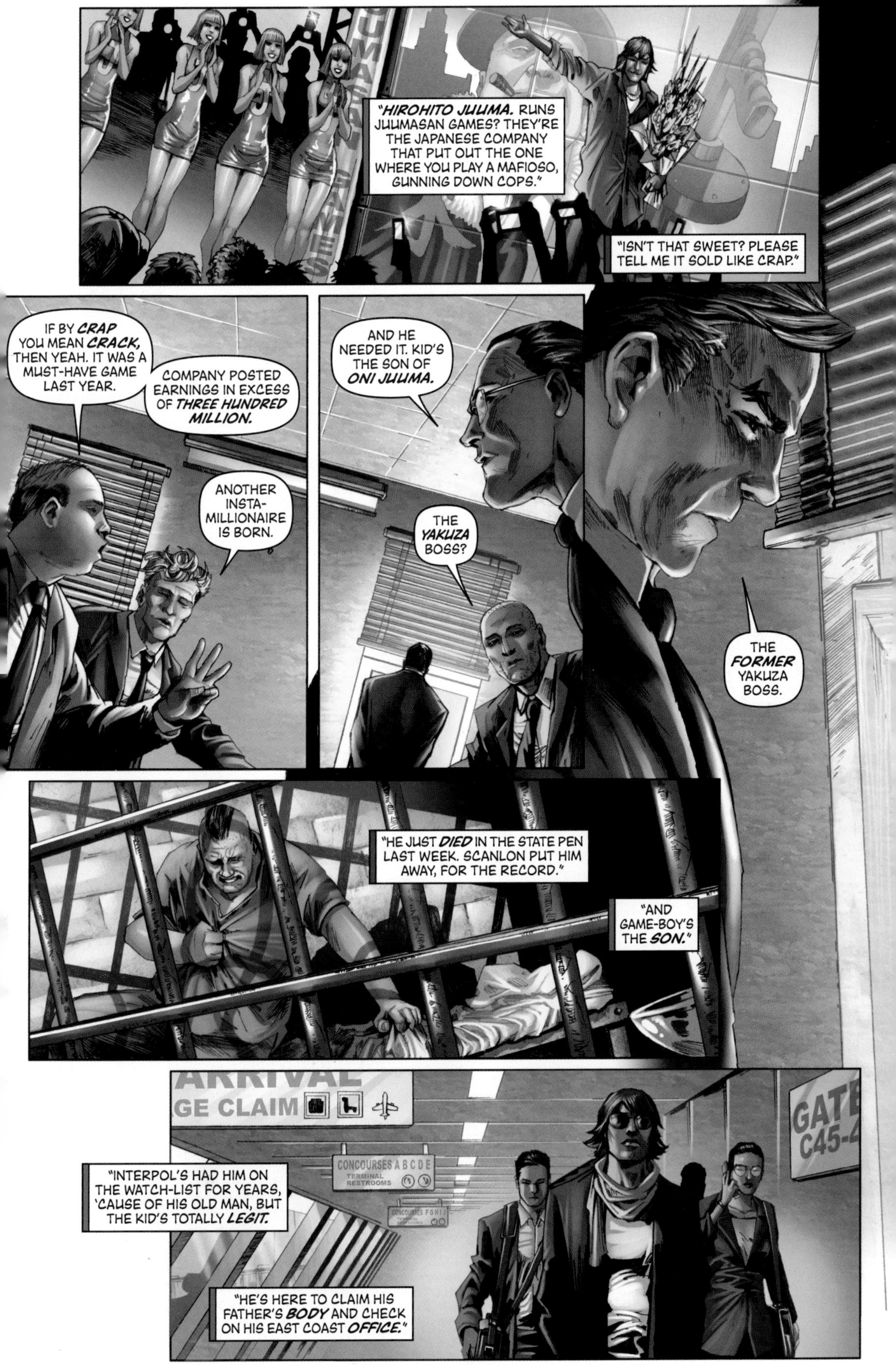

"HIROHITO JUUMA. RUNS JUUMASAN GAMES? THEY'RE THE JAPANESE COMPANY THAT PUT OUT THE ONE WHERE YOU PLAY A MAFIOSO, GUNNING DOWN COPS."
"ISN'T THAT SWEET? PLEASE TELL ME IT SOLD LIKE CRAP."
IF BY CRAP YOU MEAN CRACK, THEN YEAH. IT WAS A MUST-HAVE GAME LAST YEAR.
COMPANY POSTED EARNINGS IN EXCESS OF THREE HUNDRED MILLION.
ANOTHER INSTA-MILLIONAIRE IS BORN.
AND HE NEEDED IT. KID'S THE SON OF ONI JUUMA.
THE YAKUZA BOSS?
THE FORMER YAKUZA BOSS.
"HE JUST DIED IN THE STATE PEN LAST WEEK. SCANLON PUT HIM AWAY, FOR THE RECORD."
"AND GAME-BOY'S THE SON."
ARRIVAL
GE CLAIM
CONCOURSES A B C D E
TERMINAL
RESTROOMS
GATE
C45-4
"INTERPOL'S HAD HIM ON THE WATCH-LIST FOR YEARS, 'CAUSE OF HIS OLD MAN, BUT THE KID'S TOTALLY LEGIT.
"HE'S HERE TO CLAIM HIS FATHER'S BODY AND CHECK ON HIS EAST COAST OFFICE."

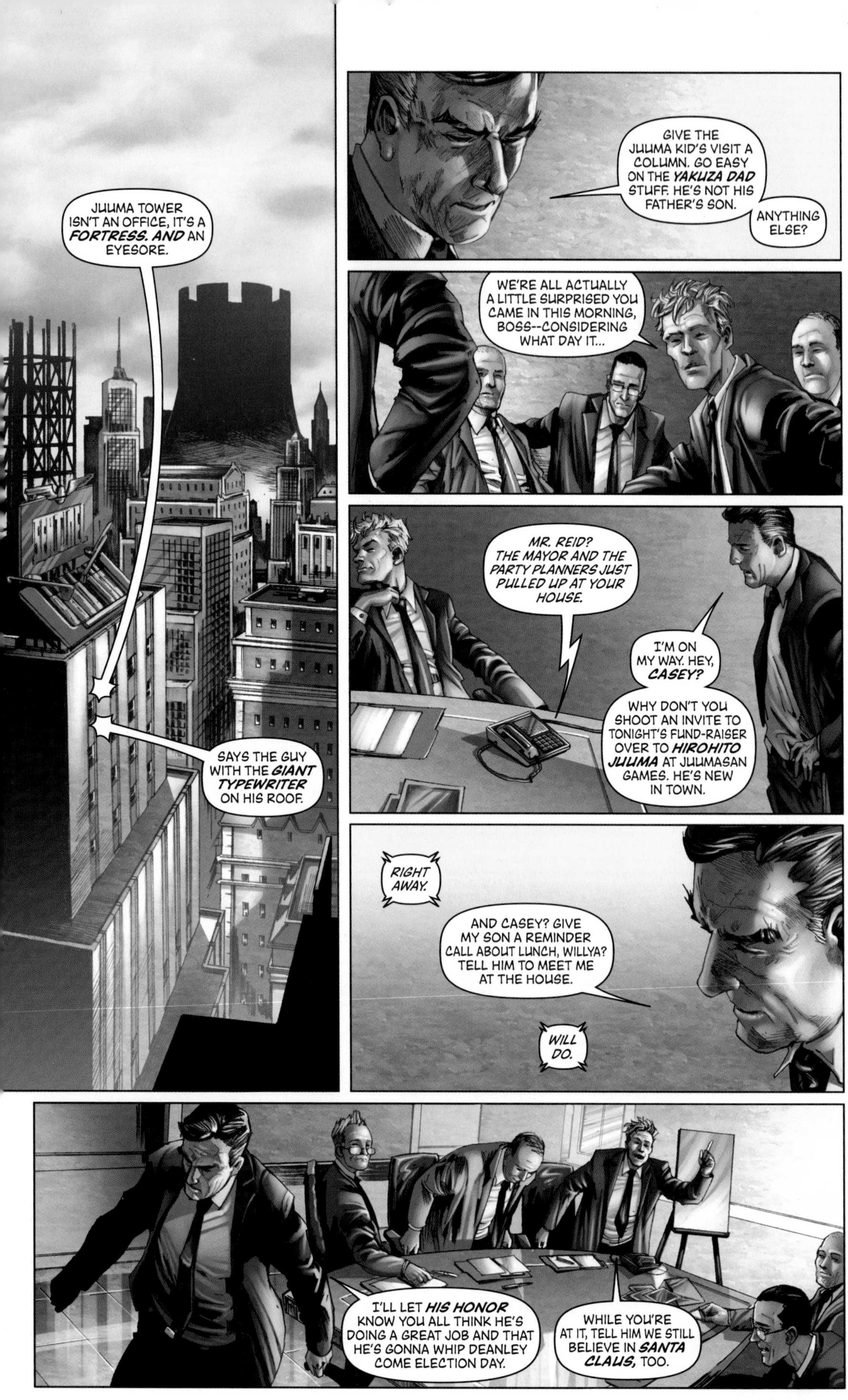

JUUMA TOWER ISN'T AN OFFICE, IT'S A ***FORTRESS. AND*** AN EYESORE.
SAYS THE GUY WITH THE ***GIANT TYPEWRITER*** ON HIS ROOF.
GIVE THE JUUMA KID'S VISIT A COLUMN. GO EASY ON THE ***YAKUZA DAD*** STUFF. HE'S NOT HIS FATHER'S SON.
ANYTHING ELSE?
WE'RE ALL ACTUALLY A LITTLE SURPRISED YOU CAME IN THIS MORNING, BOSS--CONSIDERING WHAT DAY IT...
MR. REID? THE MAYOR AND THE PARTY PLANNERS JUST PULLED UP AT YOUR HOUSE.
I'M ON MY WAY. HEY, ***CASEY?***
WHY DON'T YOU SHOOT AN INVITE TO TONIGHT'S FUND-RAISER OVER TO ***HIROHITO JUUMA*** AT JUUMASAN GAMES. HE'S NEW IN TOWN.
RIGHT AWAY.
AND CASEY? GIVE MY SON A REMINDER CALL ABOUT LUNCH, WILLYA? TELL HIM TO MEET ME AT THE HOUSE.
WILL DO.
I'LL LET ***HIS HONOR*** KNOW YOU ALL THINK HE'S DOING A GREAT JOB AND THAT HE'S GONNA WHIP DEANLEY COME ELECTION DAY.
WHILE YOU'RE AT IT, TELL HIM WE STILL BELIEVE IN ***SANTA CLAUS,*** TOO.

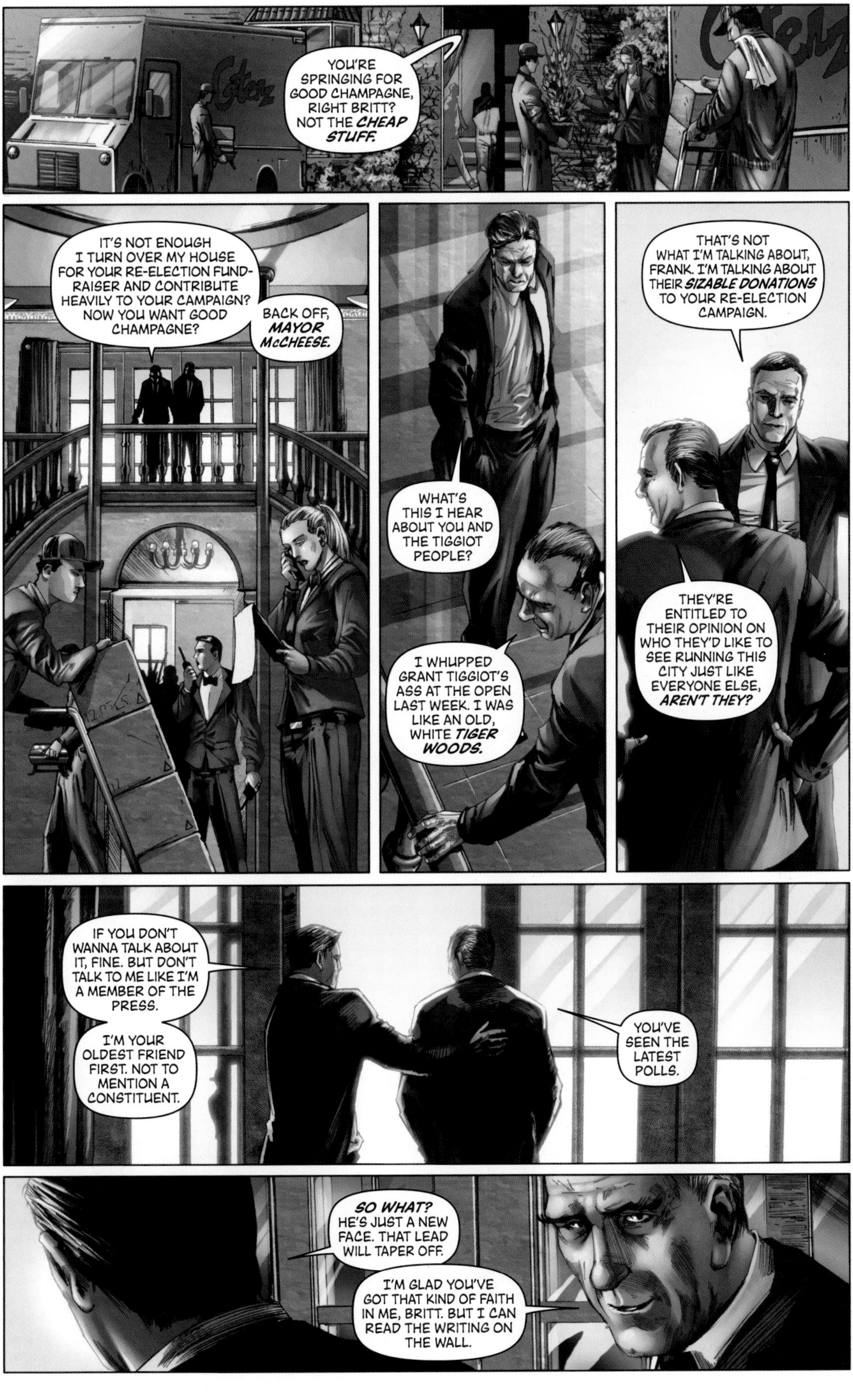
YOU'RE SPRINGING FOR GOOD CHAMPAGNE, RIGHT BRITT? NOT THE CHEAP STUFF.
IT'S NOT ENOUGH I TURN OVER MY HOUSE FOR YOUR RE-ELECTION FUND-RAISER AND CONTRIBUTE HEAVILY TO YOUR CAMPAIGN? NOW YOU WANT GOOD CHAMPAGNE?
BACK OFF, MAYOR McCHEESE.
WHAT'S THIS I HEAR ABOUT YOU AND THE TIGGIOT PEOPLE?
I WHUPPED GRANT TIGGIOT'S ASS AT THE OPEN LAST WEEK. I WAS LIKE AN OLD, WHITE TIGER WOODS.
THAT'S NOT WHAT I'M TALKING ABOUT, FRANK. I'M TALKING ABOUT THEIR SIZABLE DONATIONS TO YOUR RE-ELECTION CAMPAIGN.
THEY'RE ENTITLED TO THEIR OPINION ON WHO THEY'D LIKE TO SEE RUNNING THIS CITY JUST LIKE EVERYONE ELSE, AREN'T THEY?
IF YOU DON'T WANNA TALK ABOUT IT, FINE. BUT DON'T TALK TO ME LIKE I'M A MEMBER OF THE PRESS.
I'M YOUR OLDEST FRIEND FIRST. NOT TO MENTION A CONSTITUENT.
YOU'VE SEEN THE LATEST POLLS.
SO WHAT? HE'S JUST A NEW FACE. THAT LEAD WILL TAPER OFF.
I'M GLAD YOU'VE GOT THAT KIND OF FAITH IN ME, BRITT. BUT I CAN READ THE WRITING ON THE WALL.

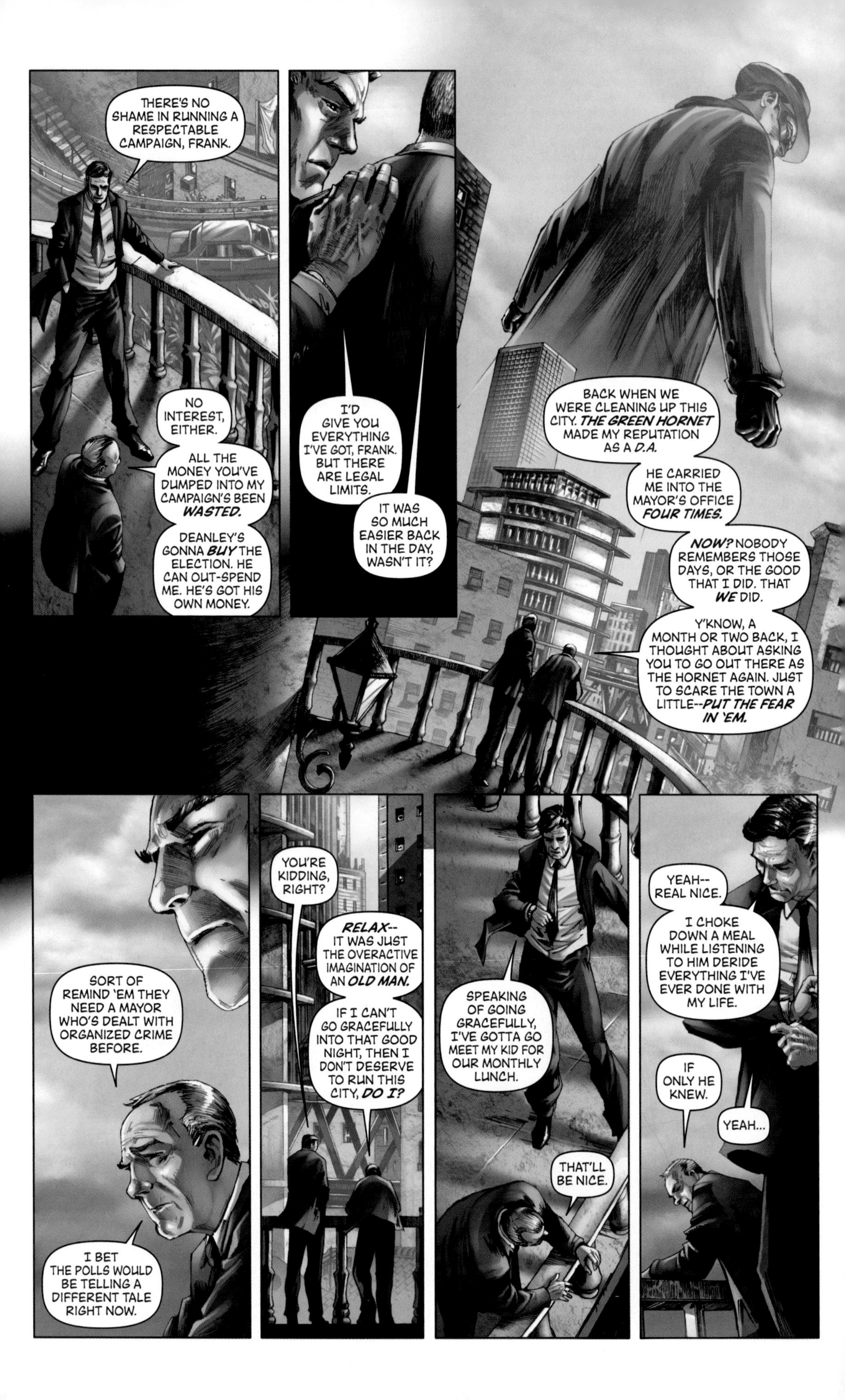

THERE'S NO SHAME IN RUNNING A RESPECTABLE CAMPAIGN, FRANK.
NO INTEREST, EITHER.
ALL THE MONEY YOU'VE DUMPED INTO MY CAMPAIGN'S BEEN WASTED.
DEANLEY'S GONNA BUY THE ELECTION. HE CAN OUT-SPEND ME. HE'S GOT HIS OWN MONEY.
I'D GIVE YOU EVERYTHING I'VE GOT, FRANK. BUT THERE ARE LEGAL LIMITS.
IT WAS SO MUCH EASIER BACK IN THE DAY, WASN'T IT?
BACK WHEN WE WERE CLEANING UP THIS CITY. THE GREEN HORNET MADE MY REPUTATION AS A D.A.
HE CARRIED ME INTO THE MAYOR'S OFFICE FOUR TIMES.
NOW? NOBODY REMEMBERS THOSE DAYS, OR THE GOOD THAT I DID. THAT WE DID.
Y'KNOW, A MONTH OR TWO BACK, I THOUGHT ABOUT ASKING YOU TO GO OUT THERE AS THE HORNET AGAIN. JUST TO SCARE THE TOWN A LITTLE--PUT THE FEAR IN 'EM.
SORT OF REMIND 'EM THEY NEED A MAYOR WHO'S DEALT WITH ORGANIZED CRIME BEFORE.
I BET THE POLLS WOULD BE TELLING A DIFFERENT TALE RIGHT NOW.
YOU'RE KIDDING, RIGHT?
RELAX--IT WAS JUST THE OVERACTIVE IMAGINATION OF AN OLD MAN.
IF I CAN'T GO GRACEFULLY INTO THAT GOOD NIGHT, THEN I DON'T DESERVE TO RUN THIS CITY, DO I?
SPEAKING OF GOING GRACEFULLY, I'VE GOTTA GO MEET MY KID FOR OUR MONTHLY LUNCH.
THAT'LL BE NICE.
YEAH--REAL NICE.
I CHOKE DOWN A MEAL WHILE LISTENING TO HIM DERIDE EVERYTHING I'VE EVER DONE WITH MY LIFE.
IF ONLY HE KNEW.
YEAH...

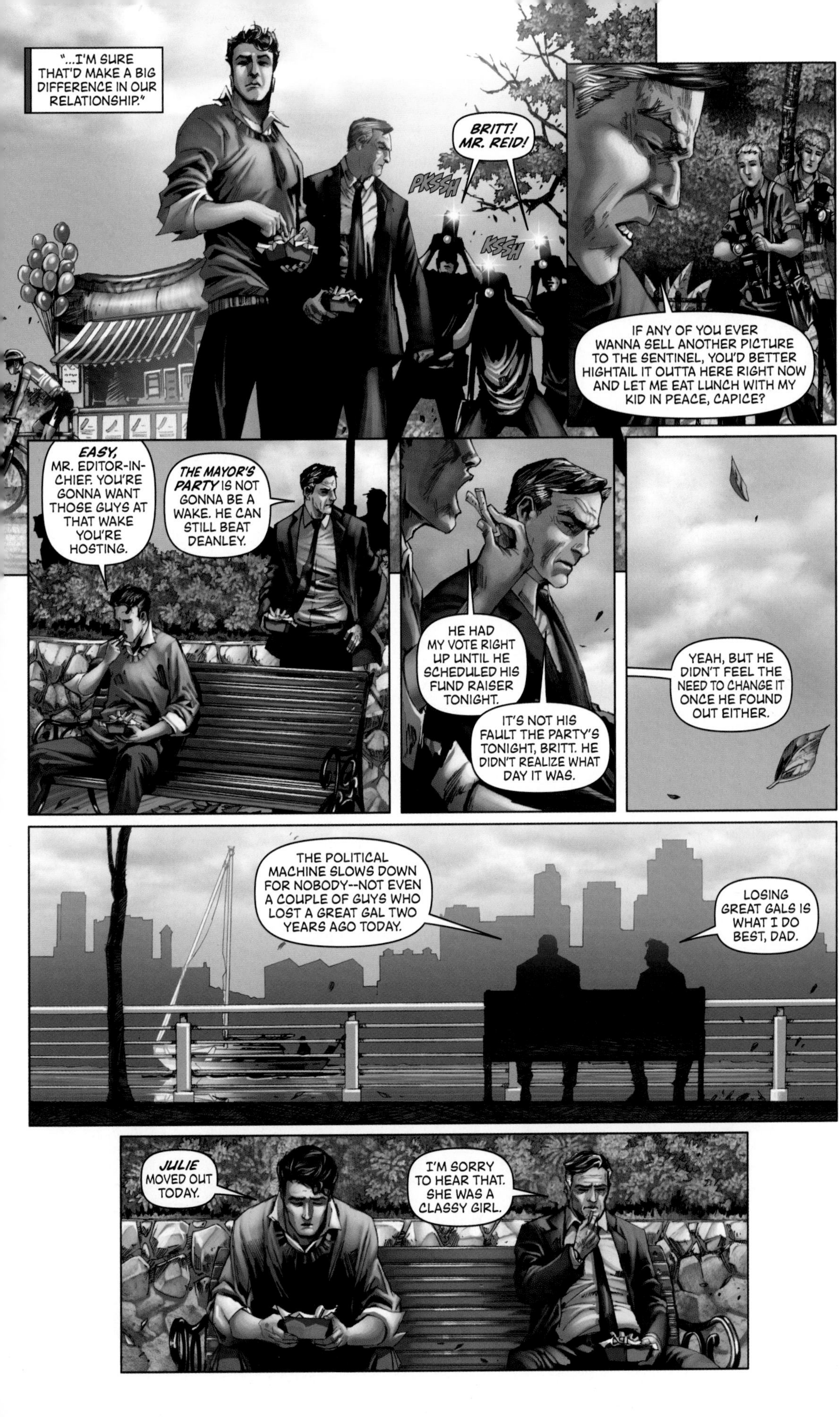
"...I'M SURE THAT'D MAKE A BIG DIFFERENCE IN OUR RELATIONSHIP."
BRITT! MR. REID!
PKSSH
KSSH
IF ANY OF YOU EVER WANNA SELL ANOTHER PICTURE TO THE SENTINEL, YOU'D BETTER HIGHTAIL IT OUTTA HERE RIGHT NOW AND LET ME EAT LUNCH WITH MY KID IN PEACE, CAPICE?
EASY, MR. EDITOR-IN-CHIEF. YOU'RE GONNA WANT THOSE GUYS AT THAT WAKE YOU'RE HOSTING.
THE MAYOR'S PARTY IS NOT GONNA BE A WAKE. HE CAN STILL BEAT DEANLEY.
HE HAD MY VOTE RIGHT UP UNTIL HE SCHEDULED HIS FUND RAISER TONIGHT.
IT'S NOT HIS FAULT THE PARTY'S TONIGHT, BRITT. HE DIDN'T REALIZE WHAT DAY IT WAS.
YEAH, BUT HE DIDN'T FEEL THE NEED TO CHANGE IT ONCE HE FOUND OUT EITHER.
THE POLITICAL MACHINE SLOWS DOWN FOR NOBODY--NOT EVEN A COUPLE OF GUYS WHO LOST A GREAT GAL TWO YEARS AGO TODAY.
LOSING GREAT GALS IS WHAT I DO BEST, DAD.
JULIE MOVED OUT TODAY.
I'M SORRY TO HEAR THAT. SHE WAS A CLASSY GIRL.

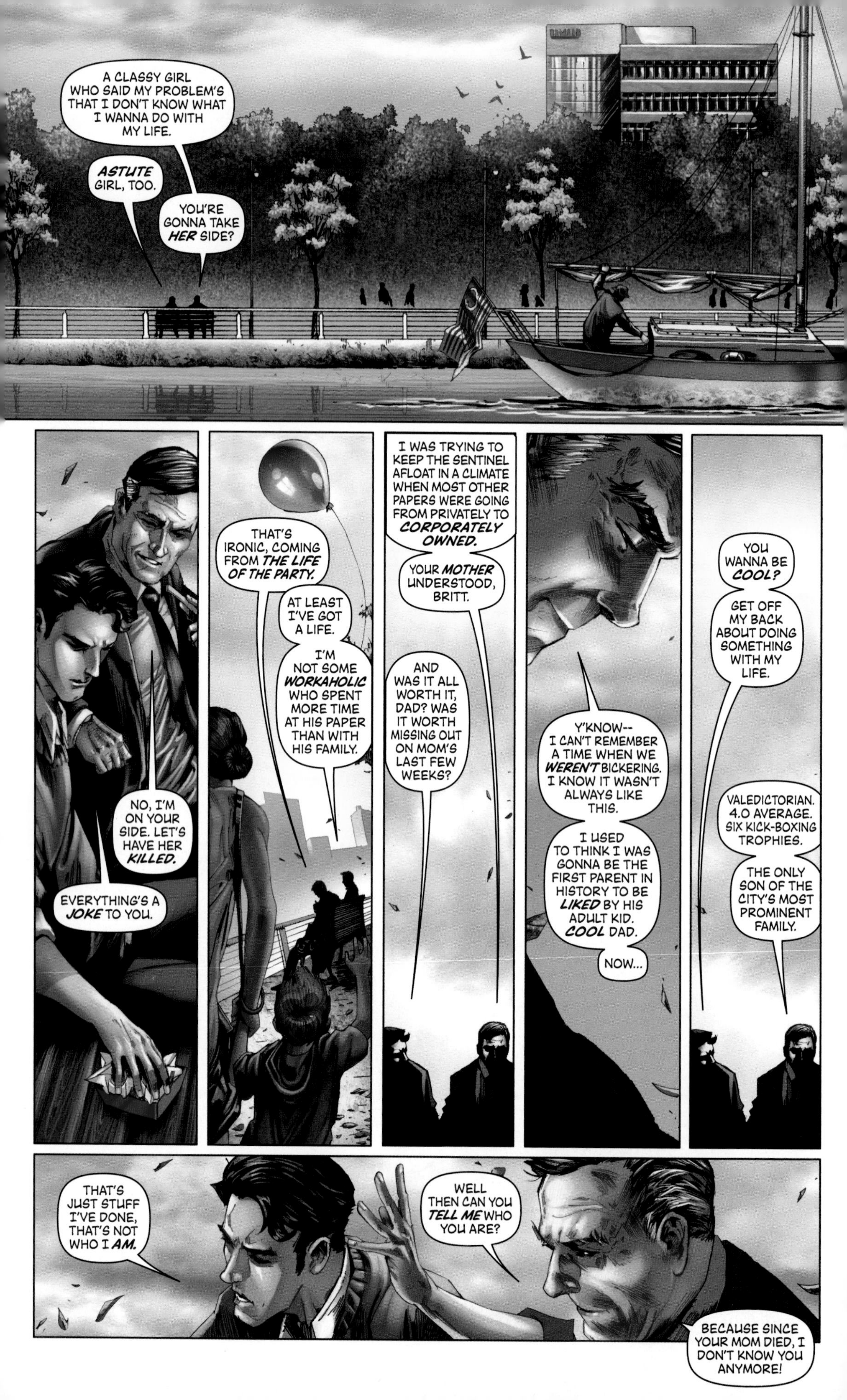
A CLASSY GIRL WHO SAID MY PROBLEM'S THAT I DON'T KNOW WHAT I WANNA DO WITH MY LIFE.
ASTUTE GIRL, TOO.
YOU'RE GONNA TAKE HER SIDE?
NO, I'M ON YOUR SIDE. LET'S HAVE HER KILLED.
EVERYTHING'S A JOKE TO YOU.
THAT'S IRONIC, COMING FROM THE LIFE OF THE PARTY.
AT LEAST I'VE GOT A LIFE.
I'M NOT SOME WORKAHOLIC WHO SPENT MORE TIME AT HIS PAPER THAN WITH HIS FAMILY.
I WAS TRYING TO KEEP THE SENTINEL AFLOAT IN A CLIMATE WHEN MOST OTHER PAPERS WERE GOING FROM PRIVATELY TO CORPORATELY OWNED.
YOUR MOTHER UNDERSTOOD, BRITT.
AND WAS IT ALL WORTH IT, DAD? WAS IT WORTH MISSING OUT ON MOM'S LAST FEW WEEKS?
Y'KNOW-- I CAN'T REMEMBER A TIME WHEN WE WEREN'T BICKERING. I KNOW IT WASN'T ALWAYS LIKE THIS.
I USED TO THINK I WAS GONNA BE THE FIRST PARENT IN HISTORY TO BE LIKED BY HIS ADULT KID. COOL DAD.
NOW...
YOU WANNA BE COOL?
GET OFF MY BACK ABOUT DOING SOMETHING WITH MY LIFE.
VALEDICTORIAN. 4.0 AVERAGE. SIX KICK-BOXING TROPHIES.
THE ONLY SON OF THE CITY'S MOST PROMINENT FAMILY.
THAT'S JUST STUFF I'VE DONE, THAT'S NOT WHO I AM.
WELL THEN CAN YOU TELL ME WHO YOU ARE?
BECAUSE SINCE YOUR MOM DIED, I DON'T KNOW YOU ANYMORE!

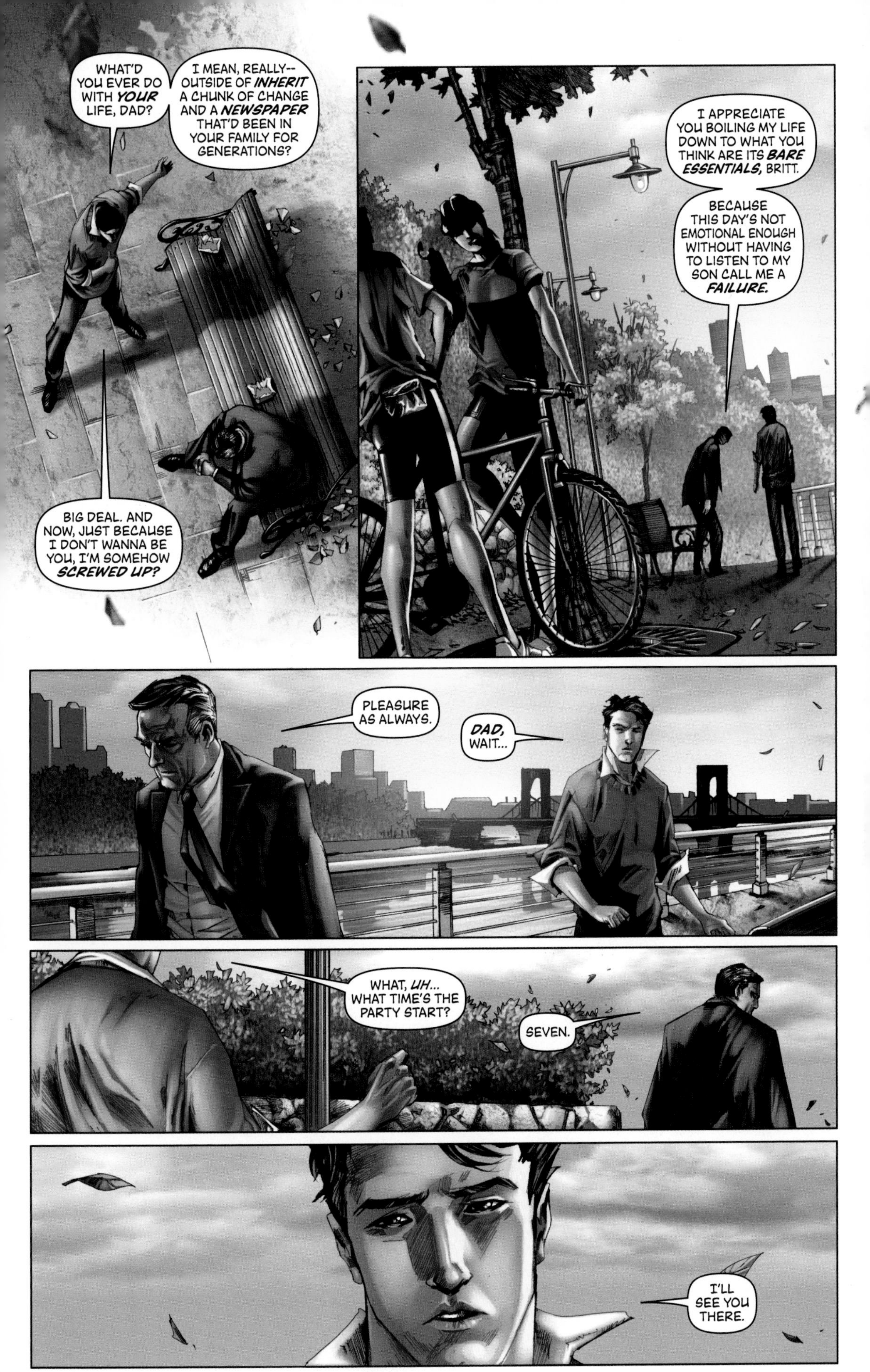
WHAT'D YOU EVER DO WITH YOUR LIFE, DAD?
I MEAN, REALLY-- OUTSIDE OF INHERIT A CHUNK OF CHANGE AND A NEWSPAPER THAT'D BEEN IN YOUR FAMILY FOR GENERATIONS?
BIG DEAL. AND NOW, JUST BECAUSE I DON'T WANNA BE YOU, I'M SOMEHOW SCREWED UP?
I APPRECIATE YOU BOILING MY LIFE DOWN TO WHAT YOU THINK ARE ITS BARE ESSENTIALS, BRITT.
BECAUSE THIS DAY'S NOT EMOTIONAL ENOUGH WITHOUT HAVING TO LISTEN TO MY SON CALL ME A FAILURE.
PLEASURE AS ALWAYS.
DAD, WAIT...
WHAT, UH... WHAT TIME'S THE PARTY START?
SEVEN.
I'LL SEE YOU THERE.

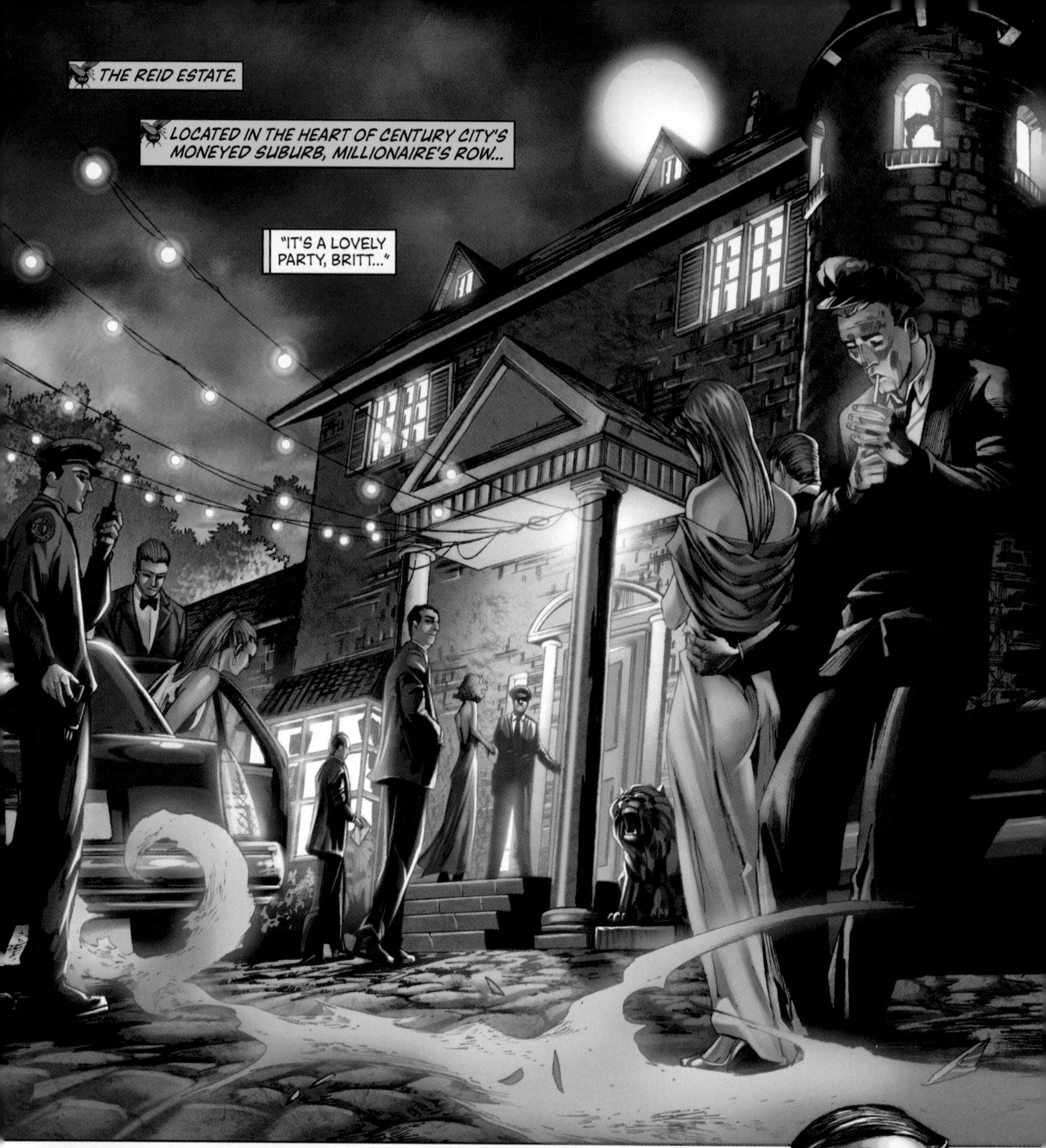
THE REID ESTATE.
LOCATED IN THE HEART OF CENTURY CITY'S MONEYED SUBURB, MILLIONAIRE'S ROW...
"IT'S A LOVELY PARTY, BRITT..."

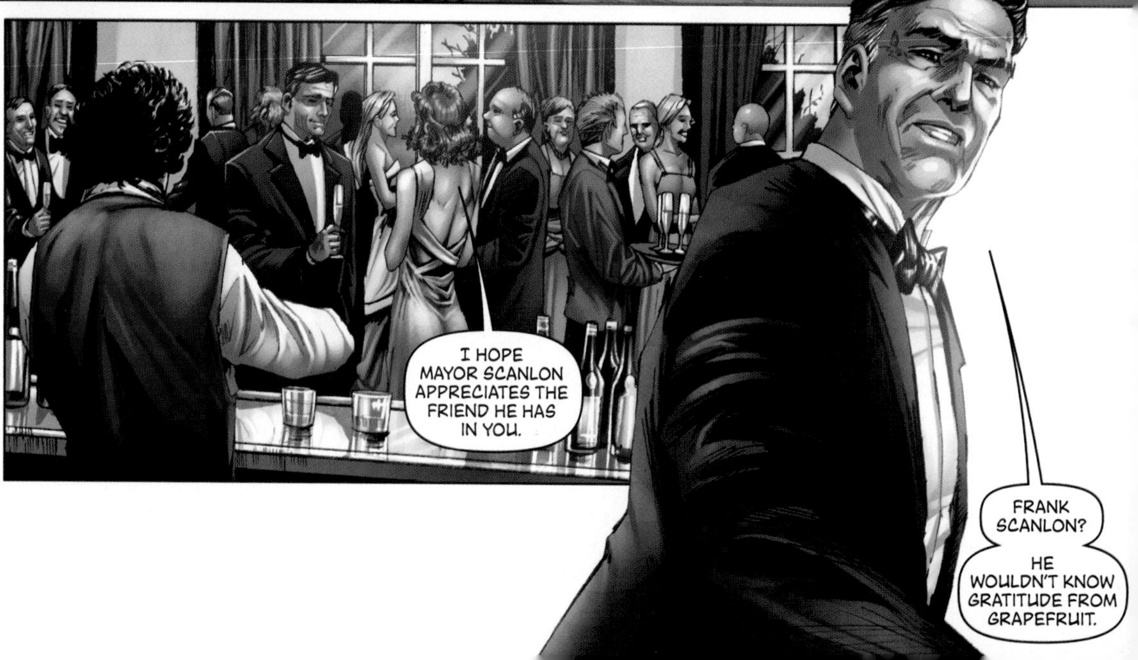
I HOPE MAYOR SCANLON APPRECIATES THE FRIEND HE HAS IN YOU.
FRANK SCANLON?
HE WOULDN'T KNOW GRATITUDE FROM GRAPEFRUIT.

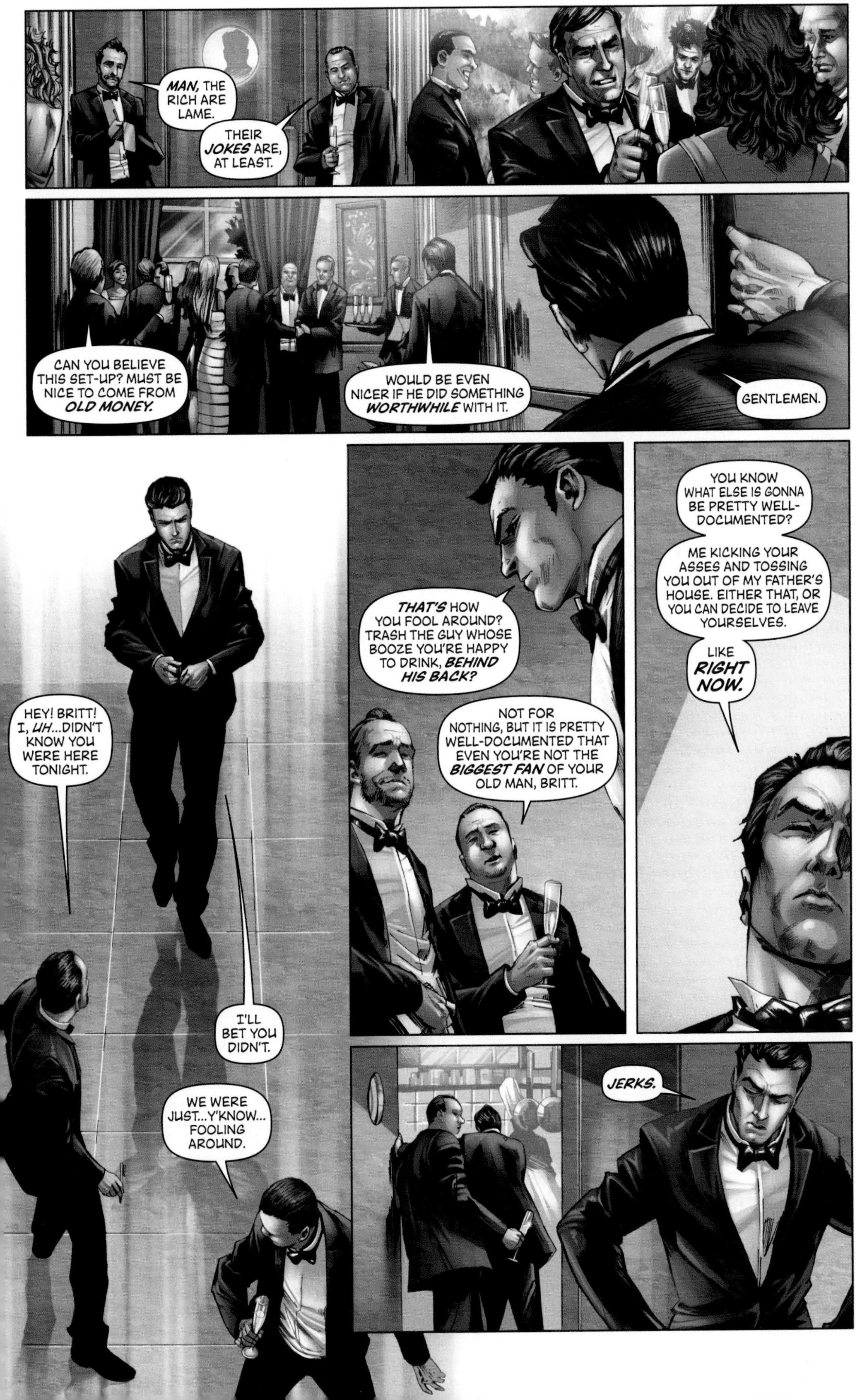
MAN, THE RICH ARE LAME.
THEIR JOKES ARE, AT LEAST.
CAN YOU BELIEVE THIS SET-UP? MUST BE NICE TO COME FROM OLD MONEY.
WOULD BE EVEN NICER IF HE DID SOMETHING WORTHWHILE WITH IT.
GENTLEMEN.
HEY! BRITT! I, UH...DIDN'T KNOW YOU WERE HERE TONIGHT.
I'LL BET YOU DIDN'T.
WE WERE JUST...Y'KNOW... FOOLING AROUND.
THAT'S HOW YOU FOOL AROUND? TRASH THE GUY WHOSE BOOZE YOU'RE HAPPY TO DRINK, BEHIND HIS BACK?
NOT FOR NOTHING, BUT IT IS PRETTY WELL-DOCUMENTED THAT EVEN YOU'RE NOT THE BIGGEST FAN OF YOUR OLD MAN, BRITT.
YOU KNOW WHAT ELSE IS GONNA BE PRETTY WELL-DOCUMENTED?
ME KICKING YOUR ASSES AND TOSSING YOU OUT OF MY FATHER'S HOUSE. EITHER THAT, OR YOU CAN DECIDE TO LEAVE YOURSELVES.
LIKE RIGHT NOW.
JERKS.

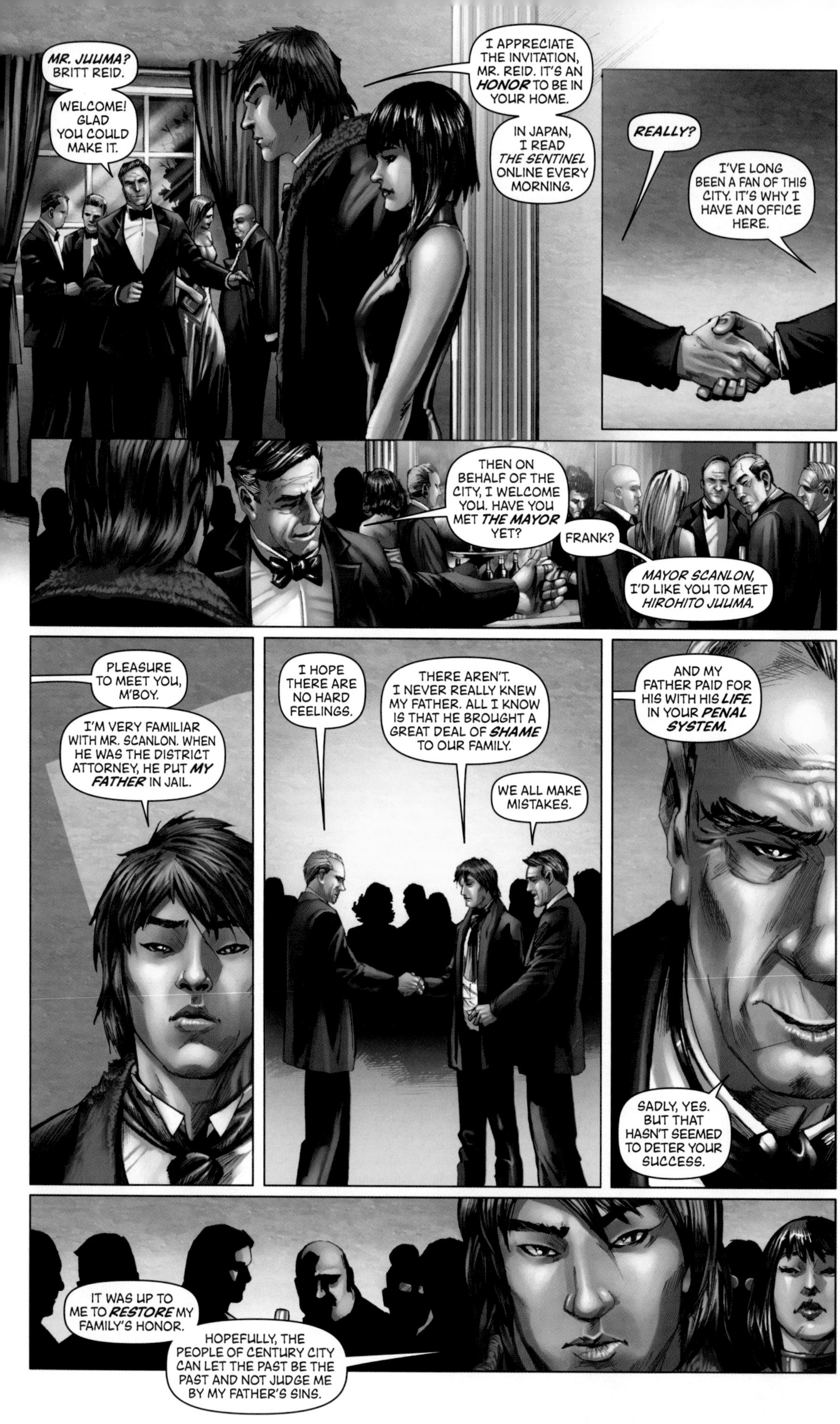
MR. JUUMA? BRITT REID.
WELCOME! GLAD YOU COULD MAKE IT.
I APPRECIATE THE INVITATION, MR. REID. IT'S AN HONOR TO BE IN YOUR HOME.
IN JAPAN, I READ THE SENTINEL ONLINE EVERY MORNING.
REALLY?
I'VE LONG BEEN A FAN OF THIS CITY. IT'S WHY I HAVE AN OFFICE HERE.
THEN ON BEHALF OF THE CITY, I WELCOME YOU. HAVE YOU MET THE MAYOR YET?
FRANK?
MAYOR SCANLON, I'D LIKE YOU TO MEET HIROHITO JUUMA.
PLEASURE TO MEET YOU, M'BOY.
I'M VERY FAMILIAR WITH MR. SCANLON. WHEN HE WAS THE DISTRICT ATTORNEY, HE PUT MY FATHER IN JAIL.
I HOPE THERE ARE NO HARD FEELINGS.
THERE AREN'T. I NEVER REALLY KNEW MY FATHER. ALL I KNOW IS THAT HE BROUGHT A GREAT DEAL OF SHAME TO OUR FAMILY.
WE ALL MAKE MISTAKES.
AND MY FATHER PAID FOR HIS WITH HIS LIFE. IN YOUR PENAL SYSTEM.
SADLY, YES. BUT THAT HASN'T SEEMED TO DETER YOUR SUCCESS.
IT WAS UP TO ME TO RESTORE MY FAMILY'S HONOR.
HOPEFULLY, THE PEOPLE OF CENTURY CITY CAN LET THE PAST BE THE PAST AND NOT JUDGE ME BY MY FATHER'S SINS.

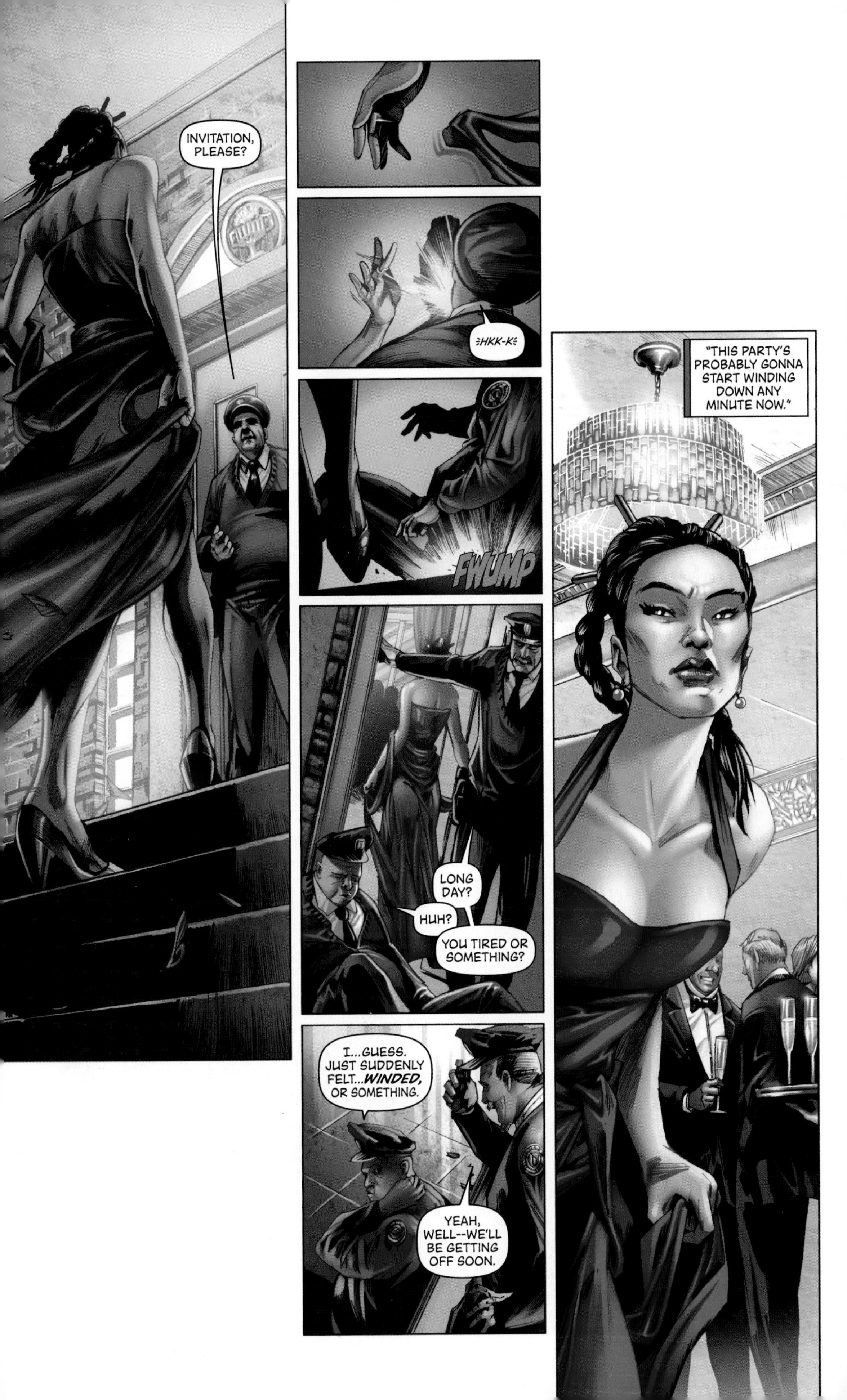
INVITATION, PLEASE?
HKK-K
FWUMP
LONG DAY?
HUH?
YOU TIRED OR SOMETHING?
I...GUESS. JUST SUDDENLY FELT...WINDED, OR SOMETHING.
YEAH, WELL--WE'LL BE GETTING OFF SOON.
"THIS PARTY'S PROBABLY GONNA START WINDING DOWN ANY MINUTE NOW."

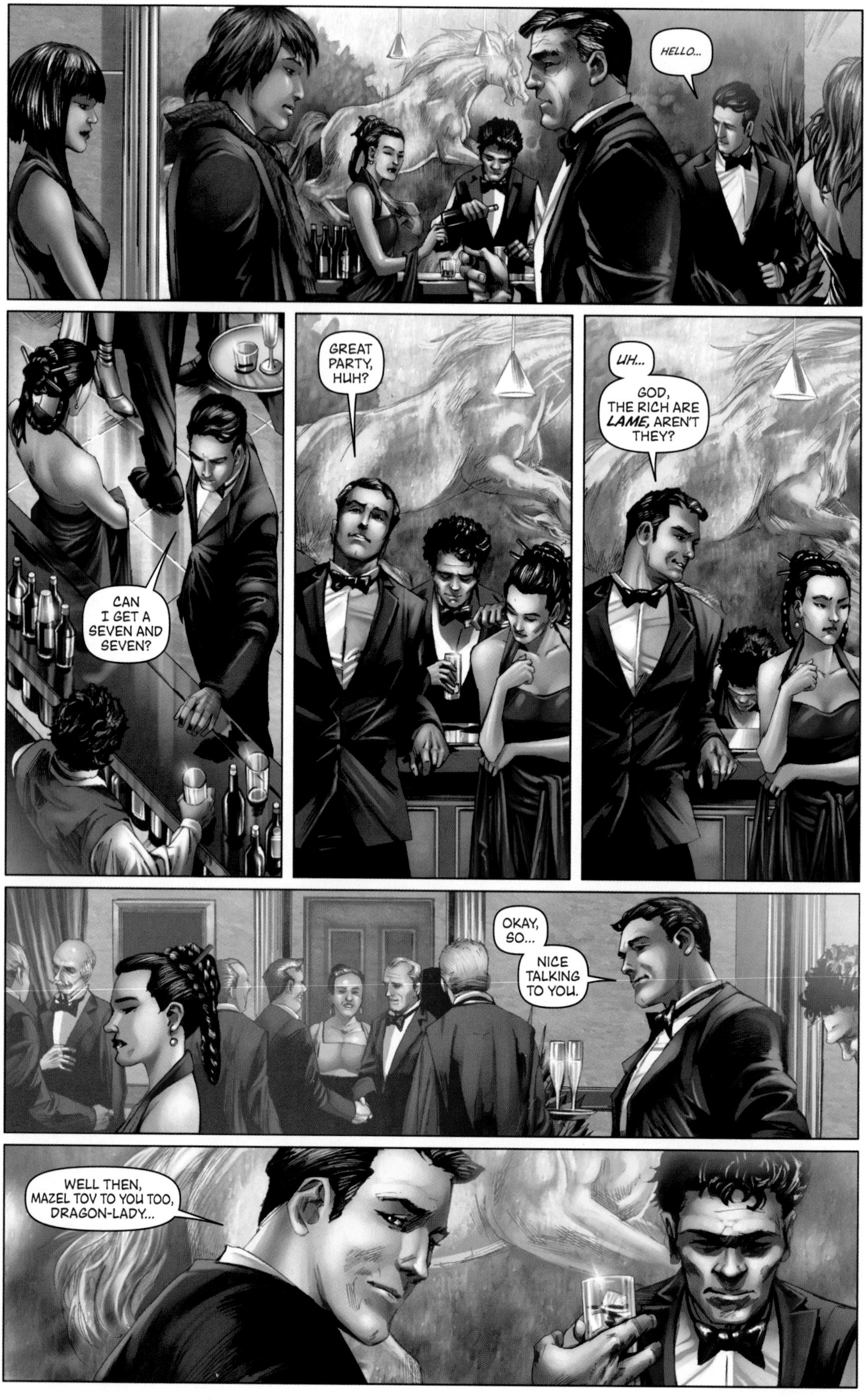
HELLO...
CAN I GET A SEVEN AND SEVEN?
GREAT PARTY, HUH?
UH...
GOD, THE RICH ARE *LAME,* AREN'T THEY?
OKAY, SO...
NICE TALKING TO YOU.
WELL THEN, MAZEL TOV TO YOU TOO, DRAGON-LADY...

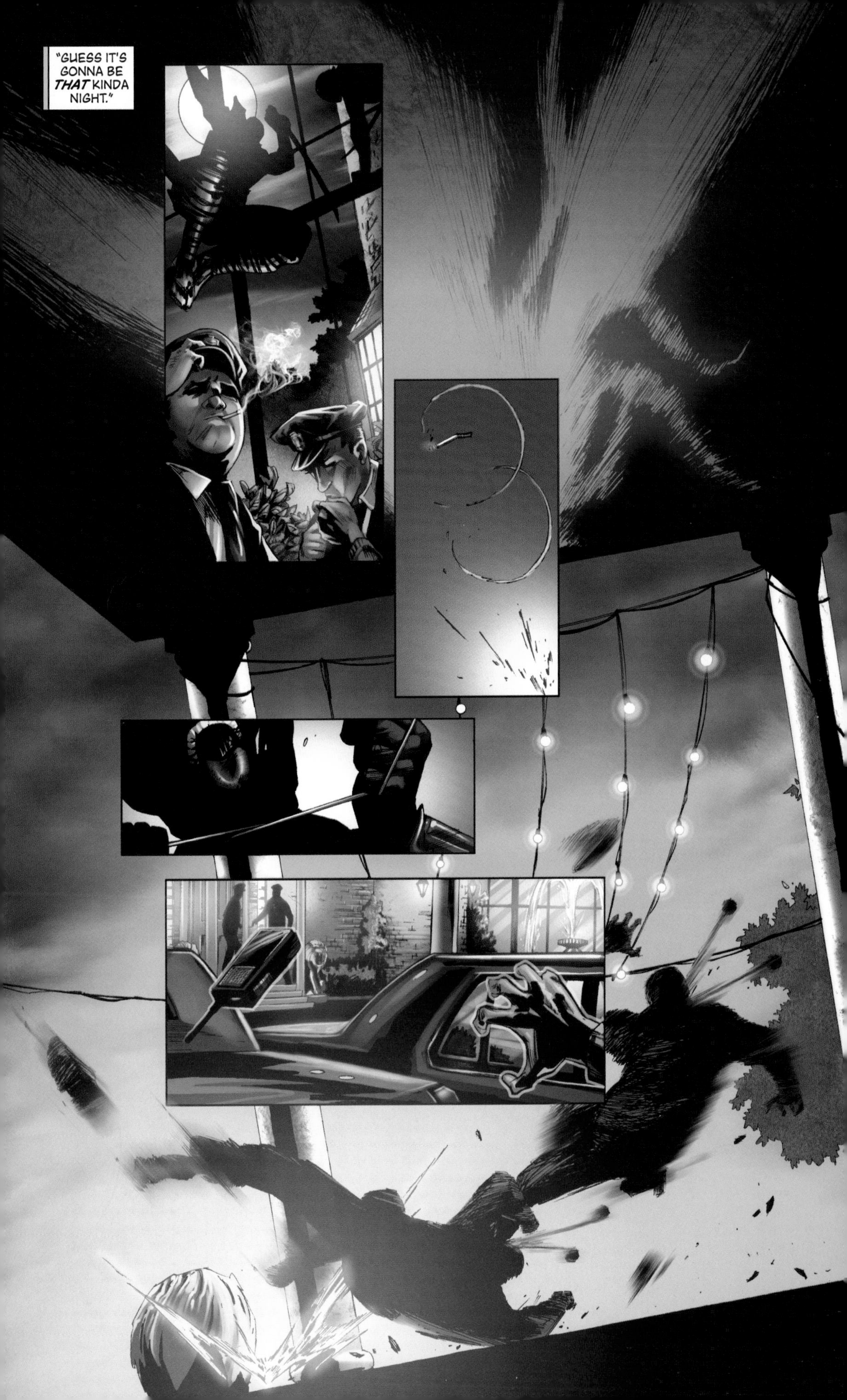
"GUESS IT'S GONNA BE THAT KINDA NIGHT."

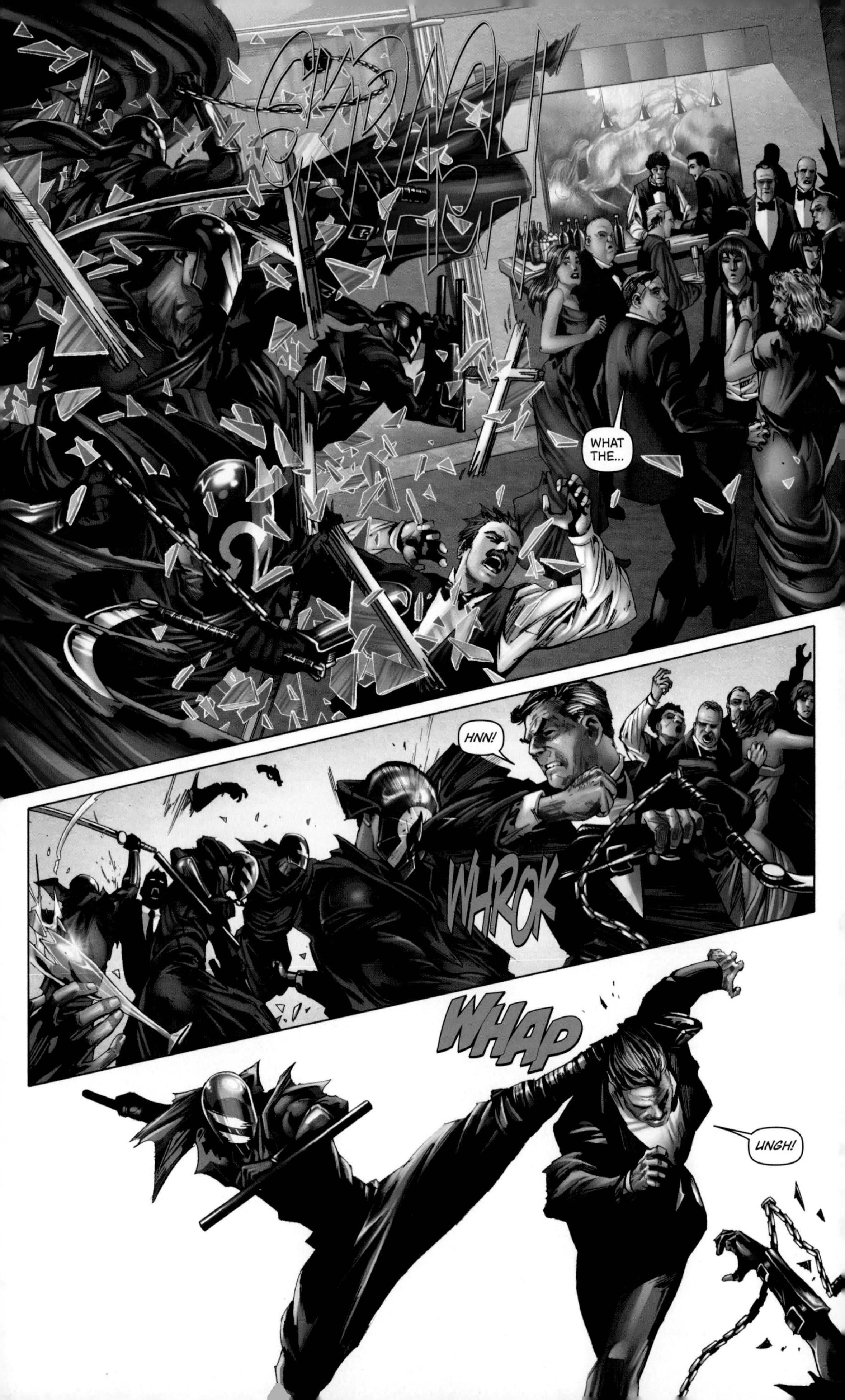
WHAT THE...
HNN!
WHROK
WHAP
UNGH!

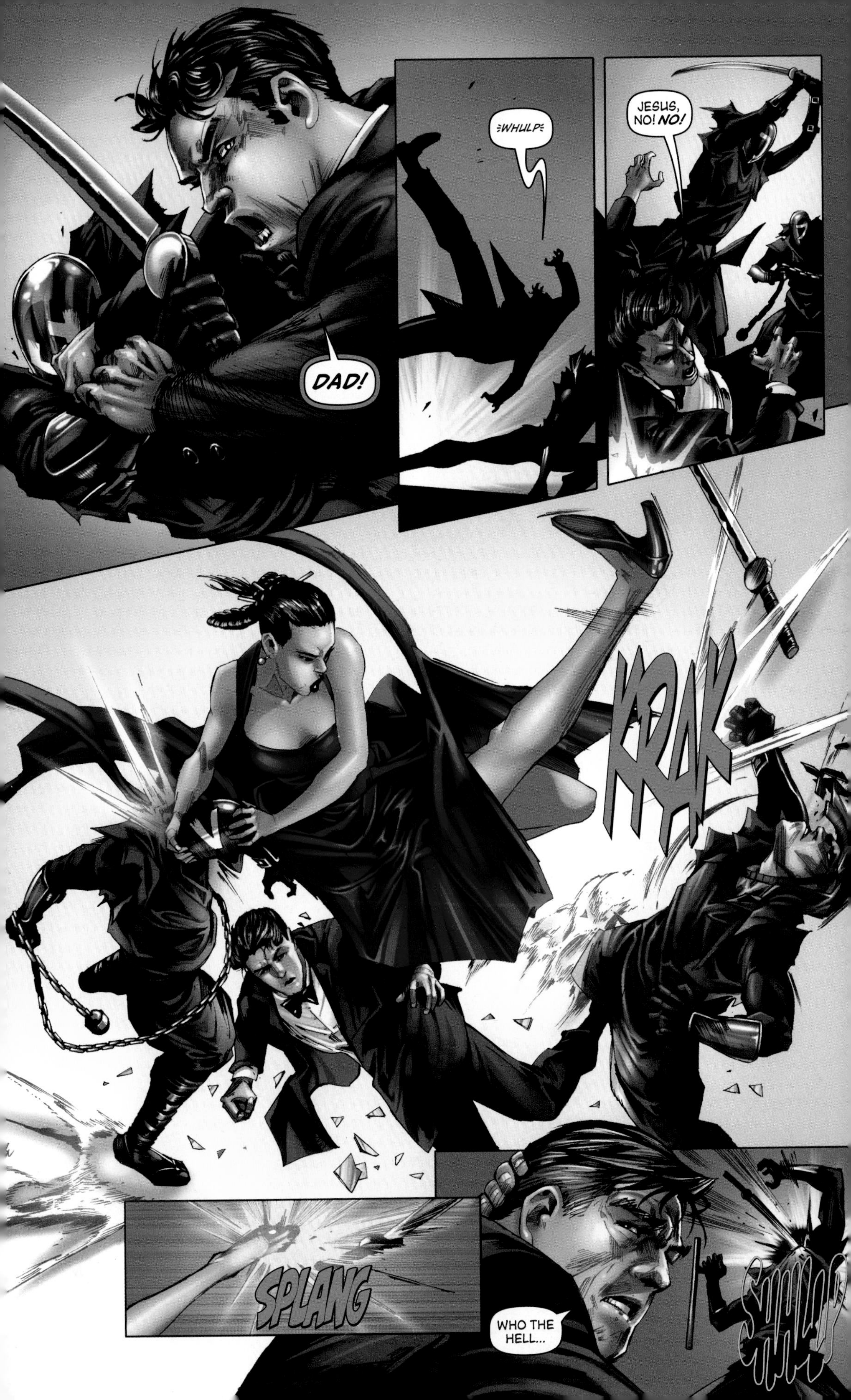
DAD!
WHULP
JESUS, NO! NO!
KRAK
SPLANG
WHO THE HELL...

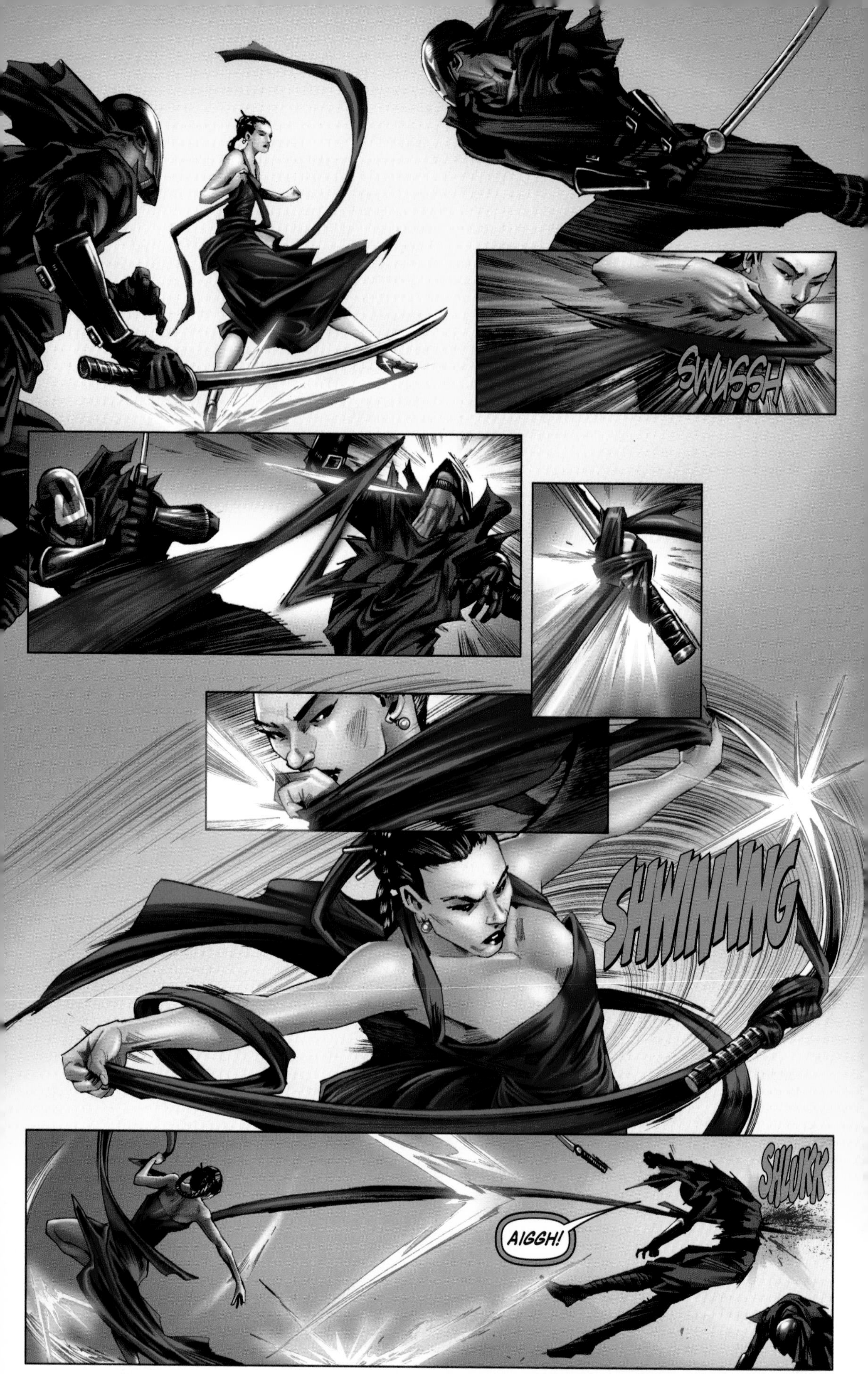
SWUSSH
SHWINNNG
AIGGH!
SHLUKK

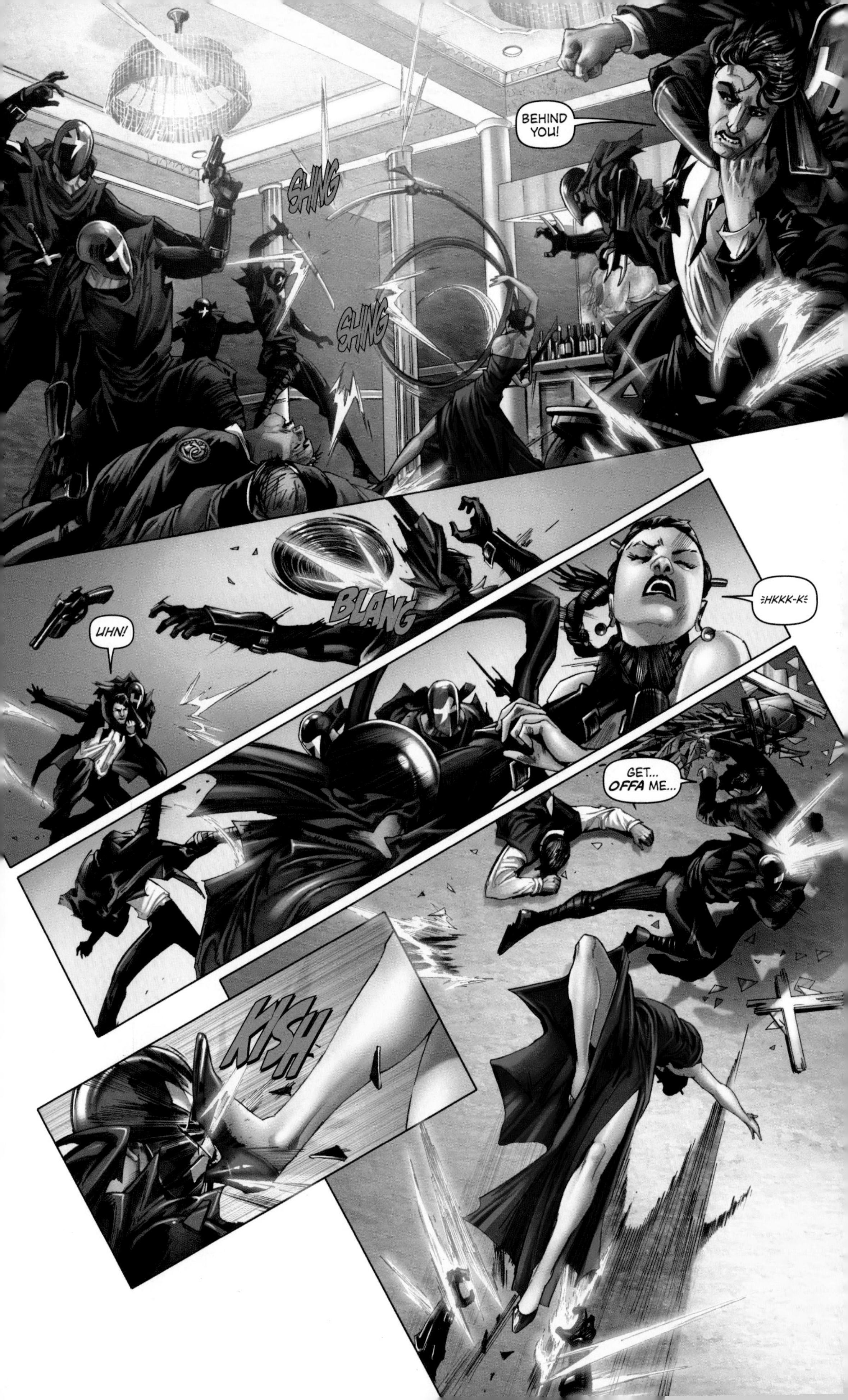

BEHIND YOU!
SHING
SHING
BLANG
UHN!
HKKK-K
GET... OFFA ME...
KISH

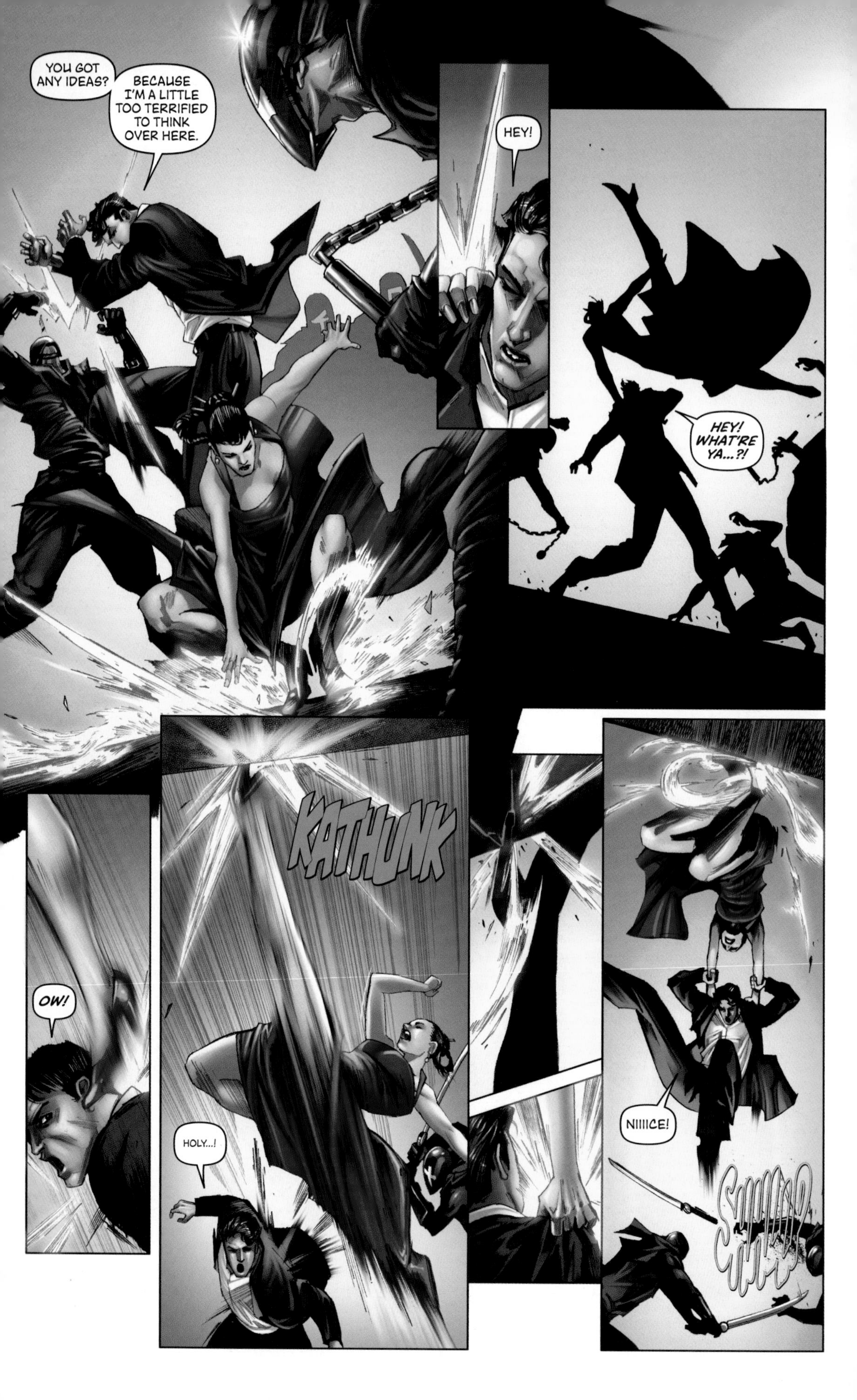
YOU GOT ANY IDEAS?
BECAUSE I'M A LITTLE TOO TERRIFIED TO THINK OVER HERE.
HEY!
HEY! WHAT'RE YA...?!
OW!
KATHUNK
HOLY...!
NIIIICE!

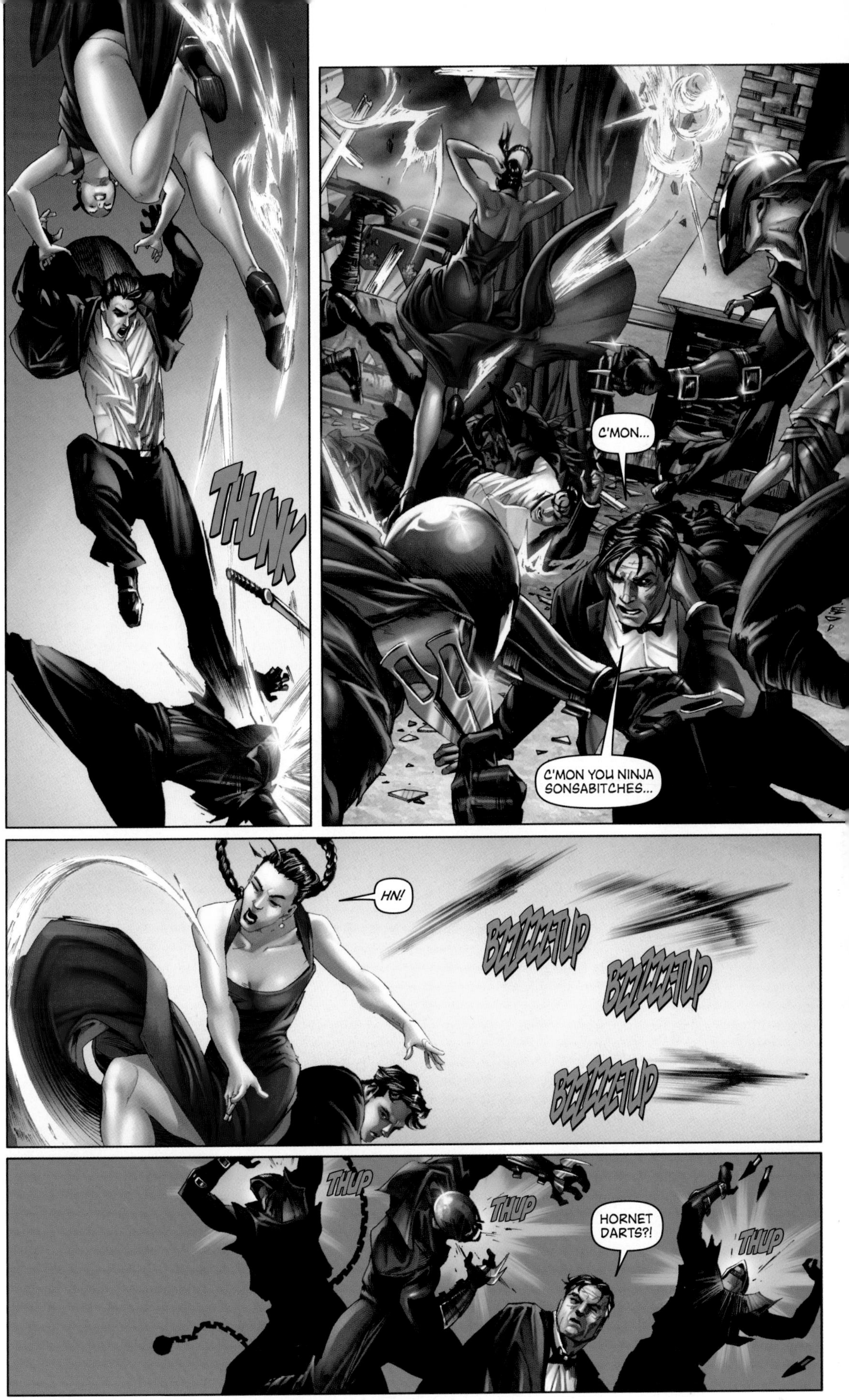
THUNK
C'MON...
C'MON YOU NINJA SONSABITCHES...
HN!
BZZZZZTUP
BZZZZZTUP
BZZZZZTUP
THUP
THUP
HORNET DARTS?!
THUP

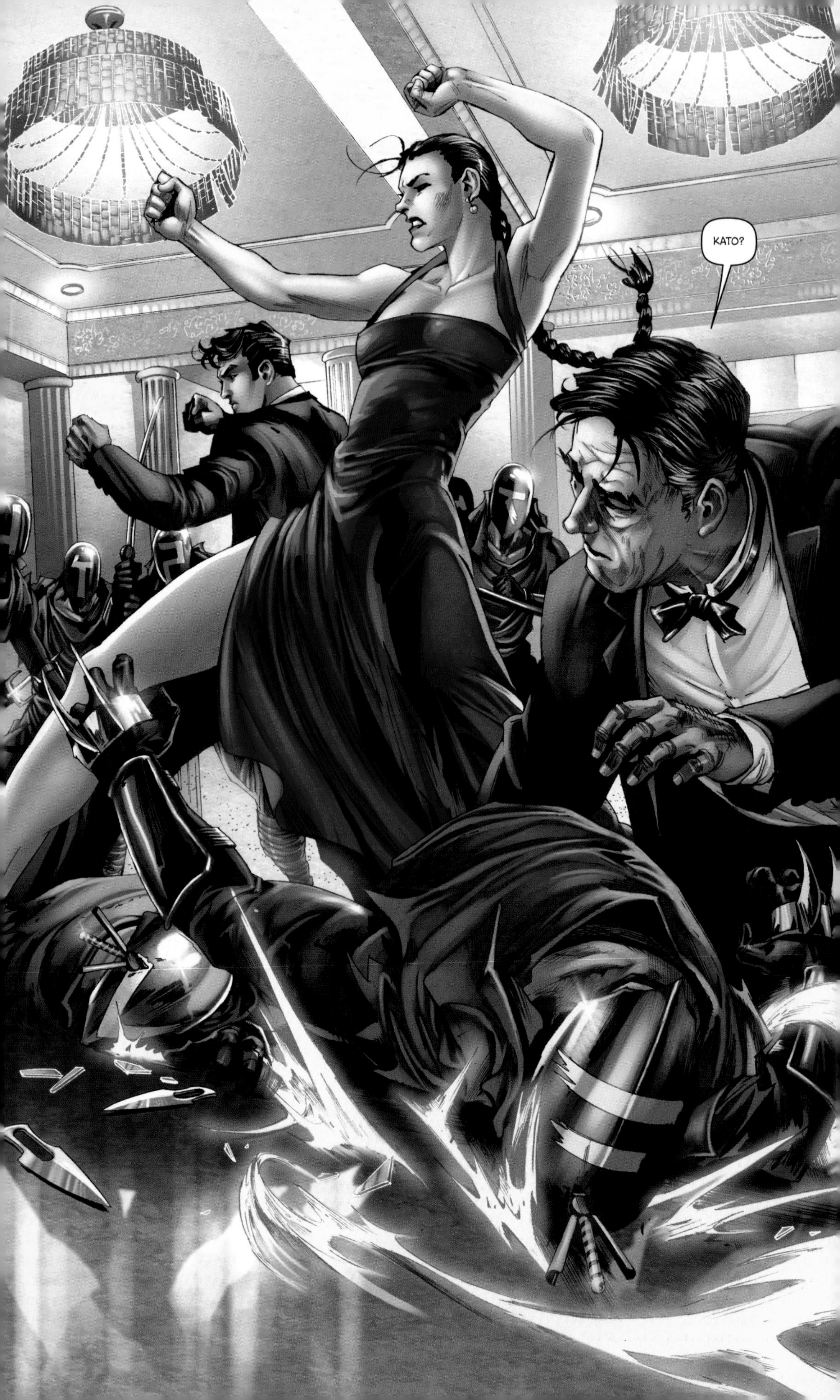
KATO?

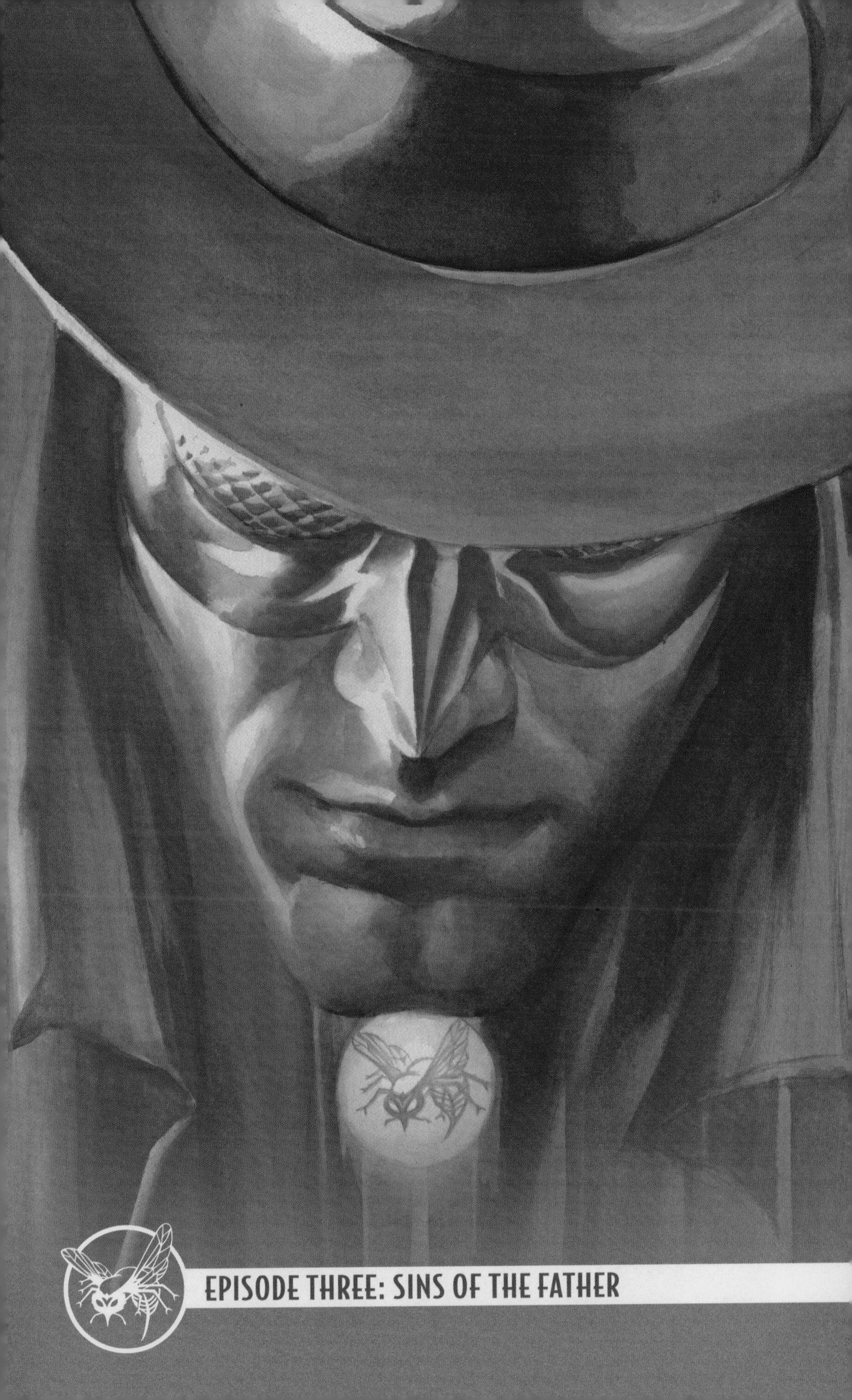

EPISODE THREE: SINS OF THE FATHER

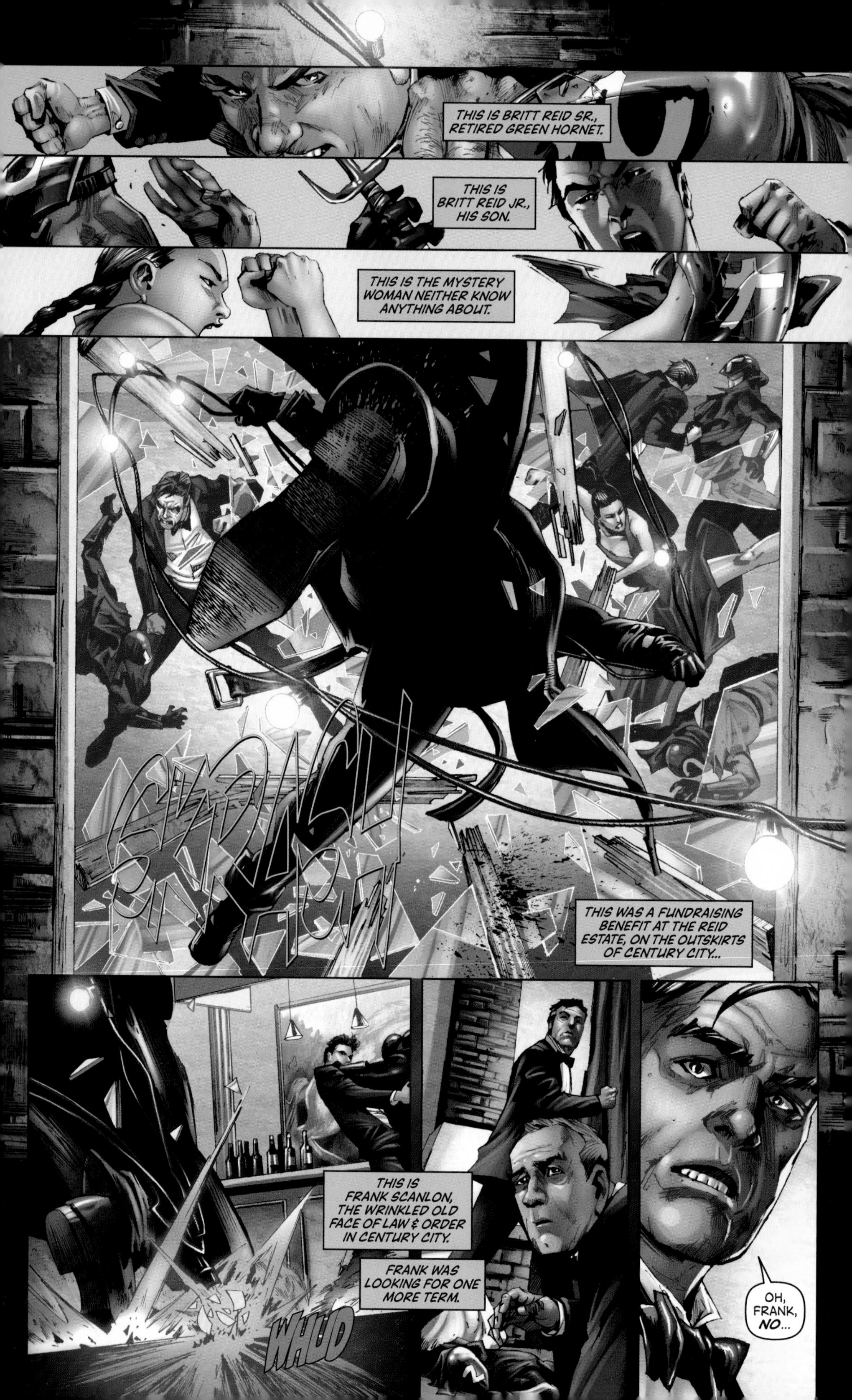
THIS IS BRITT REID SR., RETIRED GREEN HORNET.
THIS IS BRITT REID JR., HIS SON.
THIS IS THE MYSTERY WOMAN NEITHER KNOW ANYTHING ABOUT.
THIS WAS A FUNDRAISING BENEFIT AT THE REID ESTATE, ON THE OUTSKIRTS OF CENTURY CITY...
THIS IS FRANK SCANLON, THE WRINKLED OLD FACE OF LAW & ORDER IN CENTURY CITY.
FRANK WAS LOOKING FOR ONE MORE TERM.
WHUD
OH, FRANK, NO...

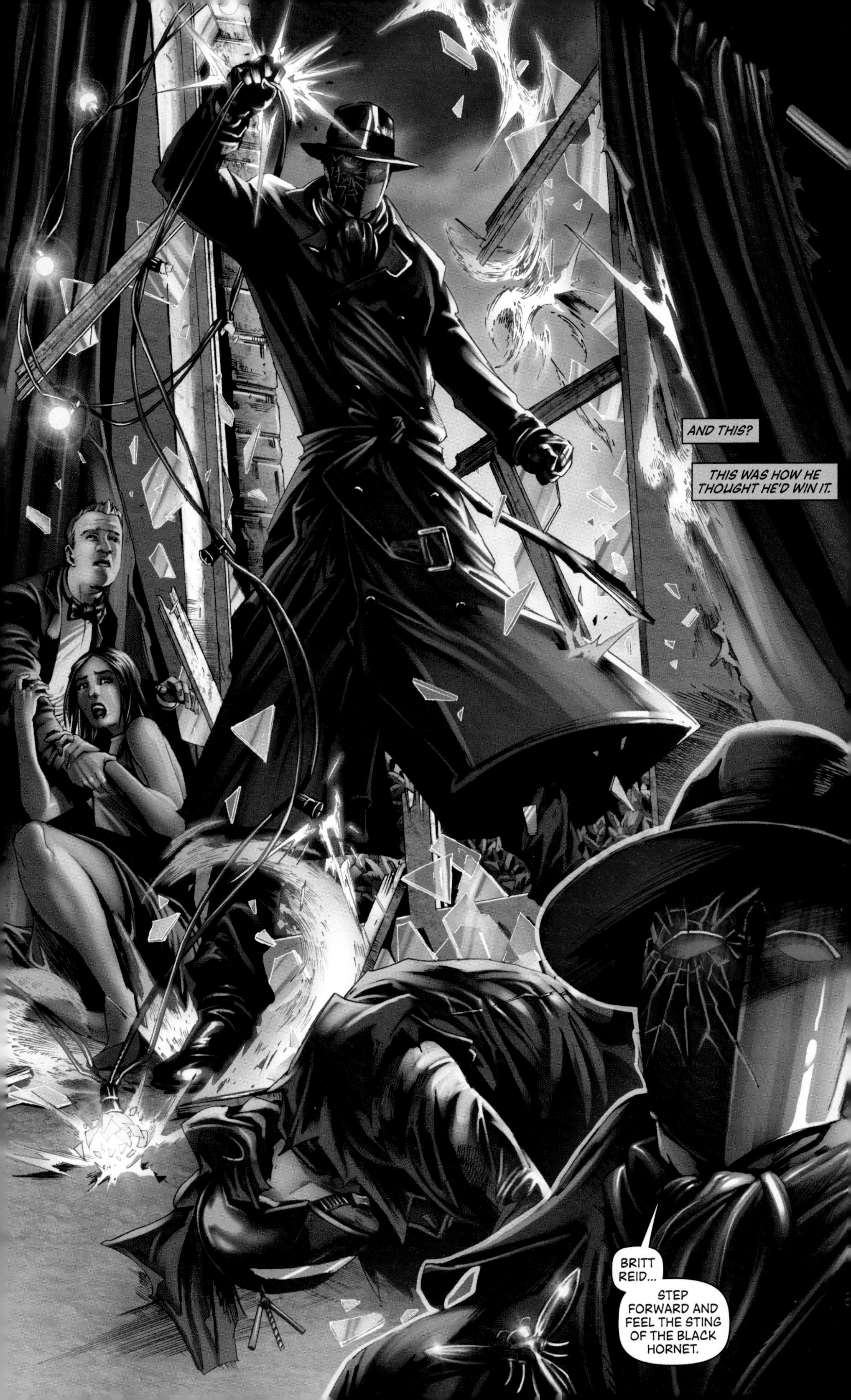
AND THIS?
THIS WAS HOW HE THOUGHT HE'D WIN IT.
BRITT REID...
STEP FORWARD AND FEEL THE STING OF THE BLACK HORNET.

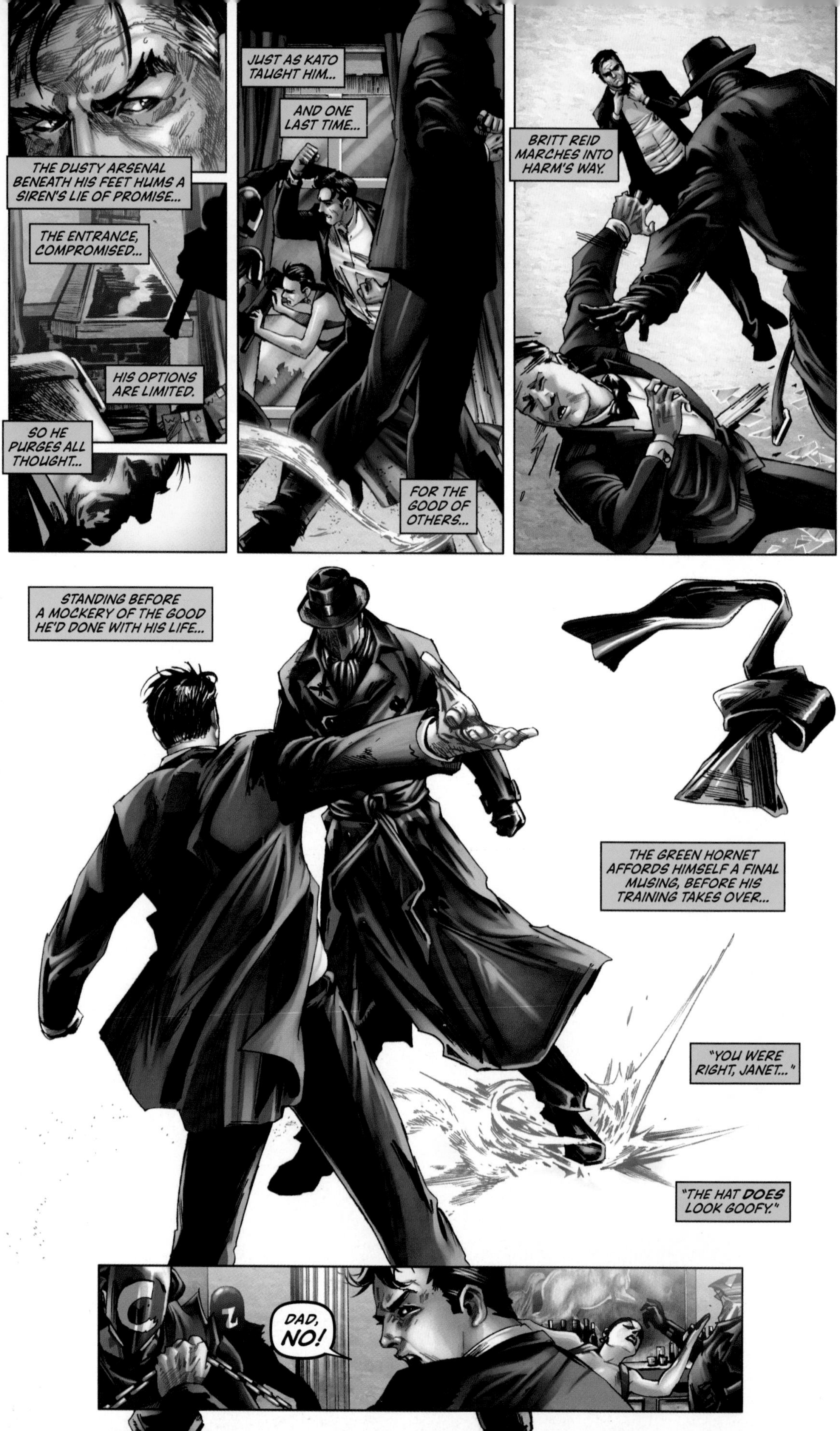
THE DUSTY ARSENAL BENEATH HIS FEET HUMS A SIREN'S LIE OF PROMISE...
THE ENTRANCE, COMPROMISED...
HIS OPTIONS ARE LIMITED.
SO HE PURGES ALL THOUGHT...
JUST AS KATO TAUGHT HIM...
AND ONE LAST TIME...
FOR THE GOOD OF OTHERS...
BRITT REID MARCHES INTO HARM'S WAY.
STANDING BEFORE A MOCKERY OF THE GOOD HE'D DONE WITH HIS LIFE...
THE GREEN HORNET AFFORDS HIMSELF A FINAL MUSING, BEFORE HIS TRAINING TAKES OVER...
"YOU WERE RIGHT, JANET..."
"THE HAT **DOES** LOOK GOOFY."
DAD, NO!

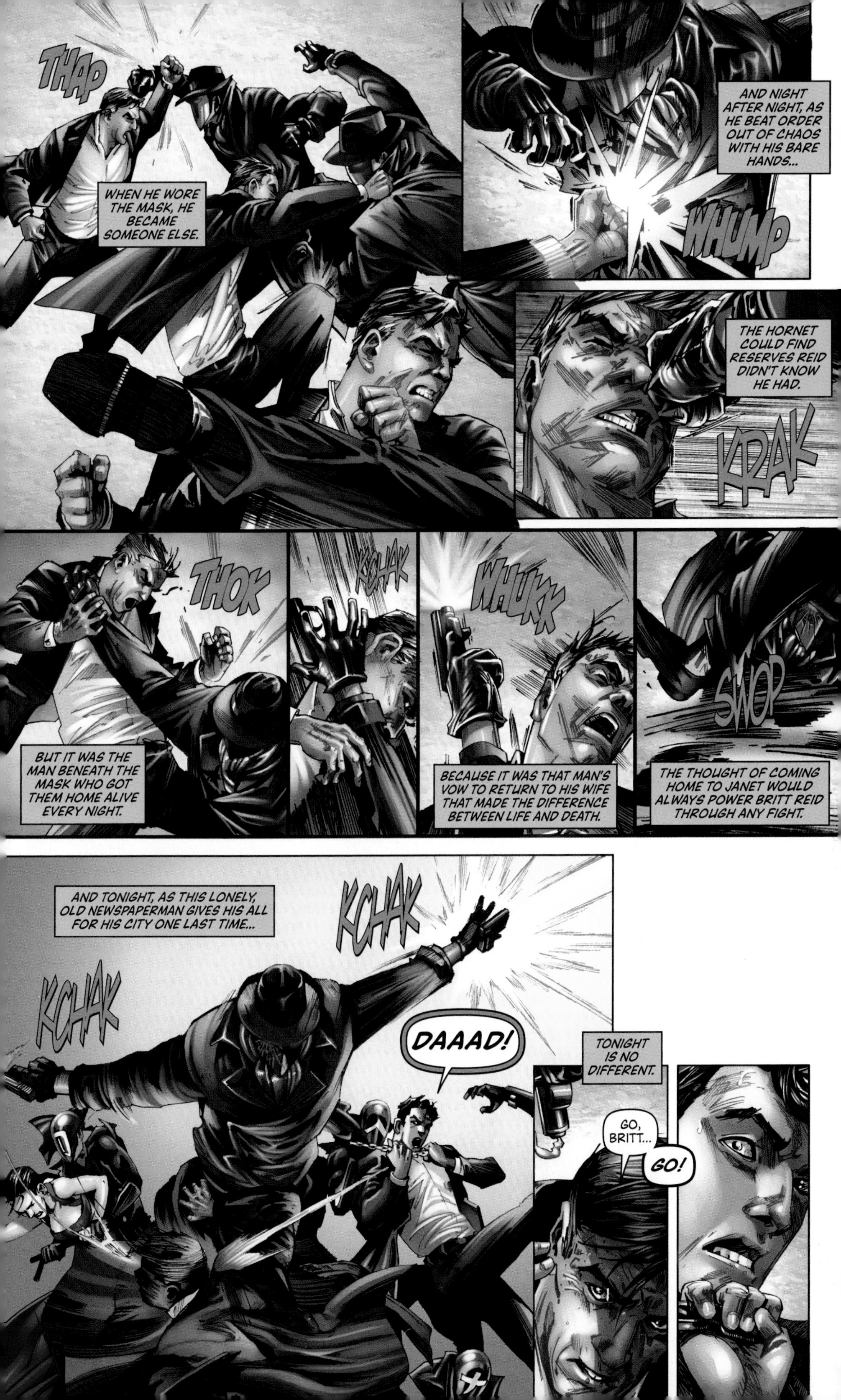
THAP
WHEN HE WORE THE MASK, HE BECAME SOMEONE ELSE.
AND NIGHT AFTER NIGHT, AS HE BEAT ORDER OUT OF CHAOS WITH HIS BARE HANDS...
WHUMP
THE HORNET COULD FIND RESERVES REID DIDN'T KNOW HE HAD.
KRAK
THOK
BUT IT WAS THE MAN BENEATH THE MASK WHO GOT THEM HOME ALIVE EVERY NIGHT.
KCHAK
WHUKK
BECAUSE IT WAS THAT MAN'S VOW TO RETURN TO HIS WIFE THAT MADE THE DIFFERENCE BETWEEN LIFE AND DEATH.
SWOP
THE THOUGHT OF COMING HOME TO JANET WOULD ALWAYS POWER BRITT REID THROUGH ANY FIGHT.
AND TONIGHT, AS THIS LONELY, OLD NEWSPAPERMAN GIVES HIS ALL FOR HIS CITY ONE LAST TIME...
KCHAK
KCHAK
DAAAD!
TONIGHT IS NO DIFFERENT.
GO, BRITT...
GO!

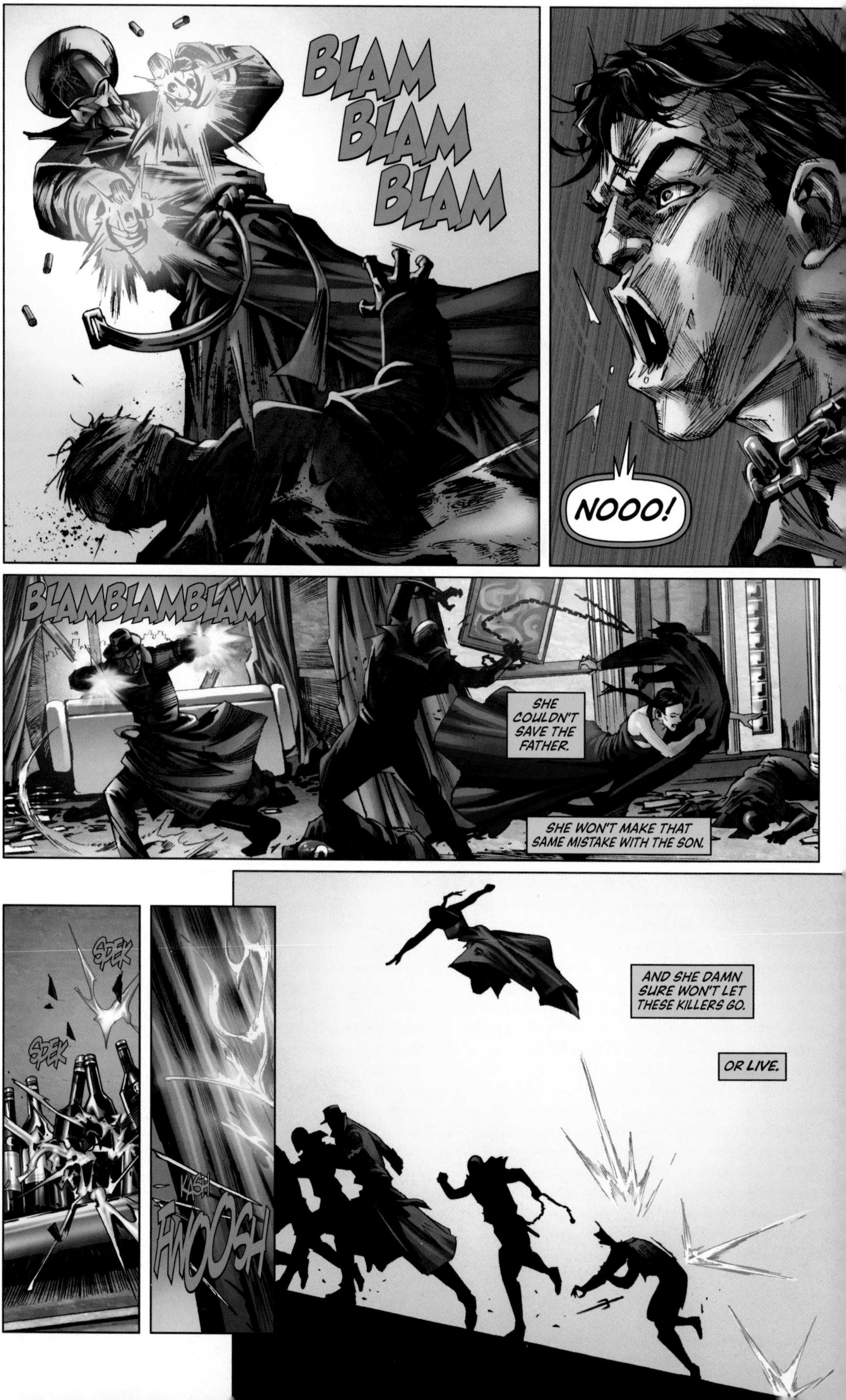
BLAM
BLAM
BLAM
NOOO!
BLAMBLAMBLAM
SHE COULDN'T SAVE THE FATHER.
SHE WON'T MAKE THAT SAME MISTAKE WITH THE SON.
SPEK
SPEK
KASH
FWOOSH
AND SHE DAMN SURE WON'T LET THESE KILLERS GO.
OR LIVE.

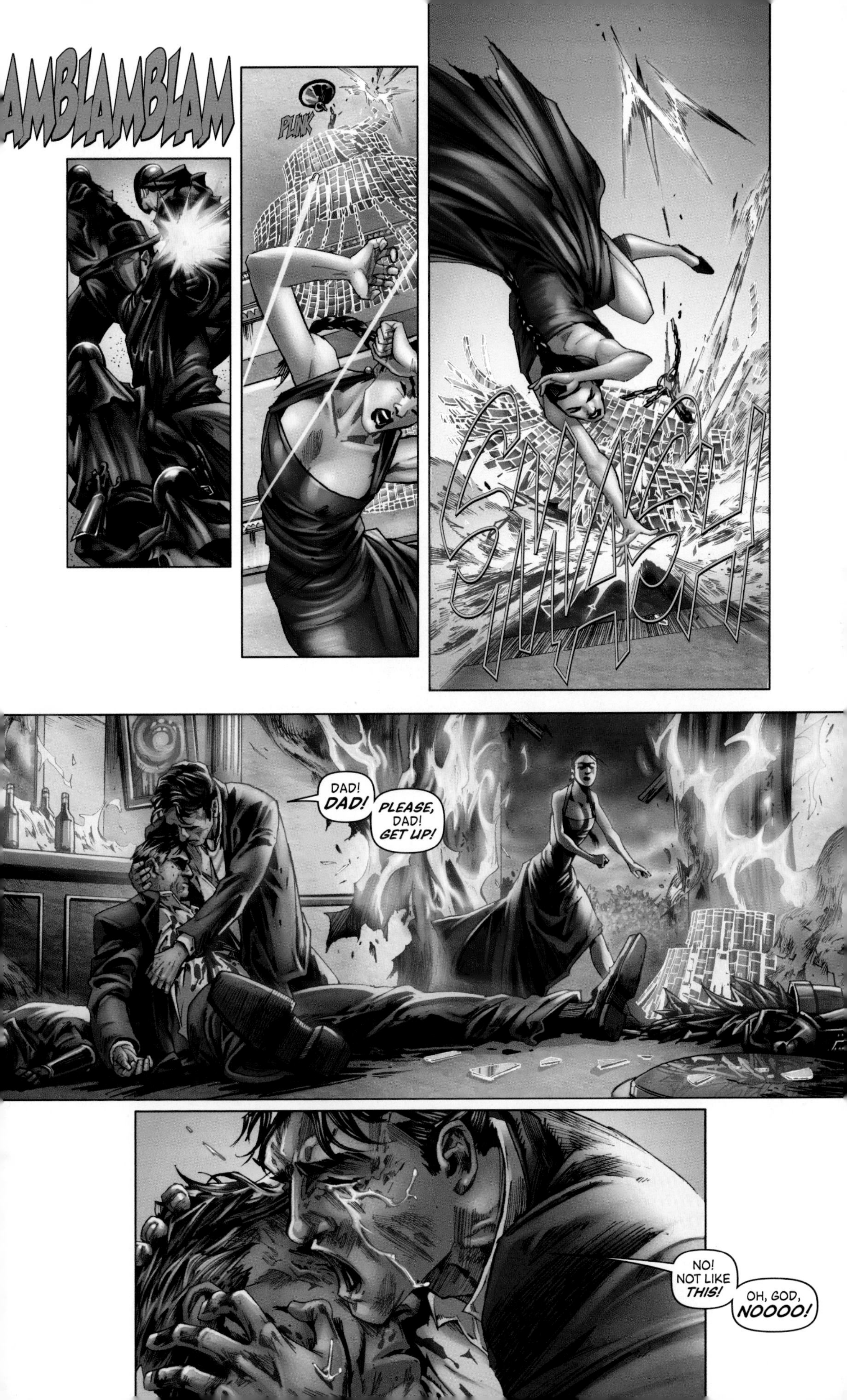
AMBLAMBLAM
PLINK
SMASH
DAD! DAD!
PLEASE, DAD! GET UP!
NO! NOT LIKE THIS!
OH, GOD, NOOOO!

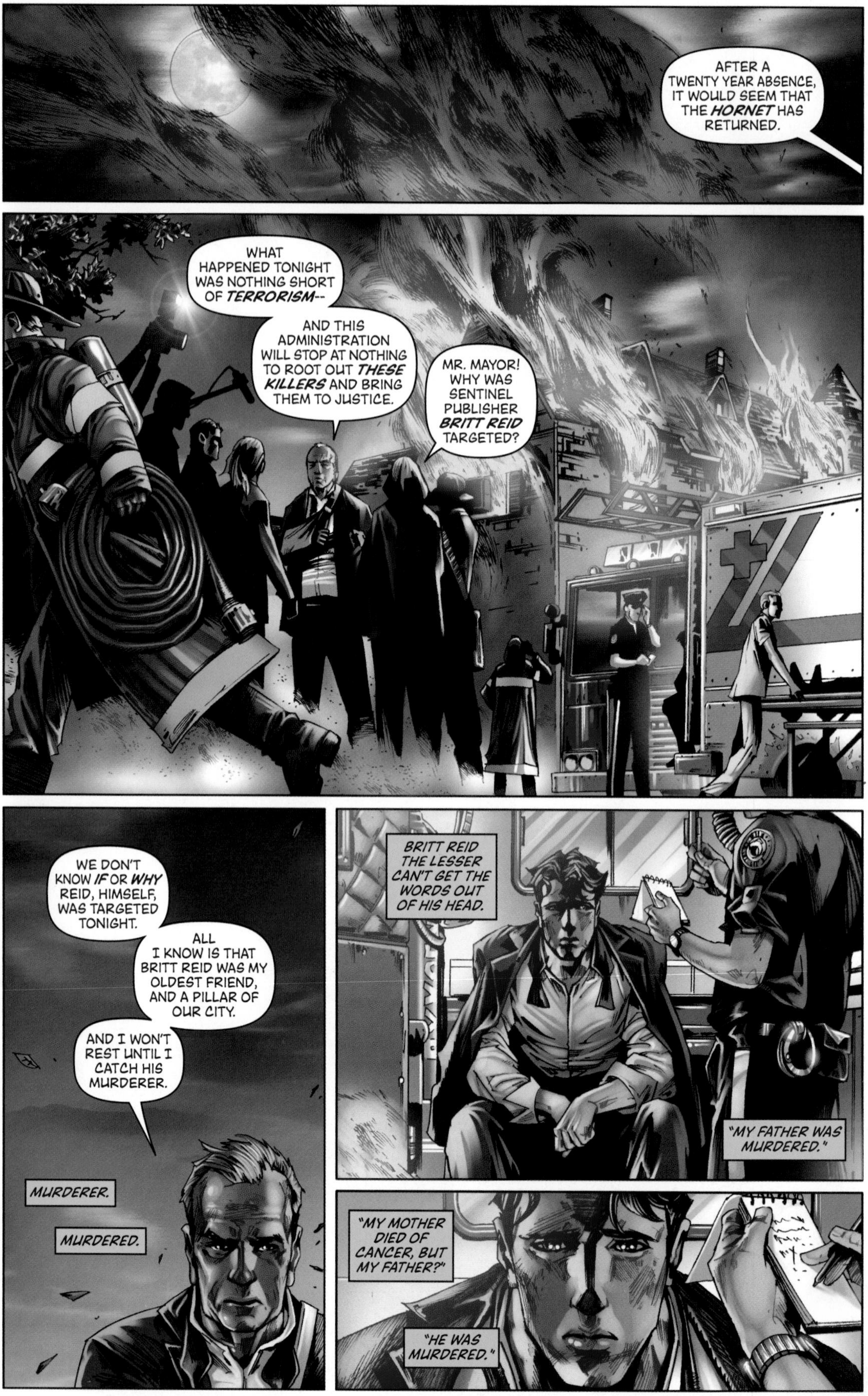

AFTER A TWENTY YEAR ABSENCE, IT WOULD SEEM THAT THE *HORNET* HAS RETURNED.
WHAT HAPPENED TONIGHT WAS NOTHING SHORT OF *TERRORISM*--
AND THIS ADMINISTRATION WILL STOP AT NOTHING TO ROOT OUT *THESE KILLERS* AND BRING THEM TO JUSTICE.
MR. MAYOR! WHY WAS SENTINEL PUBLISHER *BRITT REID* TARGETED?
WE DON'T KNOW *IF* OR *WHY* REID, HIMSELF, WAS TARGETED TONIGHT.
ALL I KNOW IS THAT BRITT REID WAS MY OLDEST FRIEND, AND A PILLAR OF OUR CITY.
AND I WON'T REST UNTIL I CATCH HIS MURDERER.
MURDERER.
MURDERED.
BRITT REID THE LESSER CAN'T GET THE WORDS OUT OF HIS HEAD.
"MY FATHER WAS MURDERED."
"MY MOTHER DIED OF CANCER, BUT MY FATHER?"
"HE WAS MURDERED."

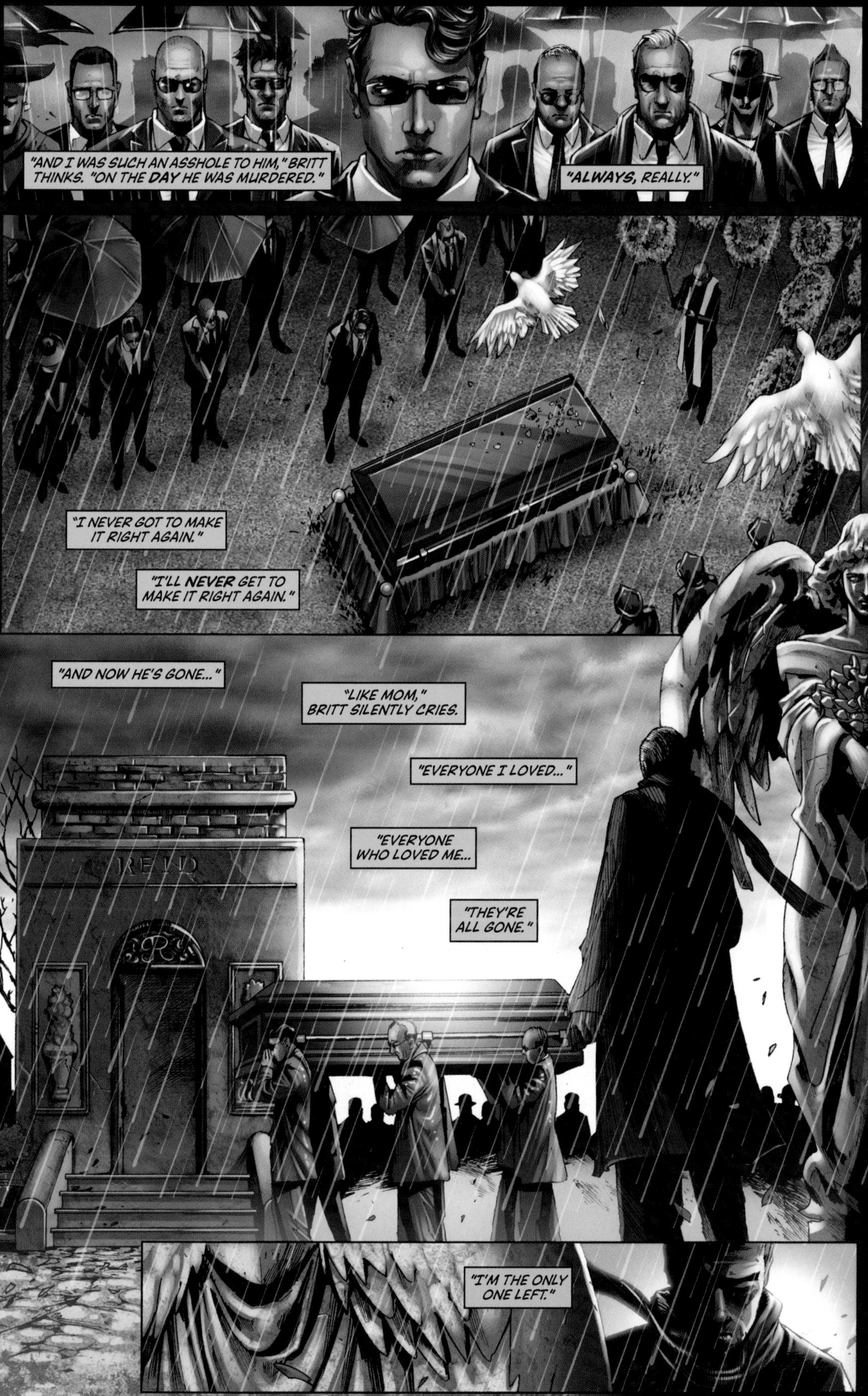
"AND I WAS SUCH AN ASSHOLE TO HIM," BRITT THINKS. "ON THE DAY HE WAS MURDERED."
"ALWAYS, REALLY."
"I NEVER GOT TO MAKE IT RIGHT AGAIN."
"I'LL NEVER GET TO MAKE IT RIGHT AGAIN."
"AND NOW HE'S GONE..."
"LIKE MOM," BRITT SILENTLY CRIES.
"EVERYONE I LOVED..."
"EVERYONE WHO LOVED ME...
"THEY'RE ALL GONE."
REID
"I'M THE ONLY ONE LEFT."

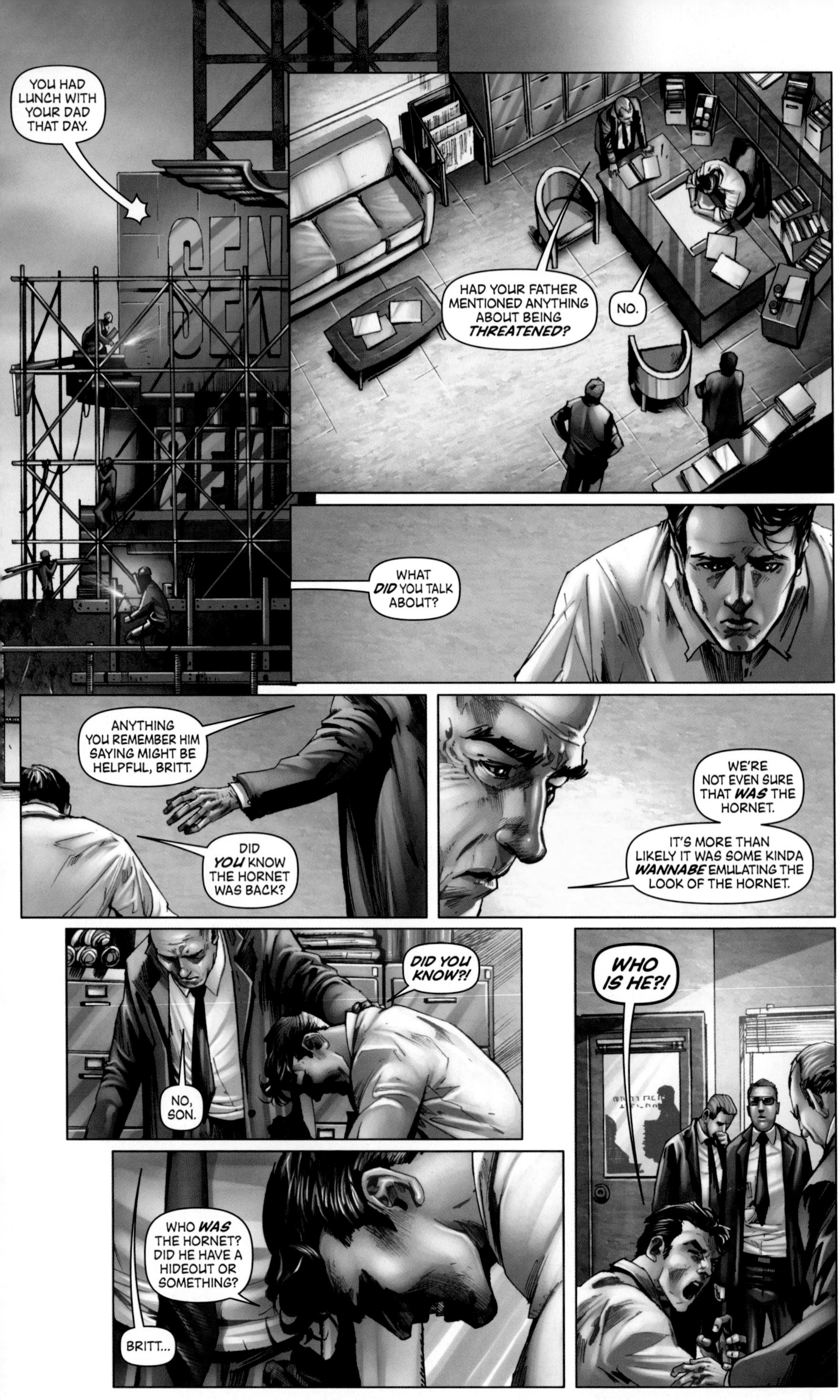
YOU HAD LUNCH WITH YOUR DAD THAT DAY.
HAD YOUR FATHER MENTIONED ANYTHING ABOUT BEING THREATENED?
NO.
WHAT DID YOU TALK ABOUT?
ANYTHING YOU REMEMBER HIM SAYING MIGHT BE HELPFUL, BRITT.
DID YOU KNOW THE HORNET WAS BACK?
WE'RE NOT EVEN SURE THAT WAS THE HORNET.
IT'S MORE THAN LIKELY IT WAS SOME KINDA WANNABE EMULATING THE LOOK OF THE HORNET.
DID YOU KNOW?!
NO, SON.
WHO WAS THE HORNET? DID HE HAVE A HIDEOUT OR SOMETHING?
BRITT...
WHO IS HE?!

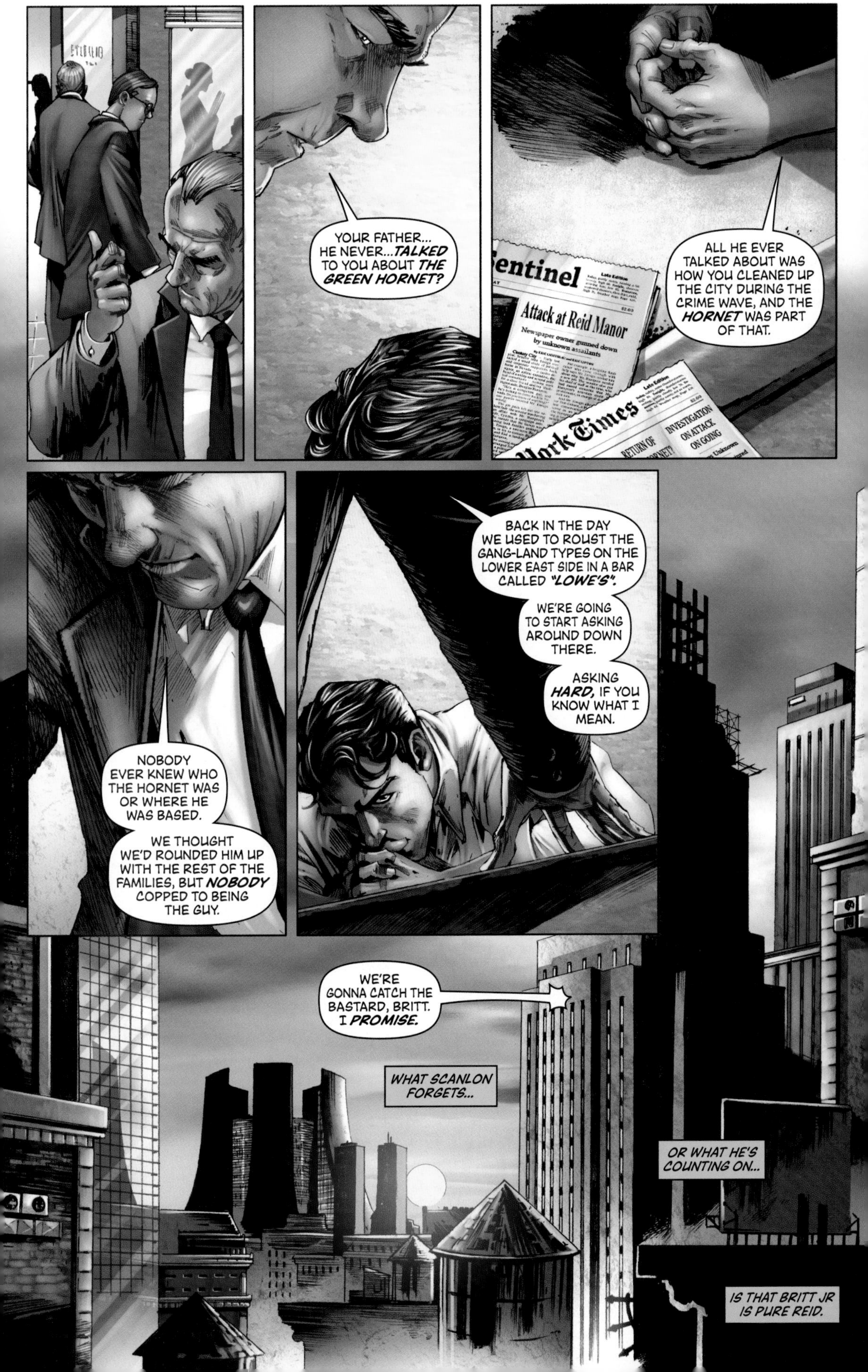

YOUR FATHER... HE NEVER...TALKED TO YOU ABOUT THE GREEN HORNET?
Sentinel
Attack at Reid Manor
Newspaper owner gunned down by unknown assailants
ALL HE EVER TALKED ABOUT WAS HOW YOU CLEANED UP THE CITY DURING THE CRIME WAVE, AND THE HORNET WAS PART OF THAT.
INVESTIGATION ON ATTACK ON GOING
NOBODY EVER KNEW WHO THE HORNET WAS OR WHERE HE WAS BASED.
WE THOUGHT WE'D ROUNDED HIM UP WITH THE REST OF THE FAMILIES, BUT NOBODY COPPED TO BEING THE GUY.
BACK IN THE DAY WE USED TO ROUST THE GANG-LAND TYPES ON THE LOWER EAST SIDE IN A BAR CALLED "LOWE'S".
WE'RE GOING TO START ASKING AROUND DOWN THERE.
ASKING HARD, IF YOU KNOW WHAT I MEAN.
WE'RE GONNA CATCH THE BASTARD, BRITT. I PROMISE.
WHAT SCANLON FORGETS...
OR WHAT HE'S COUNTING ON...
IS THAT BRITT JR IS PURE REID.

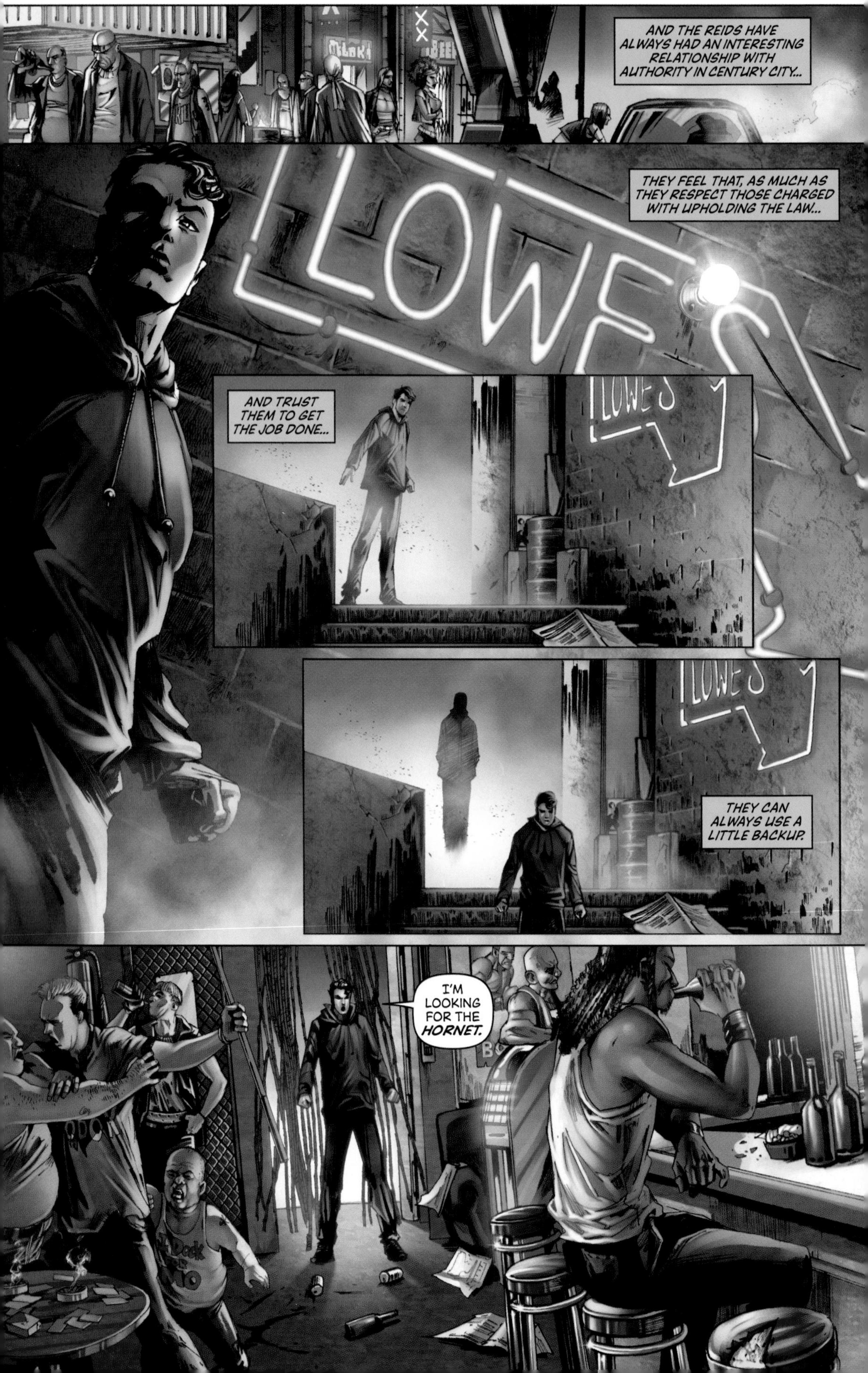
AND THE REIDS HAVE ALWAYS HAD AN INTERESTING RELATIONSHIP WITH AUTHORITY IN CENTURY CITY...
LOWE'S
THEY FEEL THAT, AS MUCH AS THEY RESPECT THOSE CHARGED WITH UPHOLDING THE LAW...
AND TRUST THEM TO GET THE JOB DONE...
THEY CAN ALWAYS USE A LITTLE BACKUP.
I'M LOOKING FOR THE *HORNET.*

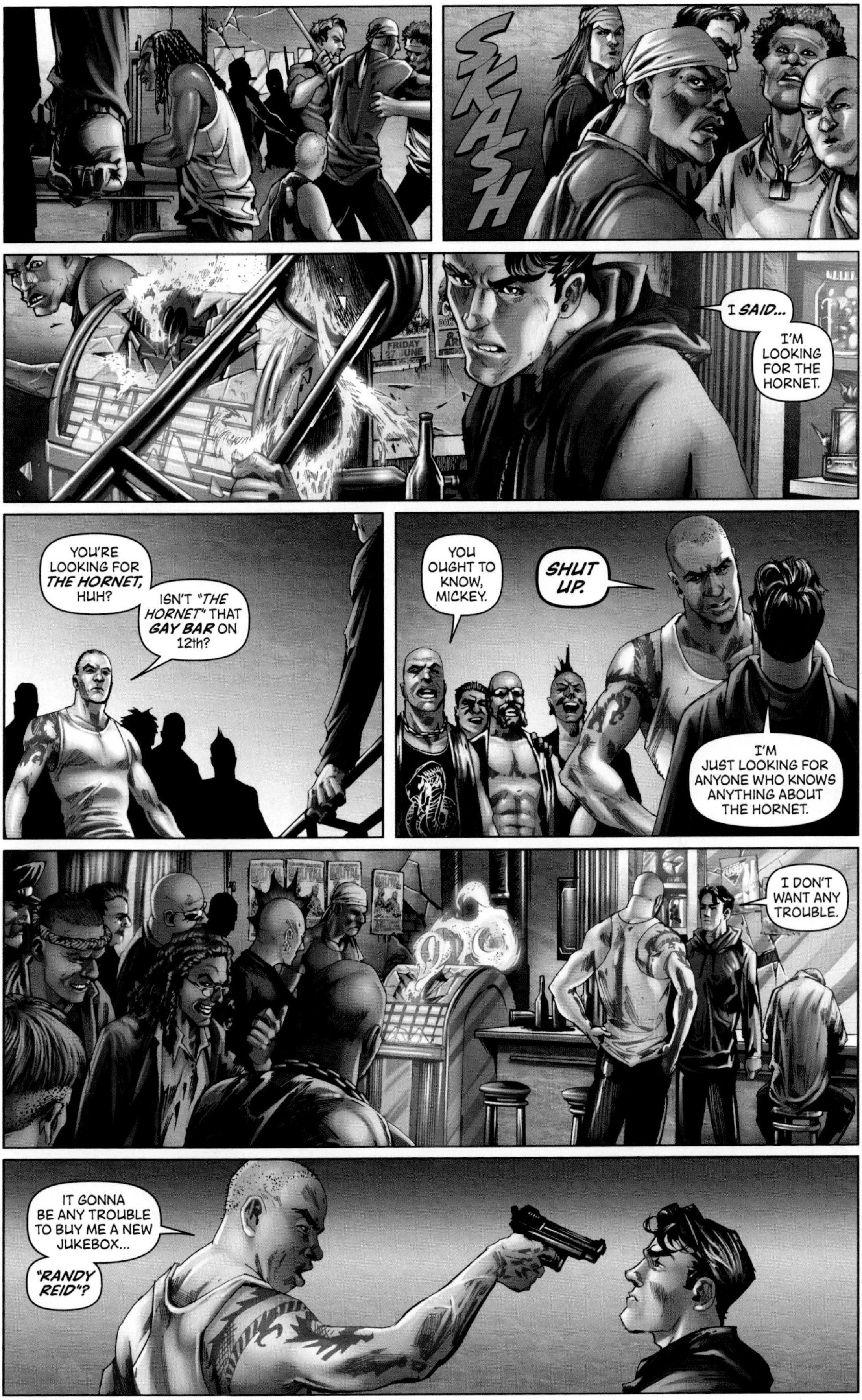
SKASH
FRIDAY 27 JUNE
I SAID...
I'M LOOKING FOR THE HORNET.
YOU'RE LOOKING FOR THE HORNET, HUH?
ISN'T "THE HORNET" THAT GAY BAR ON 12th?
YOU OUGHT TO KNOW, MICKEY.
SHUT UP.
I'M JUST LOOKING FOR ANYONE WHO KNOWS ANYTHING ABOUT THE HORNET.
BRUTAL
I DON'T WANT ANY TROUBLE.
IT GONNA BE ANY TROUBLE TO BUY ME A NEW JUKEBOX...
"RANDY REID"?

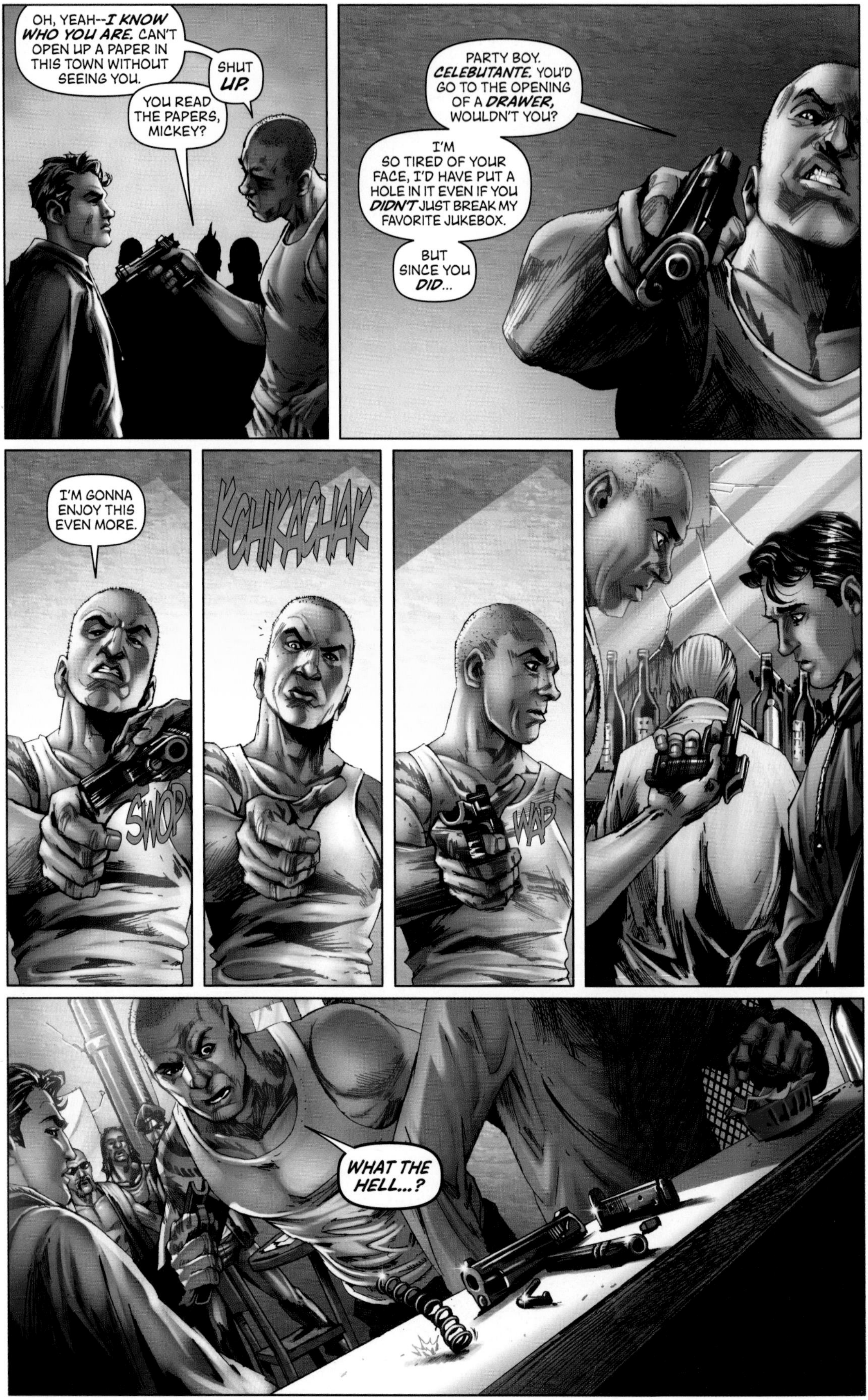
OH, YEAH--*I KNOW WHO YOU ARE.* CAN'T OPEN UP A PAPER IN THIS TOWN WITHOUT SEEING YOU.
SHUT *UP.*
YOU READ THE PAPERS, MICKEY?
PARTY BOY. *CELEBUTANTE.* YOU'D GO TO THE OPENING OF A *DRAWER,* WOULDN'T YOU?
I'M SO TIRED OF YOUR FACE, I'D HAVE PUT A HOLE IN IT EVEN IF YOU *DIDN'T* JUST BREAK MY FAVORITE JUKEBOX.
BUT SINCE YOU *DID*...
I'M GONNA ENJOY THIS EVEN MORE.
SWOP
KCHIKACHAK
WAP
WHAT THE HELL...?

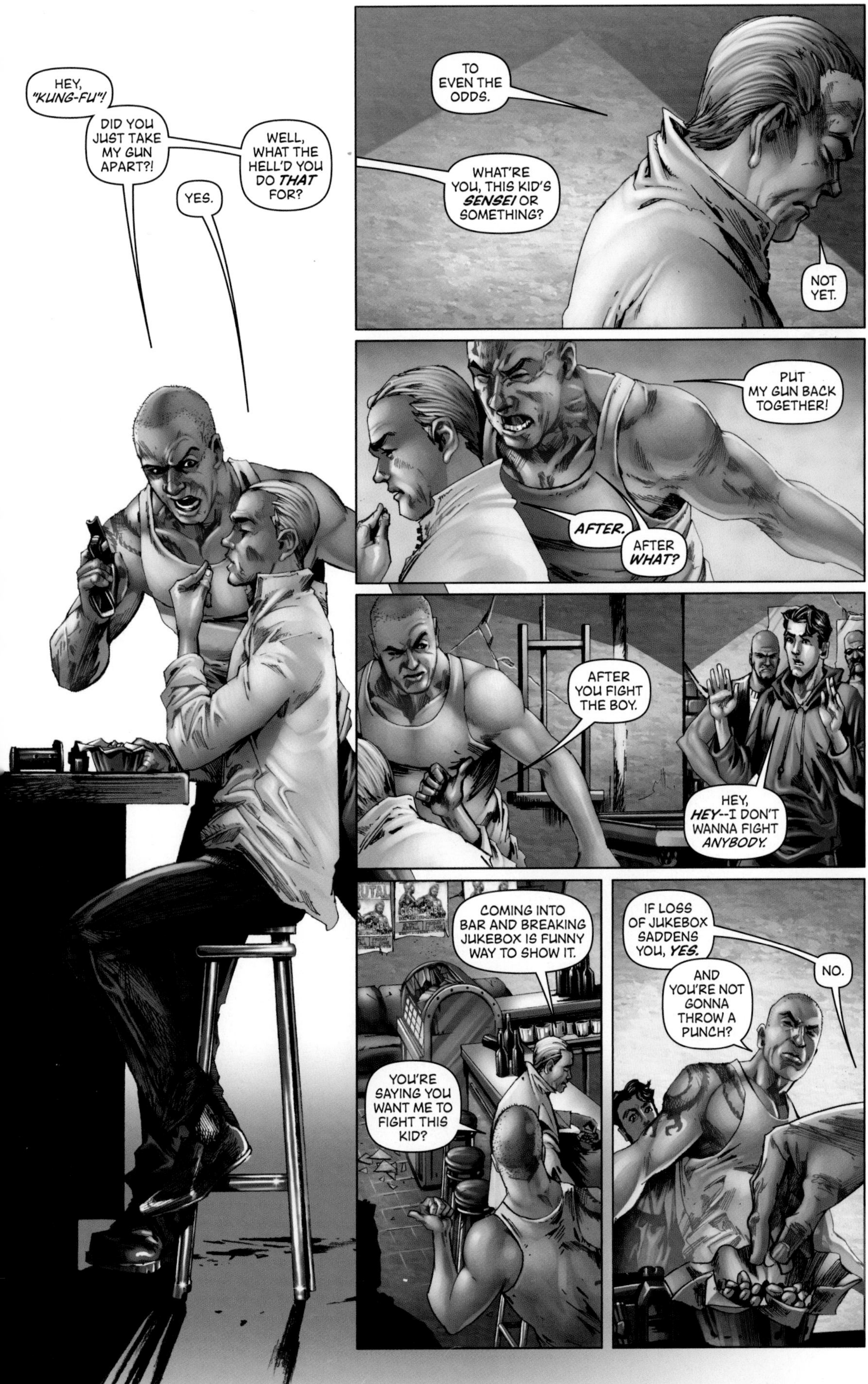

HEY, "KUNG-FU"!
DID YOU JUST TAKE MY GUN APART?!
YES.
WELL, WHAT THE HELL'D YOU DO *THAT* FOR?
TO EVEN THE ODDS.
WHAT'RE YOU, THIS KID'S *SENSEI* OR SOMETHING?
NOT YET.
PUT MY GUN BACK TOGETHER!
AFTER.
AFTER *WHAT?*
AFTER YOU FIGHT THE BOY.
HEY, *HEY*--I DON'T WANNA FIGHT *ANYBODY.*
YOU'RE SAYING YOU WANT ME TO FIGHT THIS KID?
COMING INTO BAR AND BREAKING JUKEBOX IS FUNNY WAY TO SHOW IT.
IF LOSS OF JUKEBOX SADDENS YOU, *YES.*
AND YOU'RE NOT GONNA THROW A PUNCH?
NO.

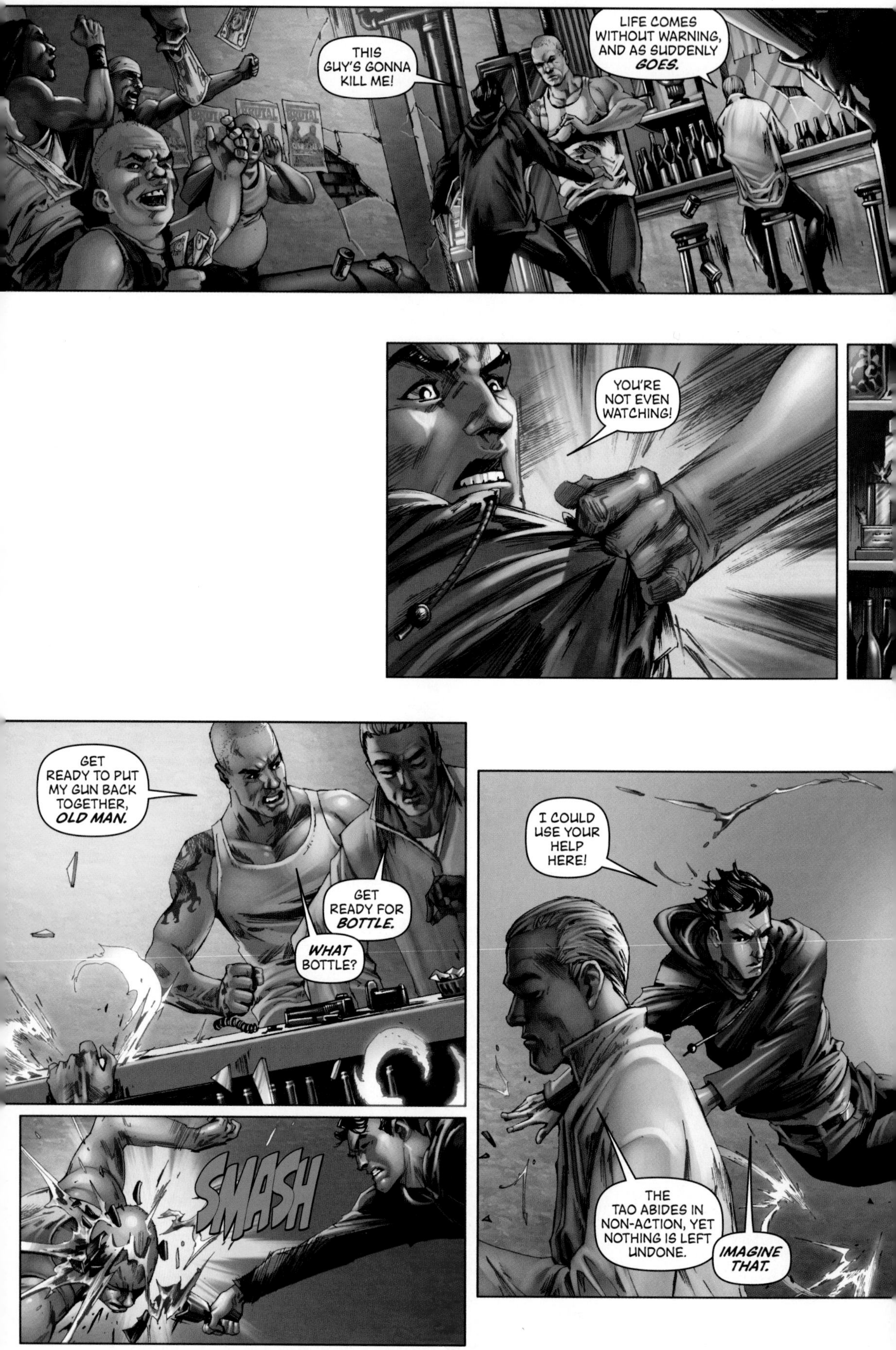
THIS GUY'S GONNA KILL ME!
LIFE COMES WITHOUT WARNING, AND AS SUDDENLY *GOES.*
YOU'RE NOT EVEN WATCHING!
GET READY TO PUT MY GUN BACK TOGETHER, *OLD MAN.*
GET READY FOR *BOTTLE.*
WHAT BOTTLE?
SMASH
I COULD USE YOUR HELP HERE!
THE TAO ABIDES IN NON-ACTION, YET NOTHING IS LEFT UNDONE.
IMAGINE THAT.

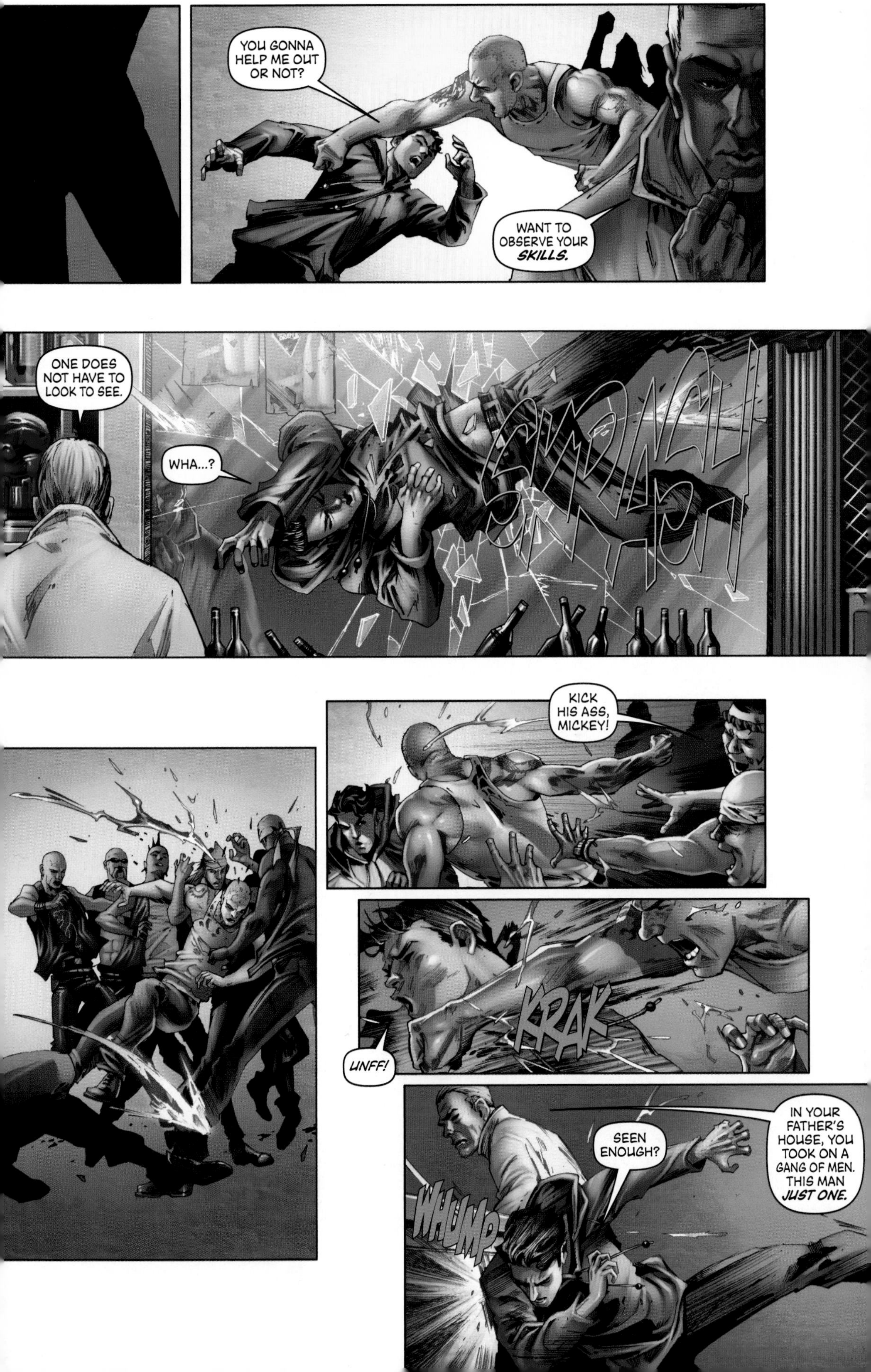
YOU GONNA HELP ME OUT OR NOT?
WANT TO OBSERVE YOUR SKILLS.
ONE DOES NOT HAVE TO LOOK TO SEE.
WHA...?
KICK HIS ASS, MICKEY!
KRAK
UNFF!
SEEN ENOUGH?
IN YOUR FATHER'S HOUSE, YOU TOOK ON A GANG OF MEN. THIS MAN JUST ONE.
WHUMP

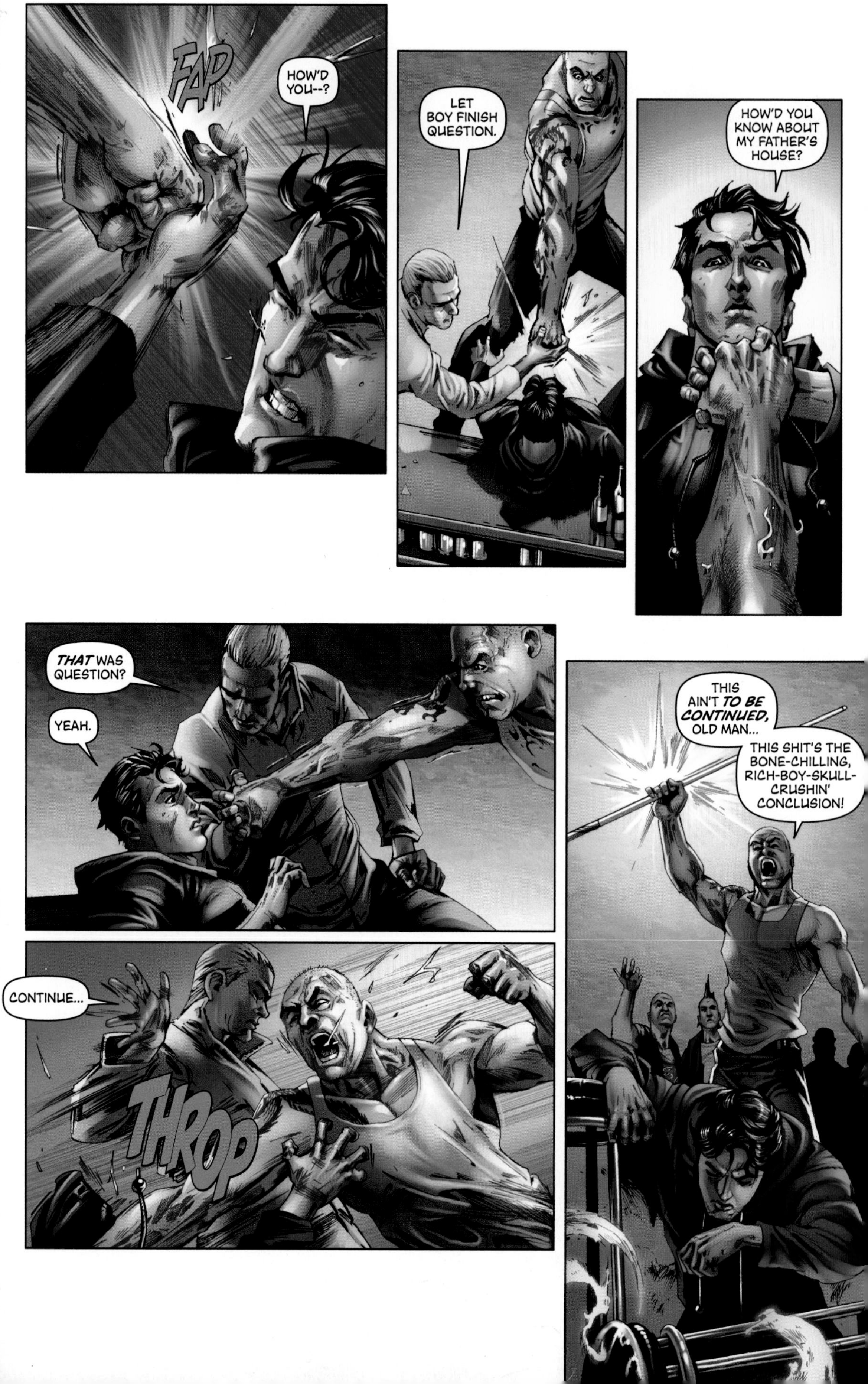
FAP
HOW'D YOU--?
LET BOY FINISH QUESTION.
HOW'D YOU KNOW ABOUT MY FATHER'S HOUSE?
THAT WAS QUESTION?
YEAH.
CONTINUE...
THROP
THIS AIN'T TO BE CONTINUED, OLD MAN...
THIS SHIT'S THE BONE-CHILLING, RICH-BOY-SKULL-CRUSHIN' CONCLUSION!

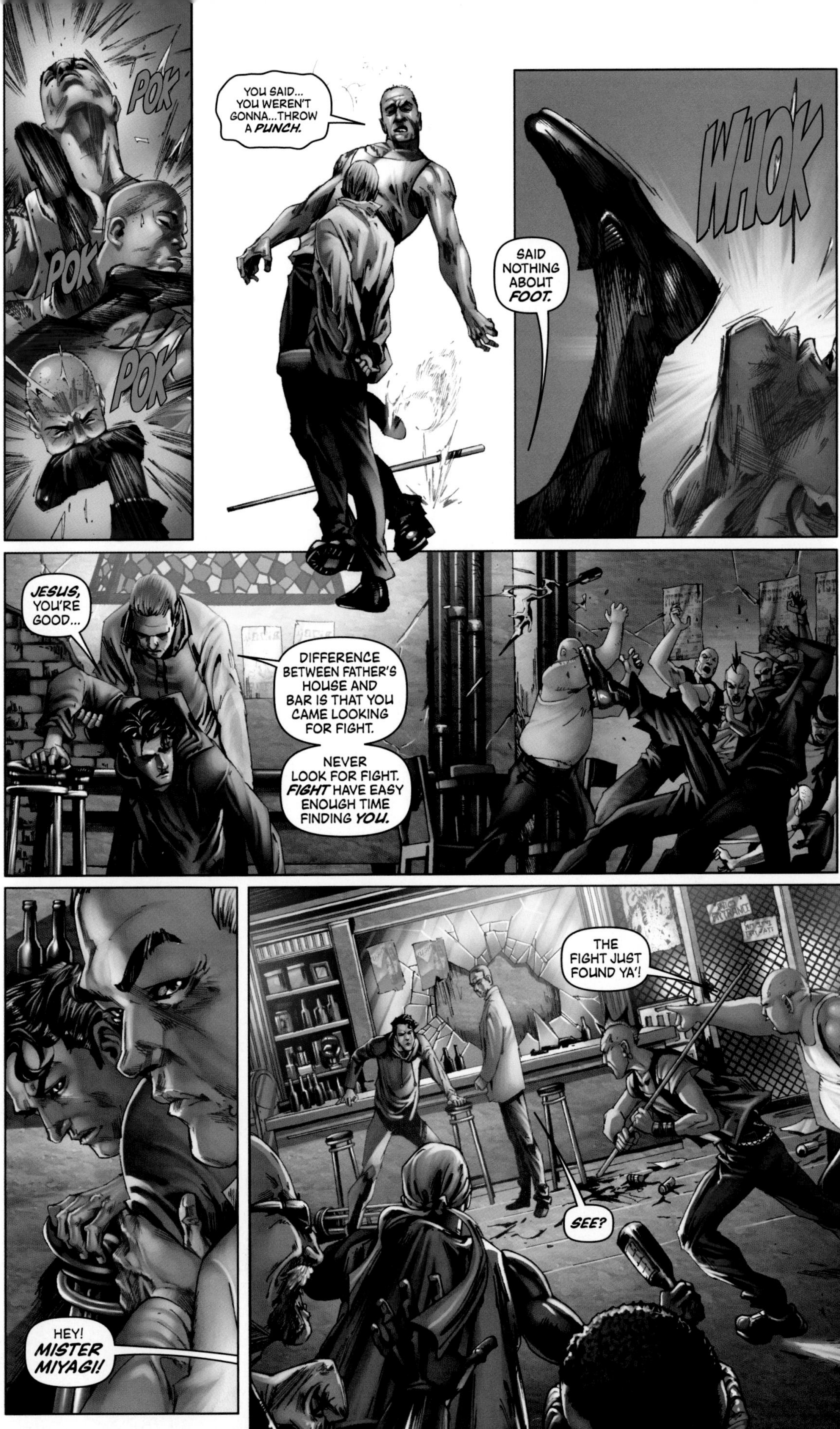
POK
POK
POK
YOU SAID... YOU WEREN'T GONNA...THROW A PUNCH.
WHOK
SAID NOTHING ABOUT FOOT.
JESUS, YOU'RE GOOD...
DIFFERENCE BETWEEN FATHER'S HOUSE AND BAR IS THAT YOU CAME LOOKING FOR FIGHT.
NEVER LOOK FOR FIGHT. FIGHT HAVE EASY ENOUGH TIME FINDING YOU.
HEY! MISTER MIYAGI!
THE FIGHT JUST FOUND YA'!
SEE?

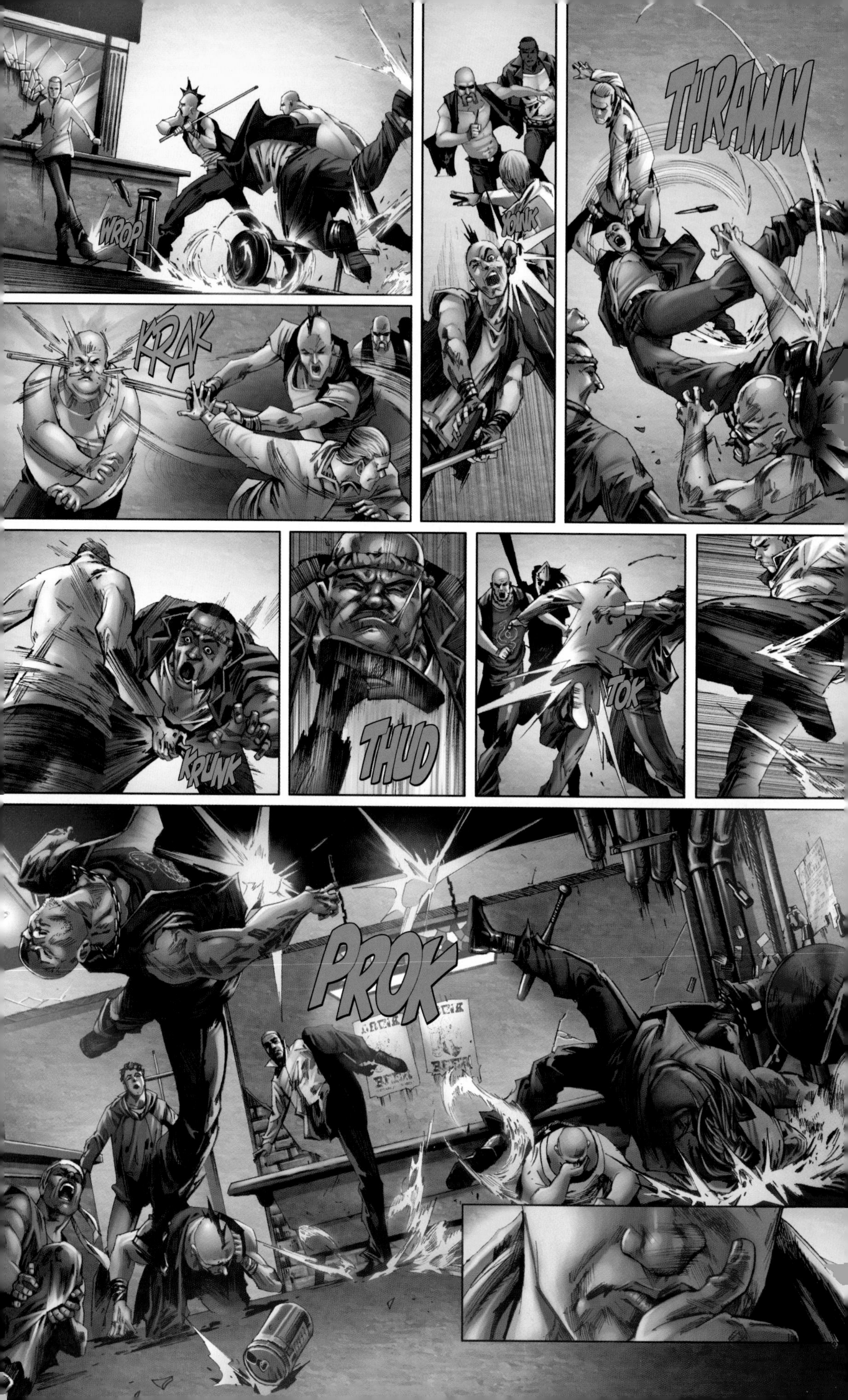
WROP
YOINK
THRAMM
KRAK
KRUNK
THUD
TOK
PROK

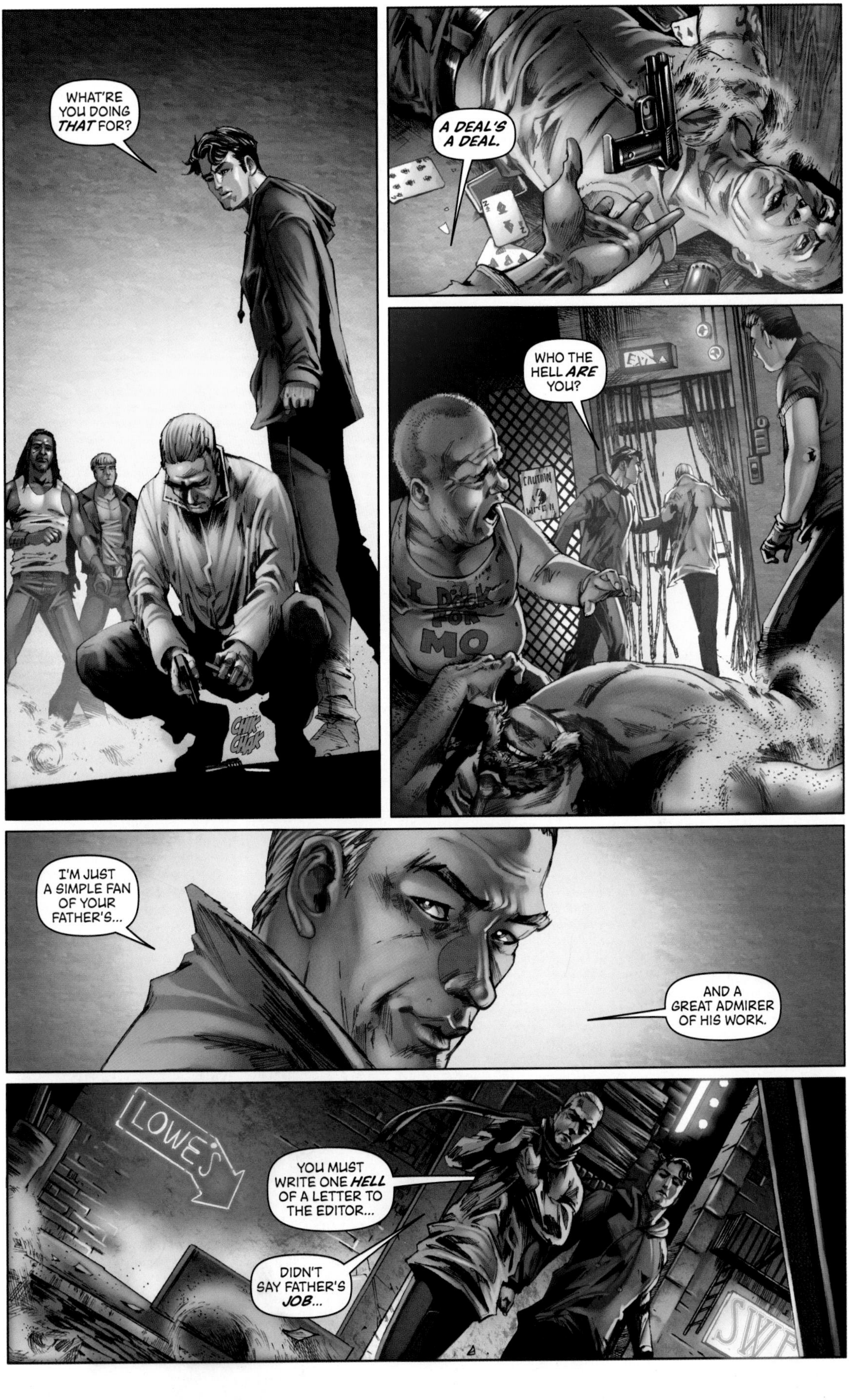
WHAT'RE YOU DOING *THAT* FOR?
CHIK CHAK
A DEAL'S A DEAL.
WHO THE HELL *ARE* YOU?
I'M JUST A SIMPLE FAN OF YOUR FATHER'S...
AND A GREAT ADMIRER OF HIS WORK.
LOWE'S
YOU MUST WRITE ONE *HELL* OF A LETTER TO THE EDITOR...
DIDN'T SAY FATHER'S *JOB*...

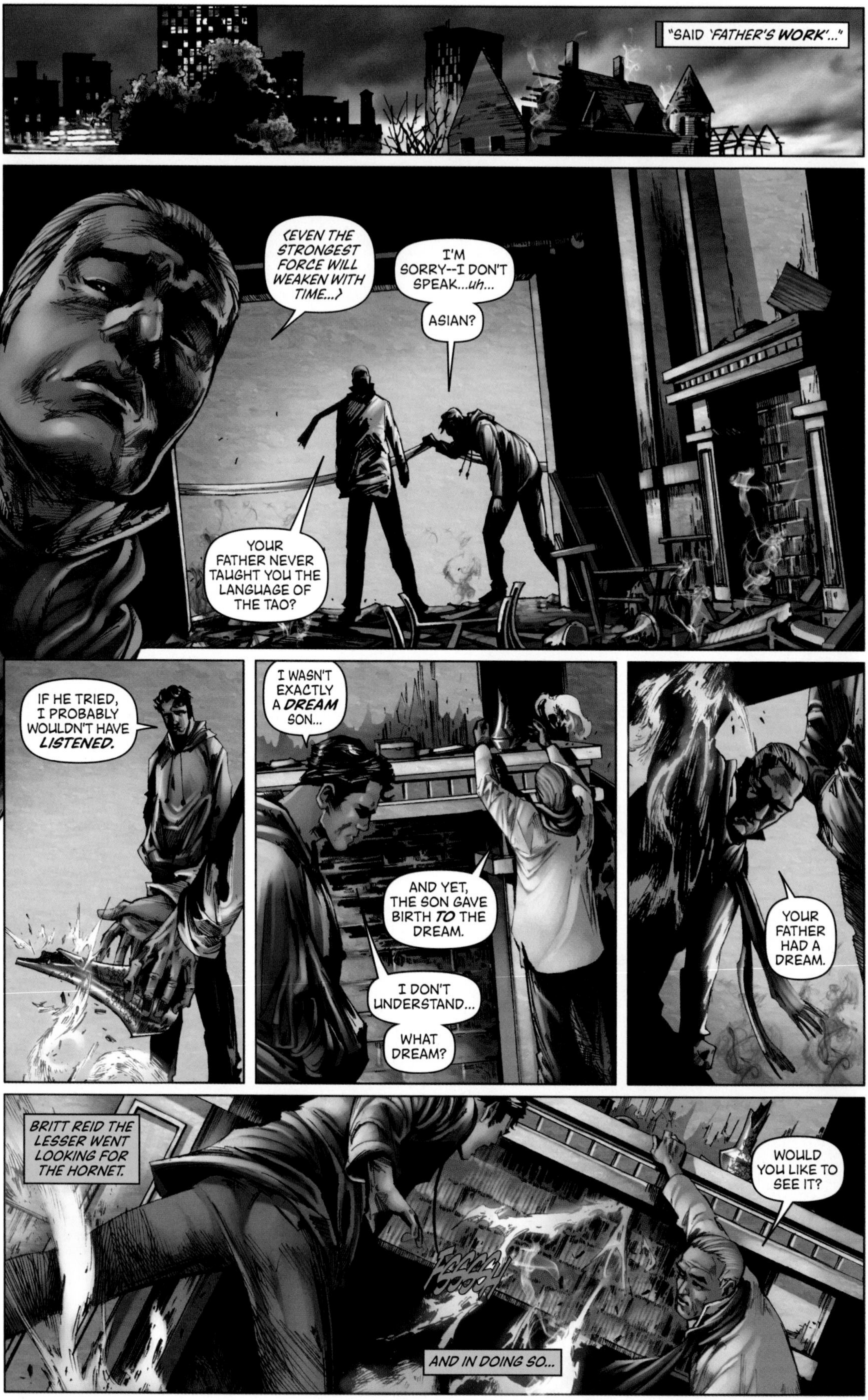
"SAID 'FATHER'S WORK'..."
<EVEN THE STRONGEST FORCE WILL WEAKEN WITH TIME...>
I'M SORRY--I DON'T SPEAK...uh...
ASIAN?
YOUR FATHER NEVER TAUGHT YOU THE LANGUAGE OF THE TAO?
IF HE TRIED, I PROBABLY WOULDN'T HAVE LISTENED.
I WASN'T EXACTLY A DREAM SON...
AND YET, THE SON GAVE BIRTH TO THE DREAM.
I DON'T UNDERSTAND...
WHAT DREAM?
YOUR FATHER HAD A DREAM.
BRITT REID THE LESSER WENT LOOKING FOR THE HORNET.
WOULD YOU LIKE TO SEE IT?
AND IN DOING SO...

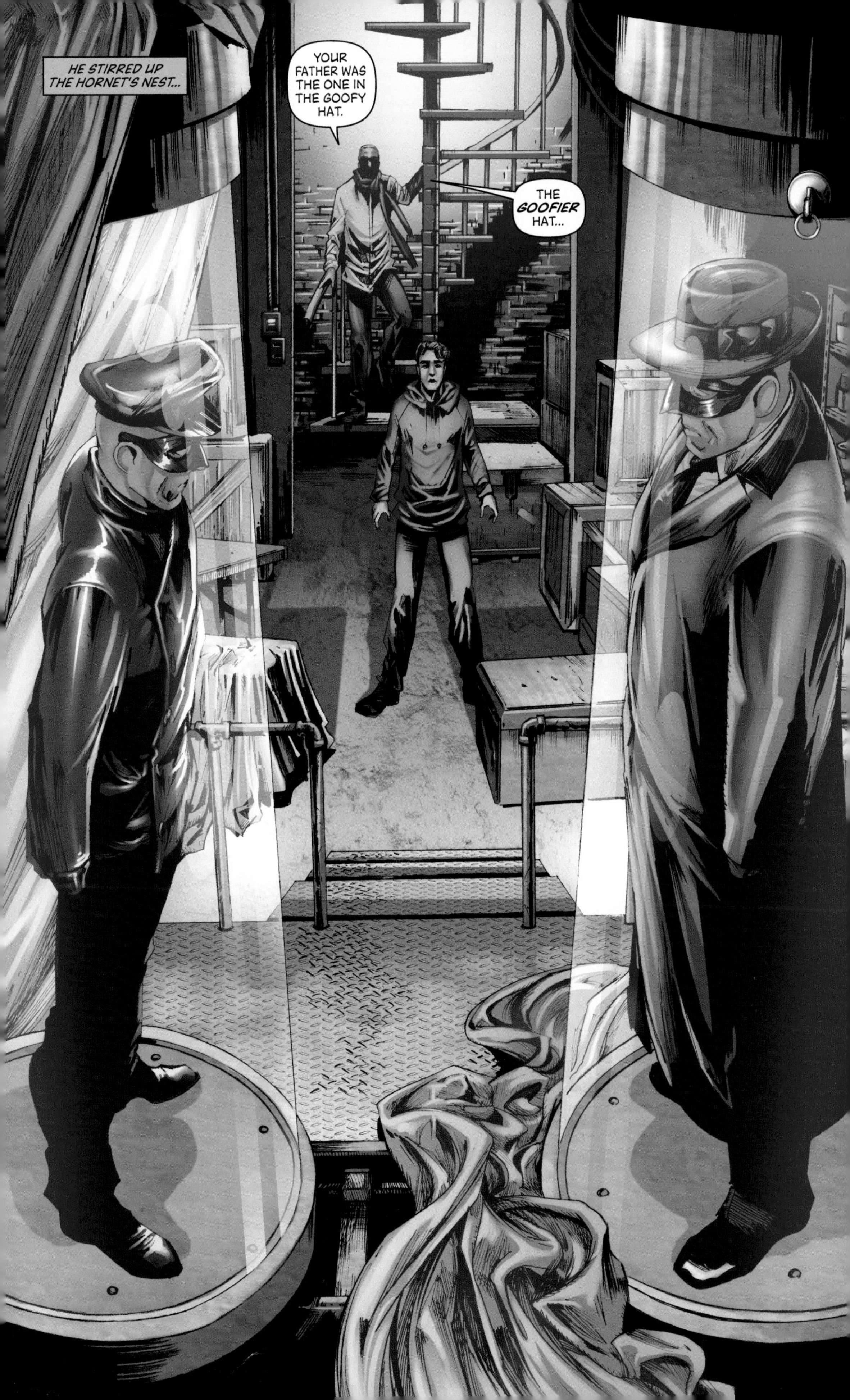
HE STIRRED UP THE HORNET'S NEST...
YOUR FATHER WAS THE ONE IN THE GOOFY HAT.
THE GOOFIER HAT...

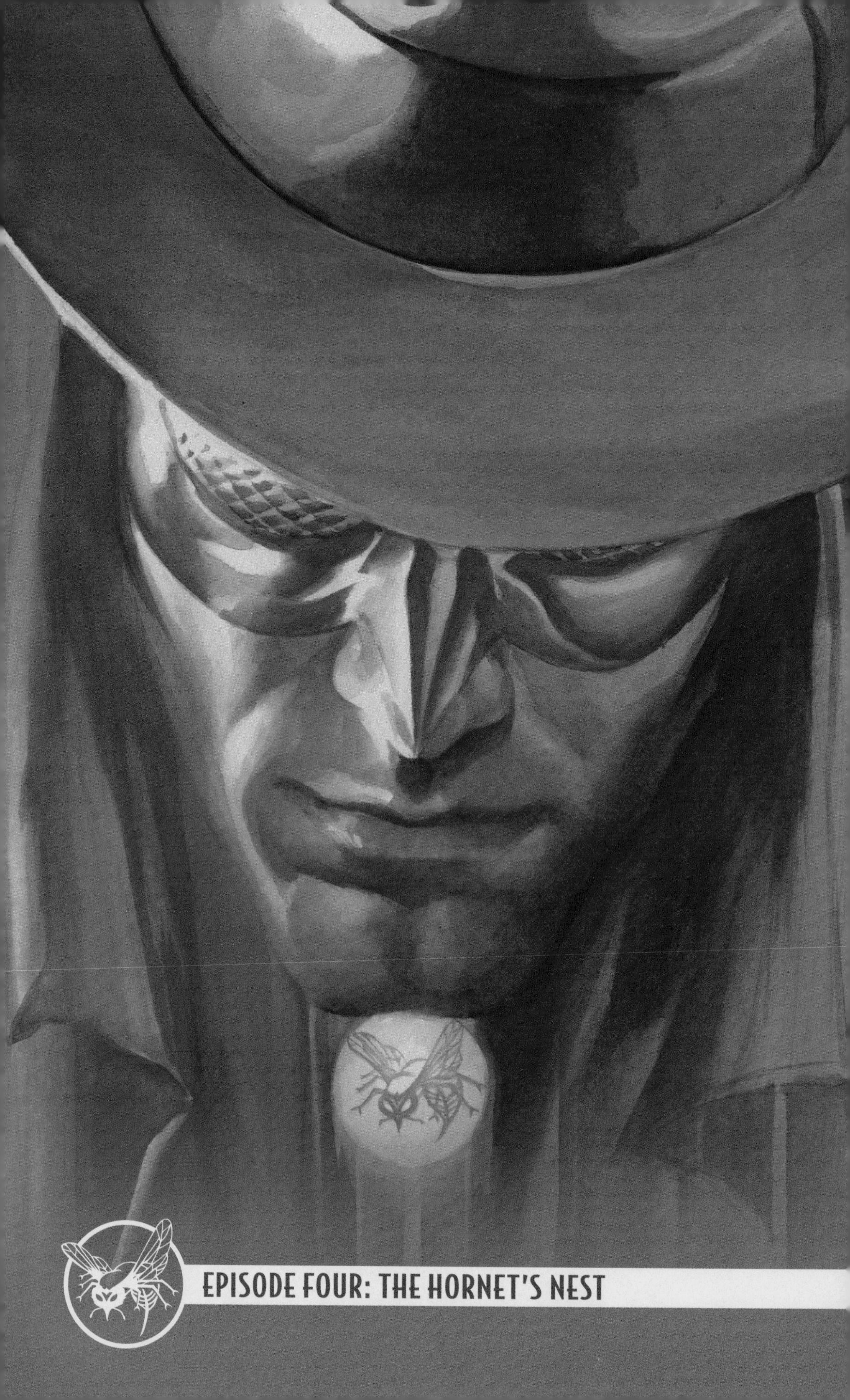

EPISODE FOUR: THE HORNET'S NEST

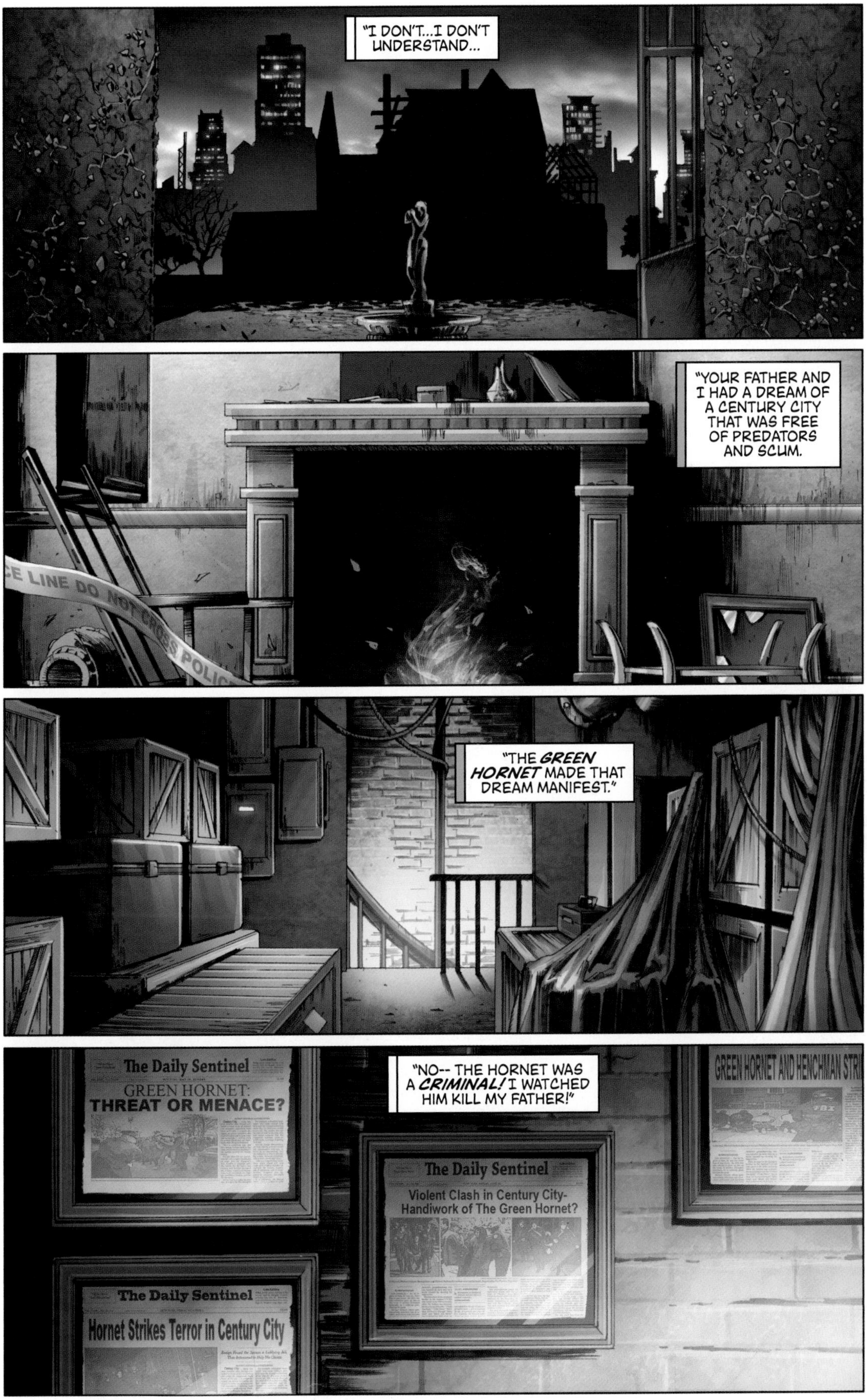
"I DON'T...I DON'T UNDERSTAND...
"YOUR FATHER AND I HAD A DREAM OF A CENTURY CITY THAT WAS FREE OF PREDATORS AND SCUM.
"THE *GREEN HORNET* MADE THAT DREAM MANIFEST."
"NO-- THE HORNET WAS A ***CRIMINAL!*** I WATCHED HIM KILL MY FATHER!"
The Daily Sentinel
GREEN HORNET: THREAT OR MENACE?
The Daily Sentinel
Violent Clash in Century City- Handiwork of The Green Hornet?
The Daily Sentinel
Hornet Strikes Terror in Century City

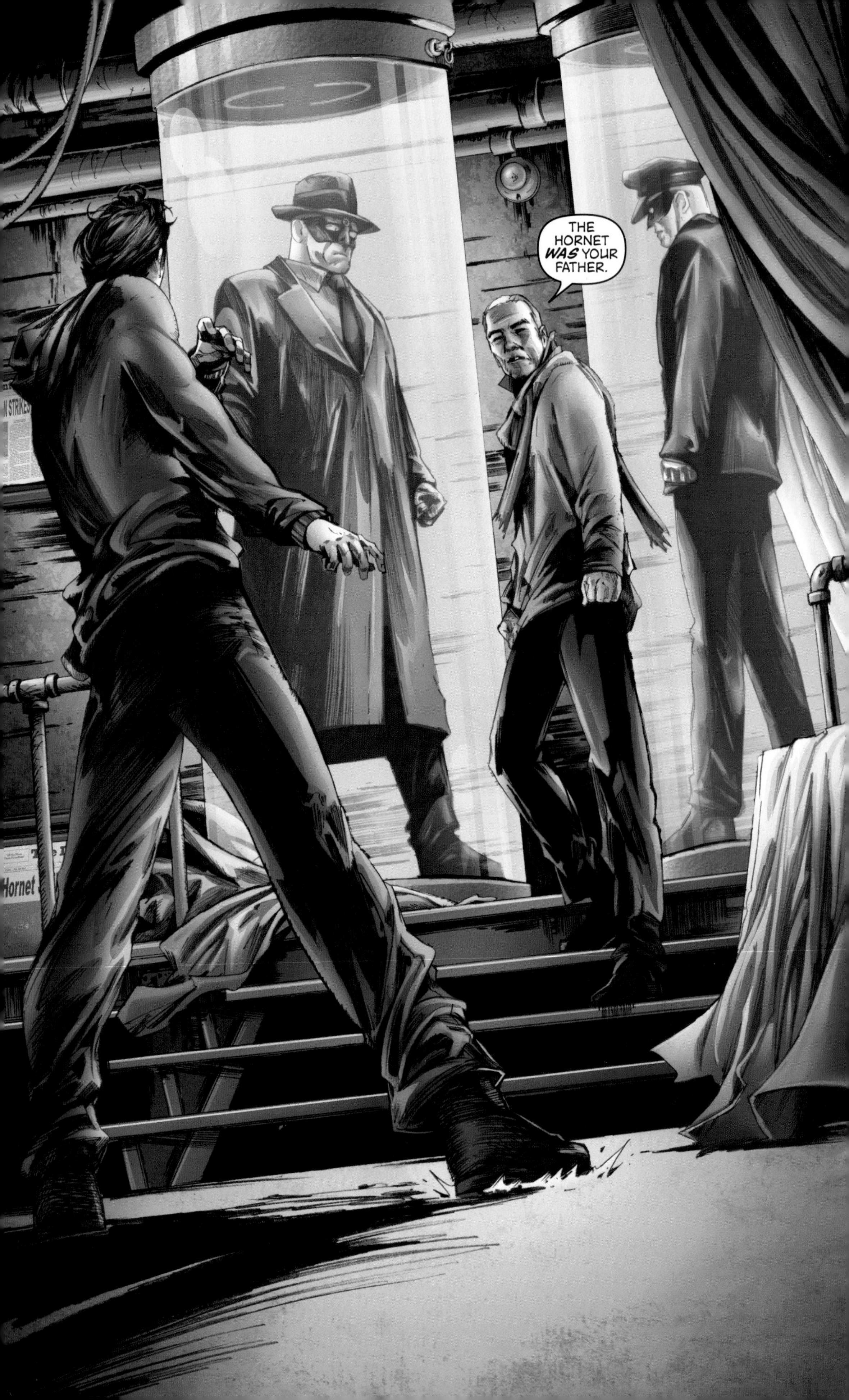
THE HORNET WAS YOUR FATHER.
Hornet

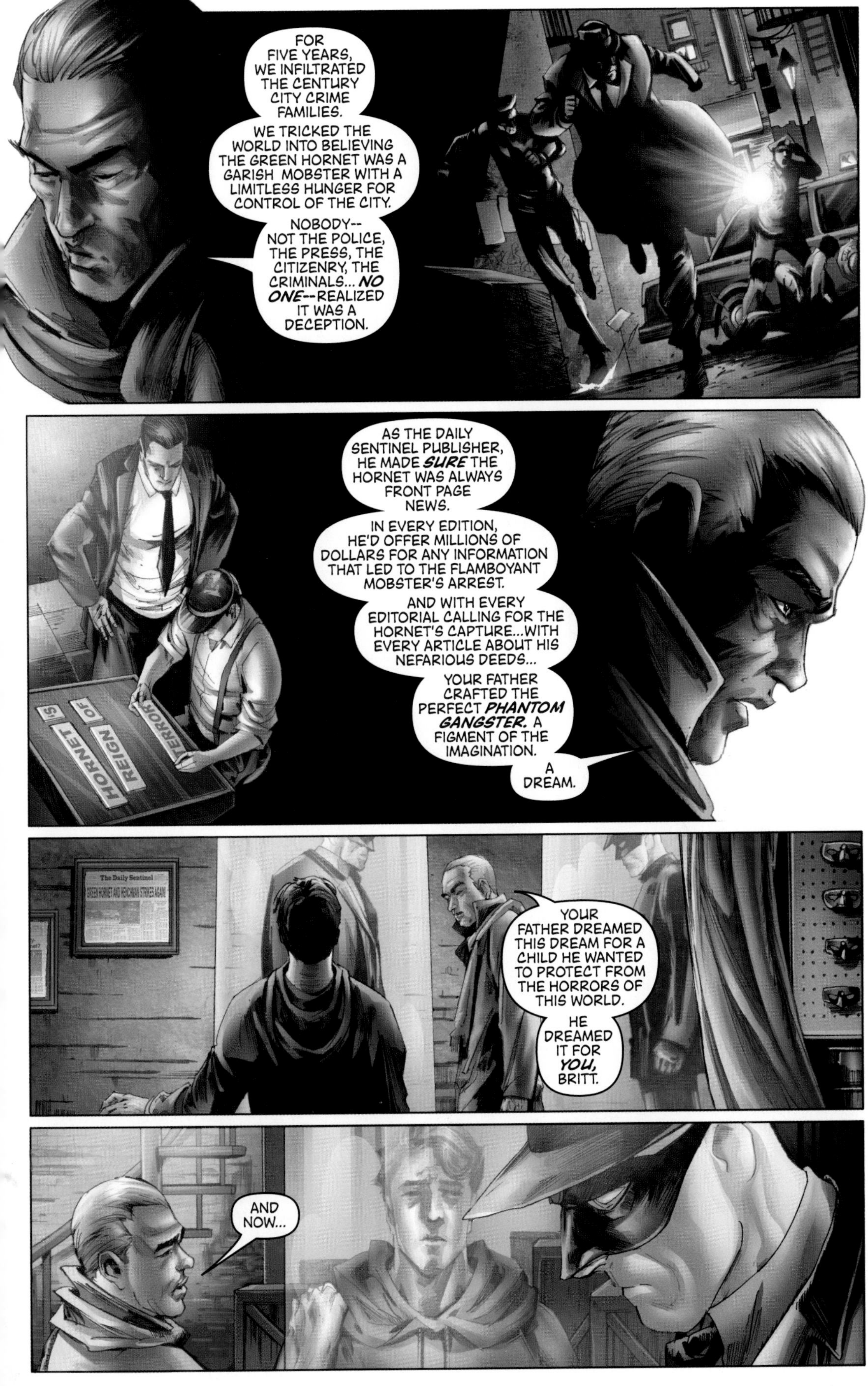

FOR FIVE YEARS, WE INFILTRATED THE CENTURY CITY CRIME FAMILIES.
WE TRICKED THE WORLD INTO BELIEVING THE GREEN HORNET WAS A GARISH MOBSTER WITH A LIMITLESS HUNGER FOR CONTROL OF THE CITY.
NOBODY-- NOT THE POLICE, THE PRESS, THE CITIZENRY, THE CRIMINALS... NO ONE--REALIZED IT WAS A DECEPTION.
IS
HORNET
OF
REIGN
TERROR
AS THE DAILY SENTINEL PUBLISHER, HE MADE SURE THE HORNET WAS ALWAYS FRONT PAGE NEWS.
IN EVERY EDITION, HE'D OFFER MILLIONS OF DOLLARS FOR ANY INFORMATION THAT LED TO THE FLAMBOYANT MOBSTER'S ARREST.
AND WITH EVERY EDITORIAL CALLING FOR THE HORNET'S CAPTURE...WITH EVERY ARTICLE ABOUT HIS NEFARIOUS DEEDS...
YOUR FATHER CRAFTED THE PERFECT PHANTOM GANGSTER. A FIGMENT OF THE IMAGINATION.
A DREAM.
The Daily Sentinel
GREEN HORNET AND HENCHMAN STRIKES AGAIN!
YOUR FATHER DREAMED THIS DREAM FOR A CHILD HE WANTED TO PROTECT FROM THE HORRORS OF THIS WORLD.
HE DREAMED IT FOR YOU, BRITT.
AND NOW...

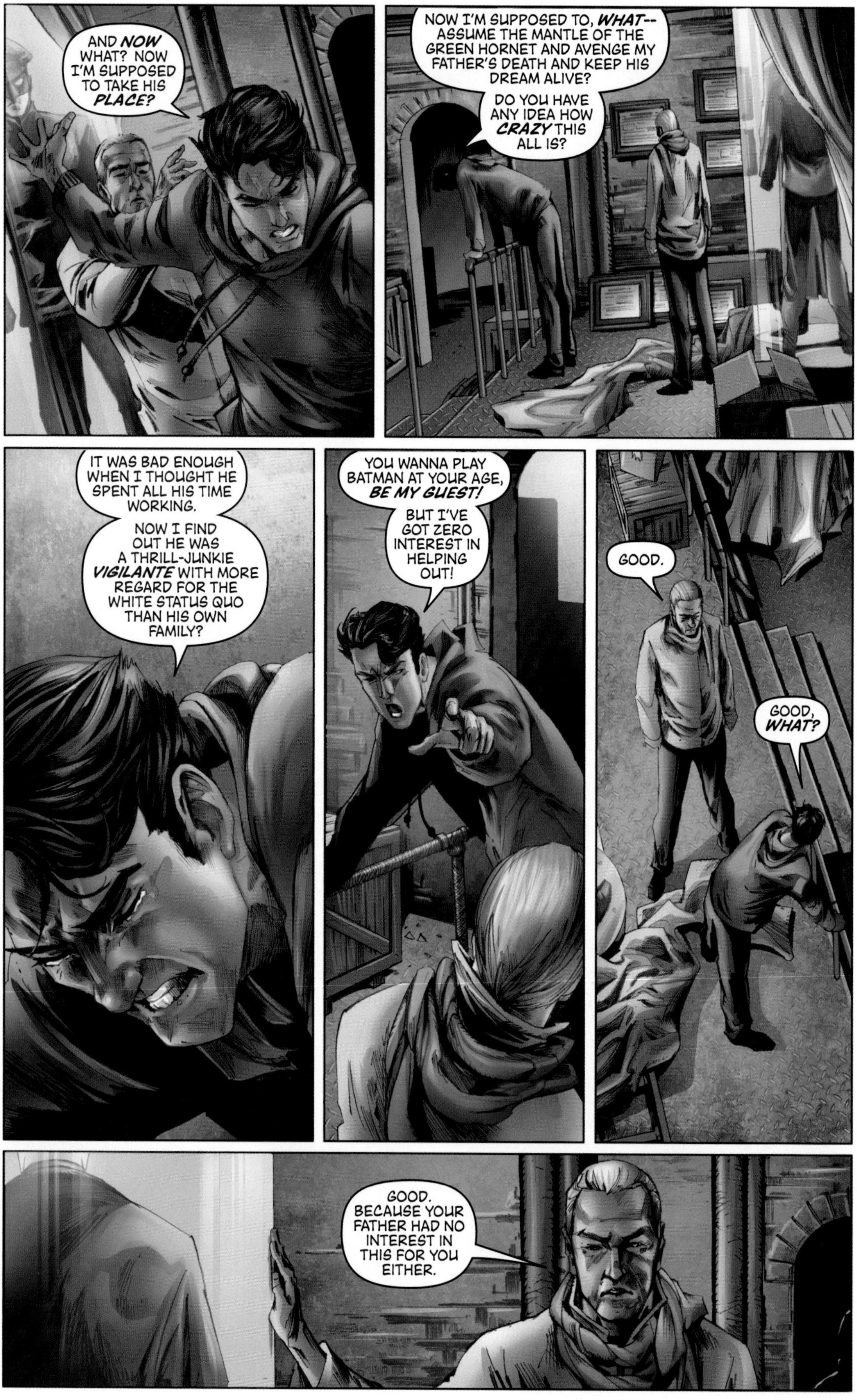
AND NOW WHAT? NOW I'M SUPPOSED TO TAKE HIS PLACE?
NOW I'M SUPPOSED TO, WHAT-- ASSUME THE MANTLE OF THE GREEN HORNET AND AVENGE MY FATHER'S DEATH AND KEEP HIS DREAM ALIVE?
DO YOU HAVE ANY IDEA HOW CRAZY THIS ALL IS?
IT WAS BAD ENOUGH WHEN I THOUGHT HE SPENT ALL HIS TIME WORKING.
NOW I FIND OUT HE WAS A THRILL-JUNKIE VIGILANTE WITH MORE REGARD FOR THE WHITE STATUS QUO THAN HIS OWN FAMILY?
YOU WANNA PLAY BATMAN AT YOUR AGE, BE MY GUEST!
BUT I'VE GOT ZERO INTEREST IN HELPING OUT!
GOOD.
GOOD, WHAT?
GOOD. BECAUSE YOUR FATHER HAD NO INTEREST IN THIS FOR YOU EITHER.

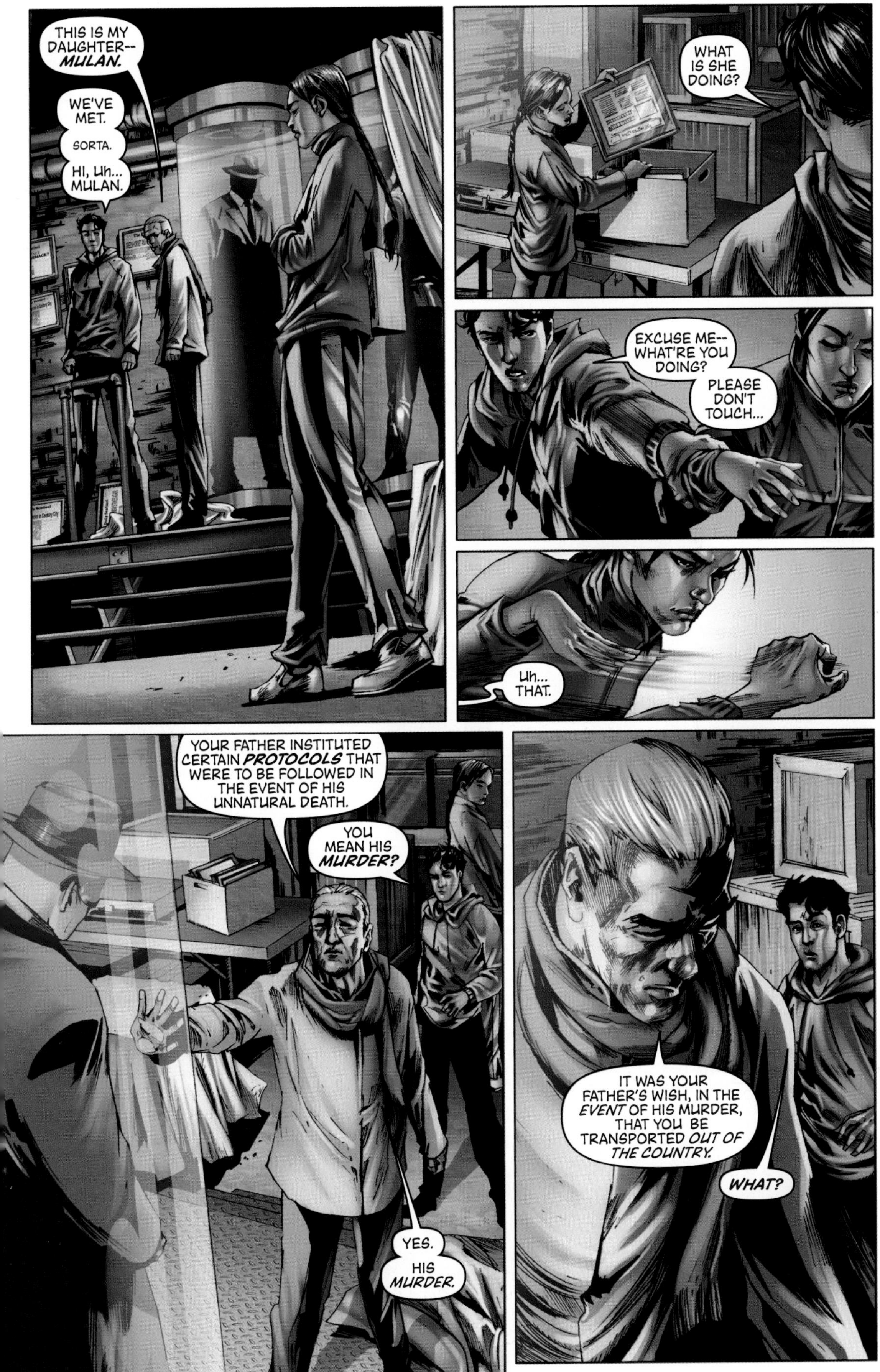
THIS IS MY DAUGHTER-- *MULAN.*
WE'VE MET.
SORTA.
HI, UH... MULAN.
WHAT IS SHE DOING?
EXCUSE ME-- WHAT'RE YOU DOING?
PLEASE DON'T TOUCH...
UH... THAT.
YOUR FATHER INSTITUTED CERTAIN *PROTOCOLS* THAT WERE TO BE FOLLOWED IN THE EVENT OF HIS UNNATURAL DEATH.
YOU MEAN HIS *MURDER?*
YES. HIS *MURDER.*
IT WAS YOUR FATHER'S WISH, IN THE *EVENT* OF HIS MURDER, THAT YOU BE TRANSPORTED *OUT OF THE COUNTRY.*
WHAT?

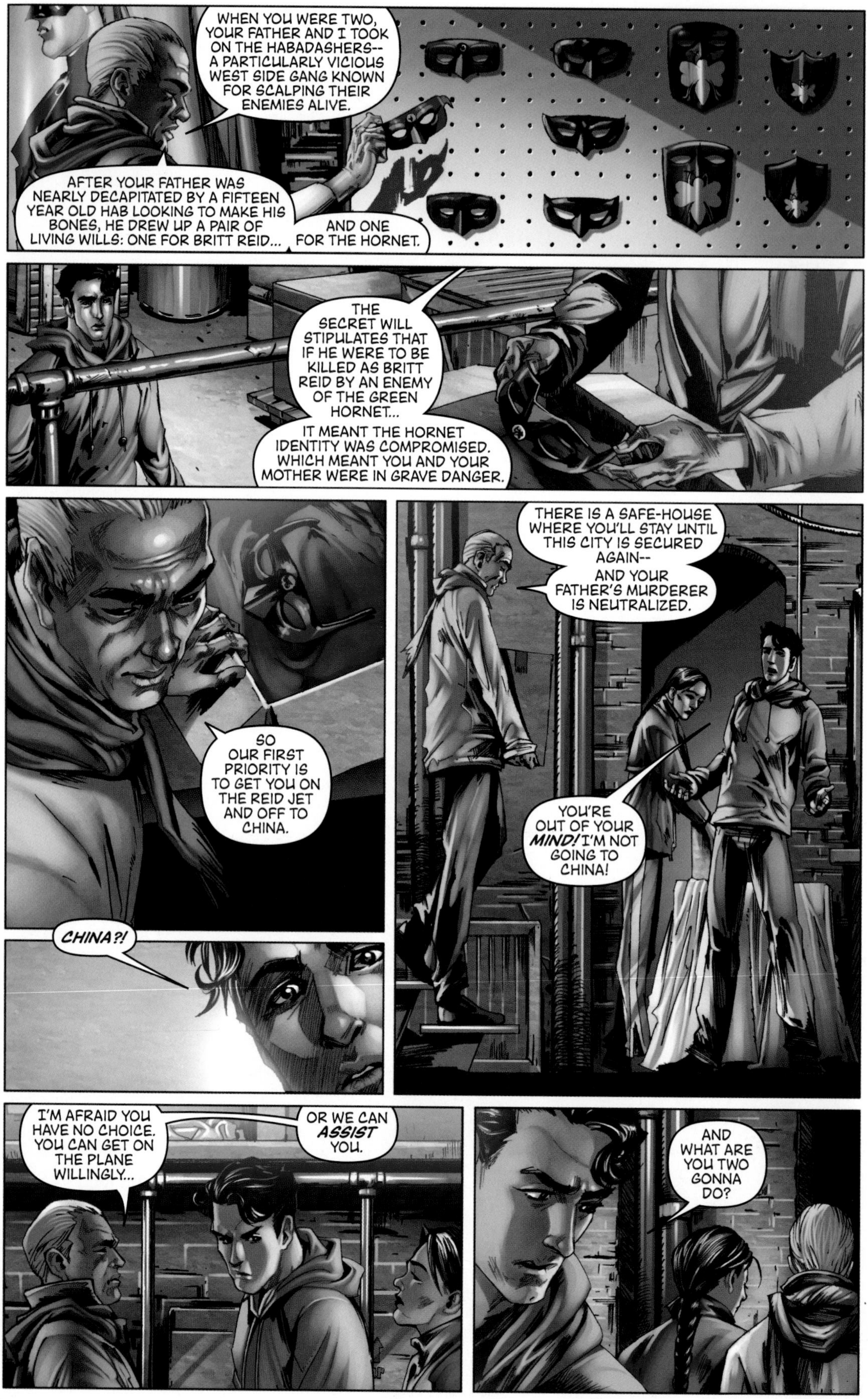
WHEN YOU WERE TWO, YOUR FATHER AND I TOOK ON THE HABADASHERS-- A PARTICULARLY VICIOUS WEST SIDE GANG KNOWN FOR SCALPING THEIR ENEMIES ALIVE.
AFTER YOUR FATHER WAS NEARLY DECAPITATED BY A FIFTEEN YEAR OLD HAB LOOKING TO MAKE HIS BONES, HE DREW UP A PAIR OF LIVING WILLS: ONE FOR BRITT REID...
AND ONE FOR THE HORNET.
THE SECRET WILL STIPULATES THAT IF HE WERE TO BE KILLED AS BRITT REID BY AN ENEMY OF THE GREEN HORNET...
IT MEANT THE HORNET IDENTITY WAS COMPROMISED. WHICH MEANT YOU AND YOUR MOTHER WERE IN GRAVE DANGER.
SO OUR FIRST PRIORITY IS TO GET YOU ON THE REID JET AND OFF TO CHINA.
CHINA?!
THERE IS A SAFE-HOUSE WHERE YOU'LL STAY UNTIL THIS CITY IS SECURED AGAIN--
AND YOUR FATHER'S MURDERER IS NEUTRALIZED.
YOU'RE OUT OF YOUR MIND! I'M NOT GOING TO CHINA!
I'M AFRAID YOU HAVE NO CHOICE. YOU CAN GET ON THE PLANE WILLINGLY...
OR WE CAN ASSIST YOU.
AND WHAT ARE YOU TWO GONNA DO?

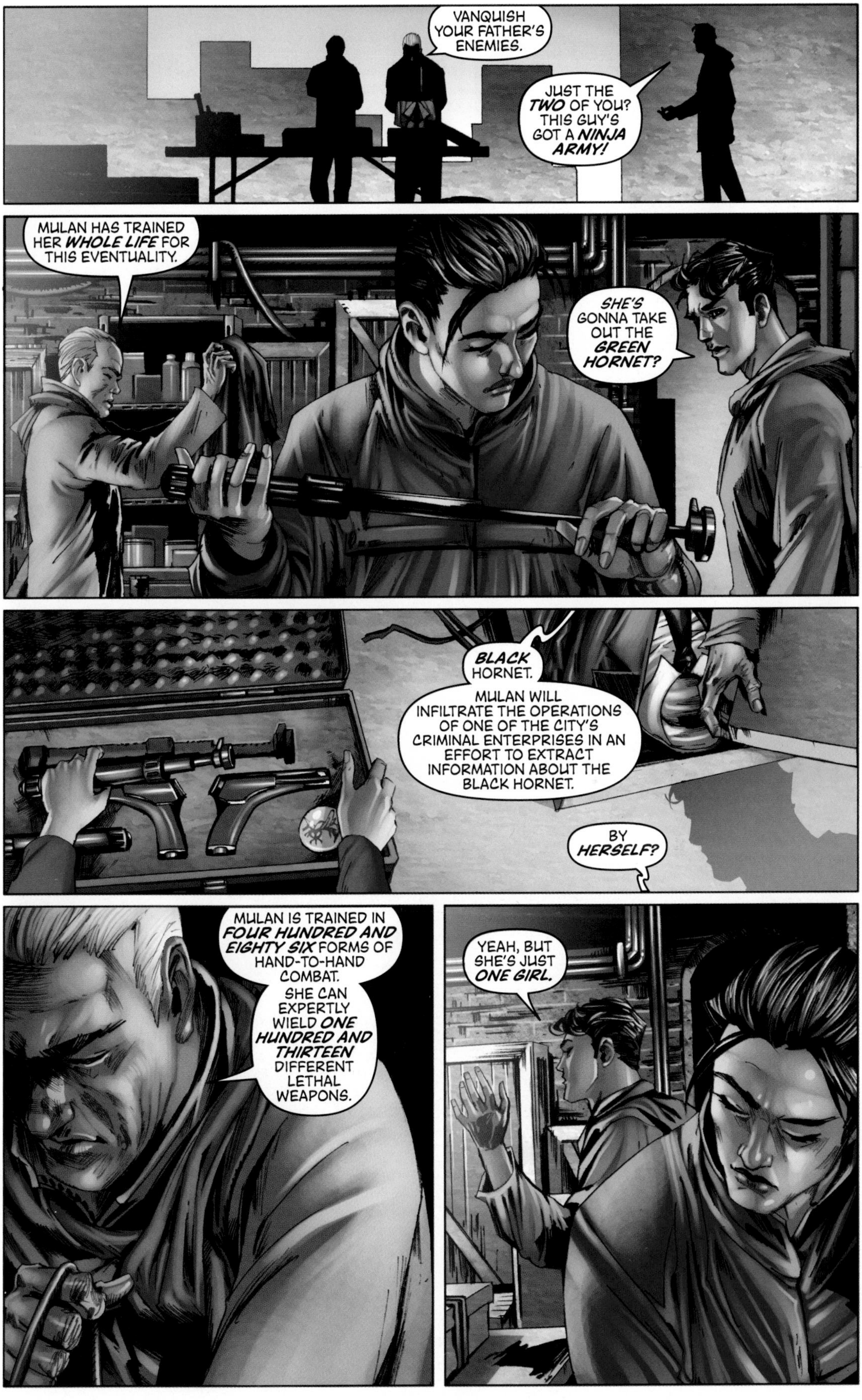
VANQUISH YOUR FATHER'S ENEMIES.
JUST THE TWO OF YOU? THIS GUY'S GOT A NINJA ARMY!
MULAN HAS TRAINED HER WHOLE LIFE FOR THIS EVENTUALITY.
SHE'S GONNA TAKE OUT THE GREEN HORNET?
BLACK HORNET.
MULAN WILL INFILTRATE THE OPERATIONS OF ONE OF THE CITY'S CRIMINAL ENTERPRISES IN AN EFFORT TO EXTRACT INFORMATION ABOUT THE BLACK HORNET.
BY HERSELF?
MULAN IS TRAINED IN FOUR HUNDRED AND EIGHTY SIX FORMS OF HAND-TO-HAND COMBAT.
SHE CAN EXPERTLY WIELD ONE HUNDRED AND THIRTEEN DIFFERENT LETHAL WEAPONS.
YEAH, BUT SHE'S JUST ONE GIRL.

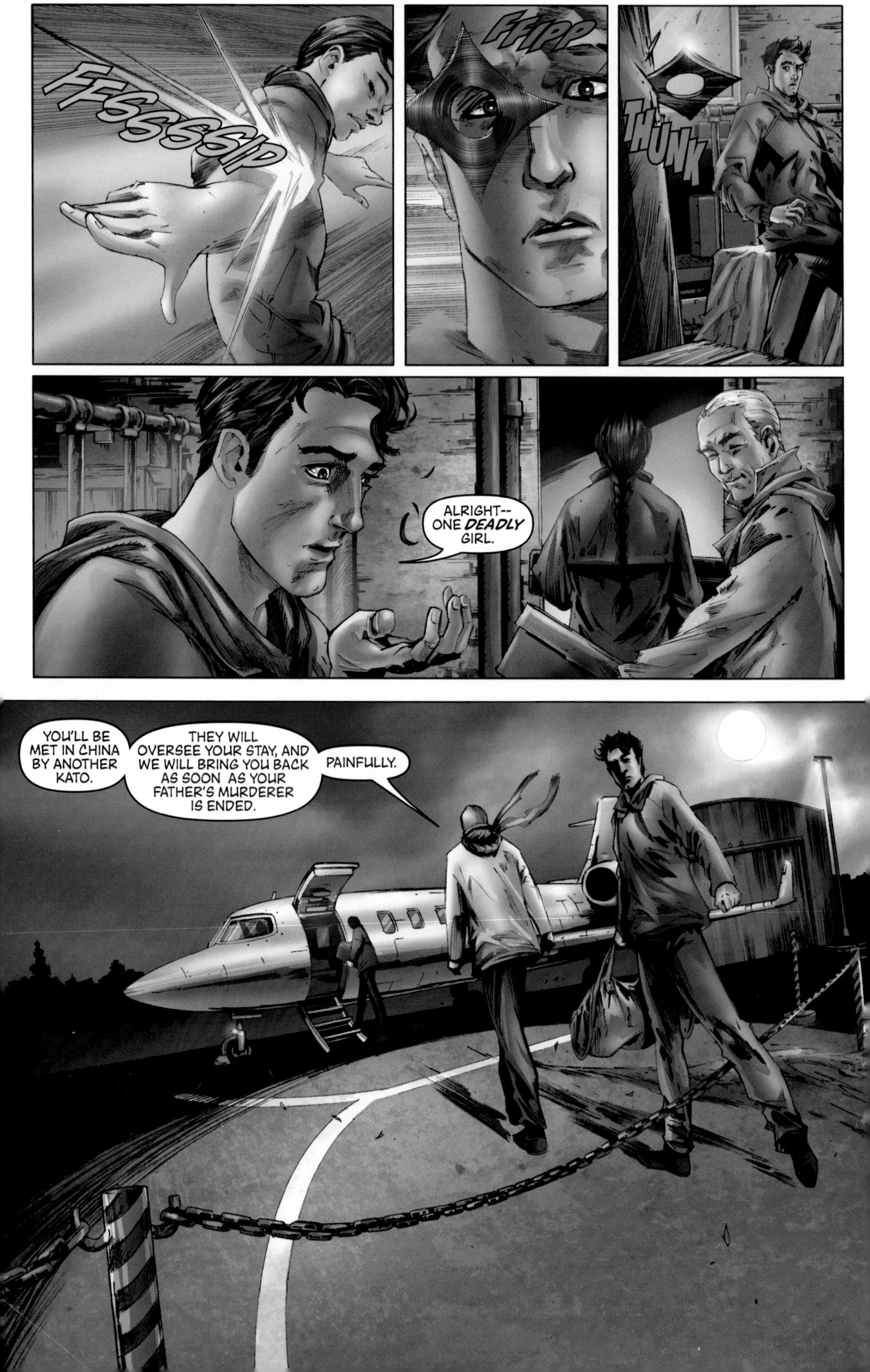
FFSSSSIP
FFIPP
THUNK
ALRIGHT-- ONE DEADLY GIRL.
YOU'LL BE MET IN CHINA BY ANOTHER KATO.
THEY WILL OVERSEE YOUR STAY, AND WE WILL BRING YOU BACK AS SOON AS YOUR FATHER'S MURDERER IS ENDED.
PAINFULLY.

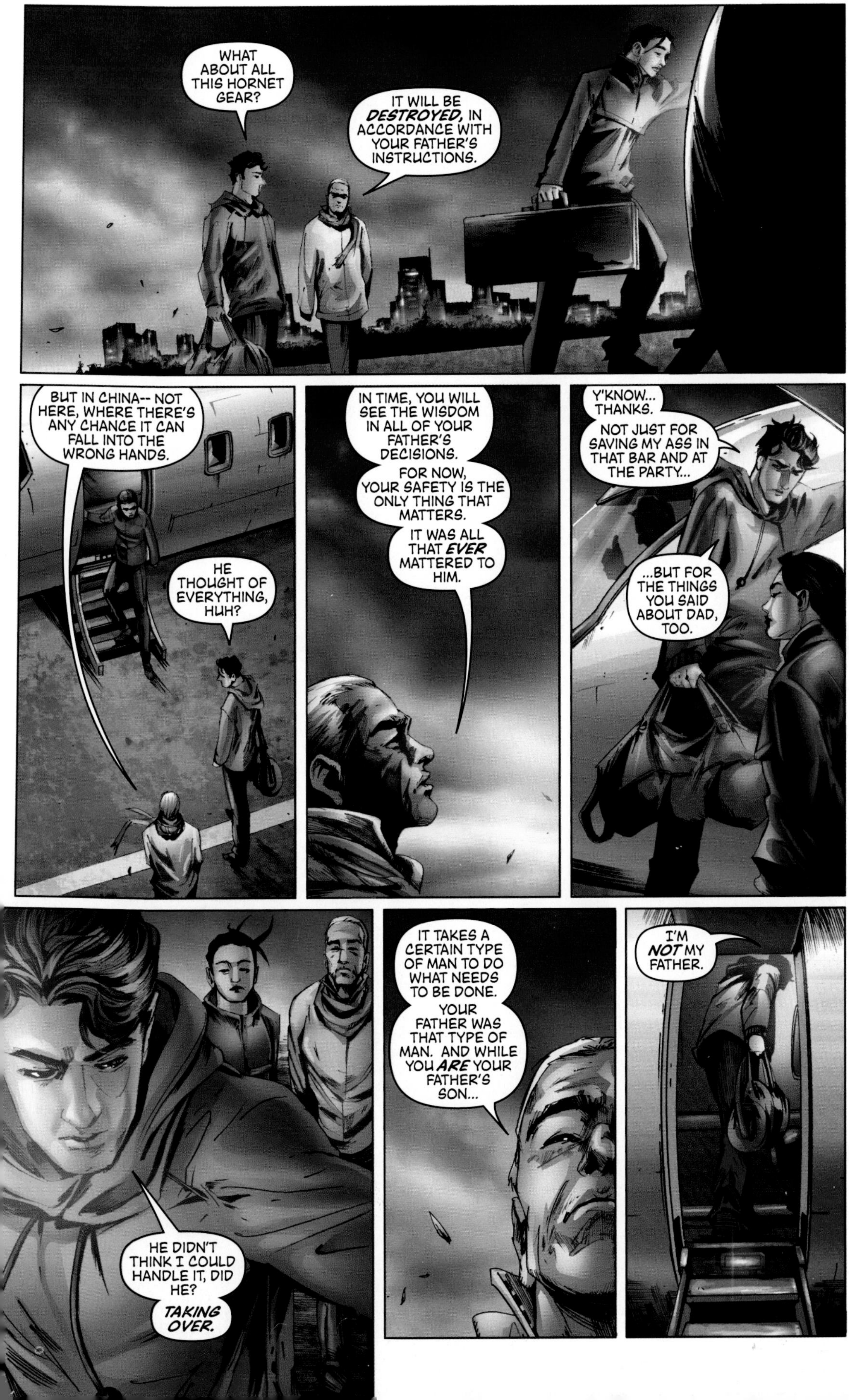
WHAT ABOUT ALL THIS HORNET GEAR?
IT WILL BE *DESTROYED,* IN ACCORDANCE WITH YOUR FATHER'S INSTRUCTIONS.
BUT IN CHINA-- NOT HERE, WHERE THERE'S ANY CHANCE IT CAN FALL INTO THE WRONG HANDS.
HE THOUGHT OF EVERYTHING, HUH?
IN TIME, YOU WILL SEE THE WISDOM IN ALL OF YOUR FATHER'S DECISIONS.
FOR NOW, YOUR SAFETY IS THE ONLY THING THAT MATTERS.
IT WAS ALL THAT *EVER* MATTERED TO HIM.
Y'KNOW... THANKS.
NOT JUST FOR SAVING MY ASS IN THAT BAR AND AT THE PARTY...
...BUT FOR THE THINGS YOU SAID ABOUT DAD, TOO.
HE DIDN'T THINK I COULD HANDLE IT, DID HE?
TAKING OVER.
IT TAKES A CERTAIN TYPE OF MAN TO DO WHAT NEEDS TO BE DONE.
YOUR FATHER WAS THAT TYPE OF MAN. AND WHILE YOU *ARE* YOUR FATHER'S SON...
I'M *NOT* MY FATHER.

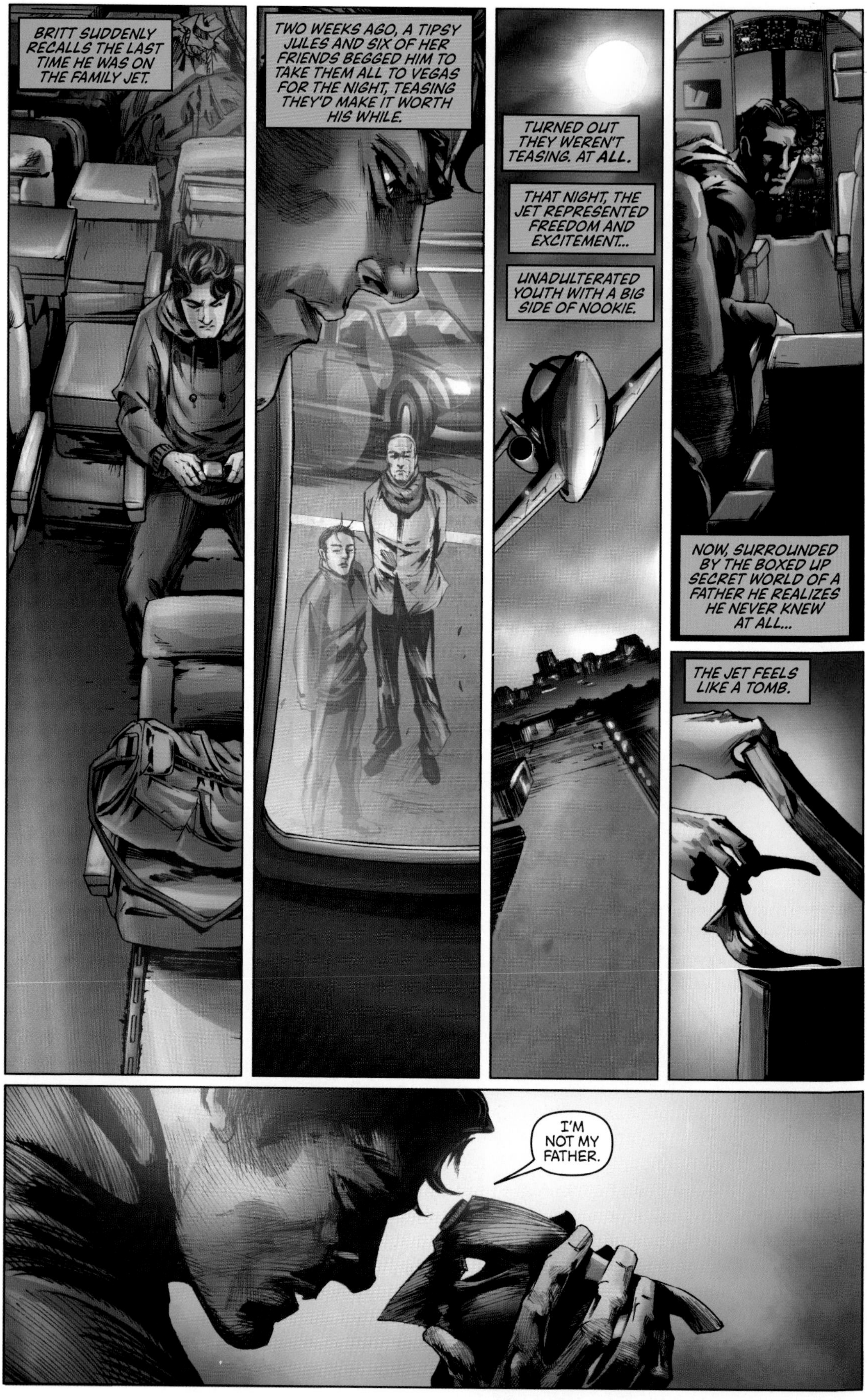
BRITT SUDDENLY RECALLS THE LAST TIME HE WAS ON THE FAMILY JET.
TWO WEEKS AGO, A TIPSY JULES AND SIX OF HER FRIENDS BEGGED HIM TO TAKE THEM ALL TO VEGAS FOR THE NIGHT, TEASING THEY'D MAKE IT WORTH HIS WHILE.
TURNED OUT THEY WEREN'T TEASING. AT ALL.
THAT NIGHT, THE JET REPRESENTED FREEDOM AND EXCITEMENT...
UNADULTERATED YOUTH WITH A BIG SIDE OF NOOKIE.
NOW, SURROUNDED BY THE BOXED UP SECRET WORLD OF A FATHER HE REALIZES HE NEVER KNEW AT ALL...
THE JET FEELS LIKE A TOMB.
I'M NOT MY FATHER.

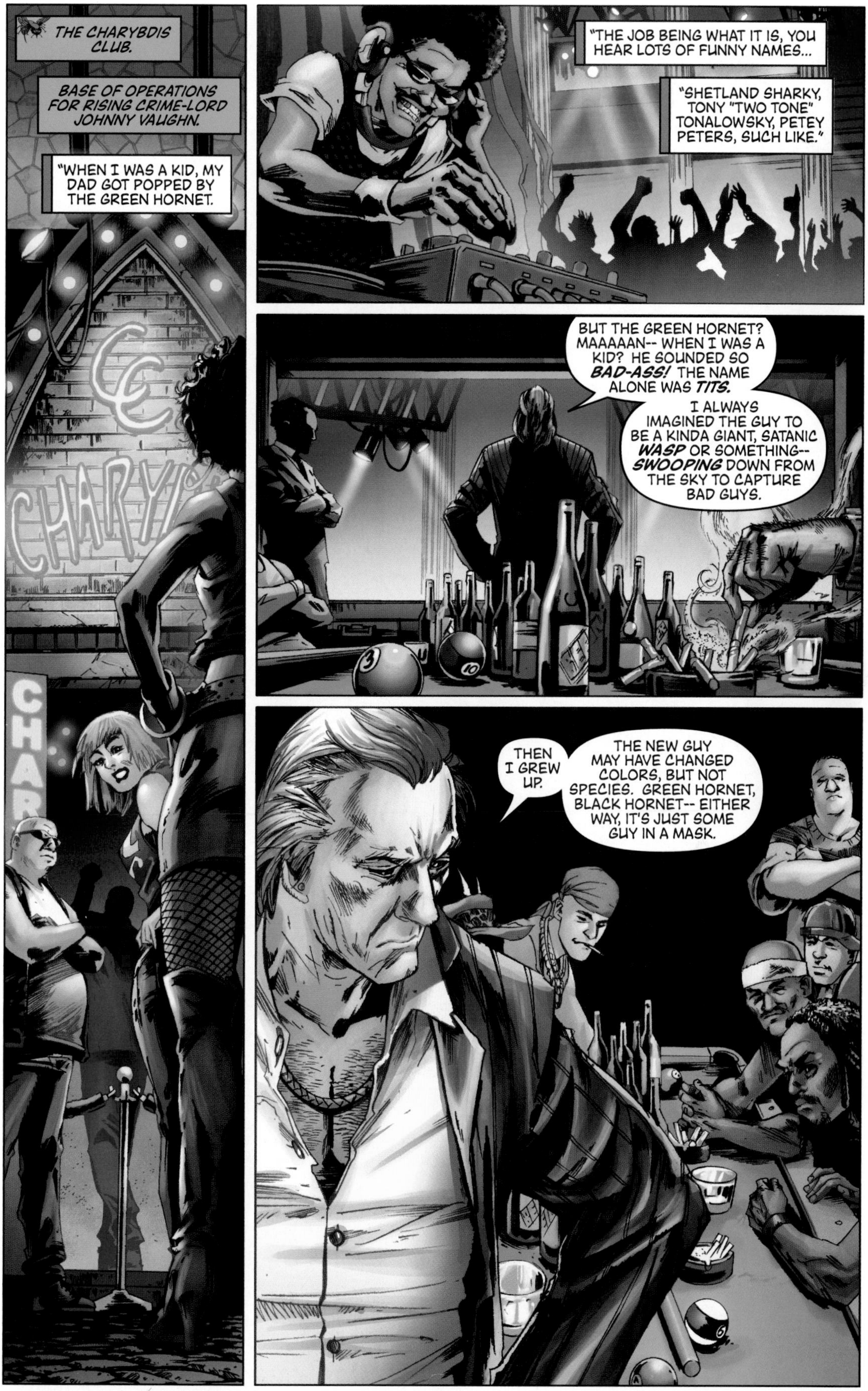
THE CHARYBDIS CLUB.
BASE OF OPERATIONS FOR RISING CRIME-LORD JOHNNY VAUGHN.
"WHEN I WAS A KID, MY DAD GOT POPPED BY THE GREEN HORNET.
"THE JOB BEING WHAT IT IS, YOU HEAR LOTS OF FUNNY NAMES...
"SHETLAND SHARKY, TONY "TWO TONE" TONALOWSKY, PETEY PETERS, SUCH LIKE."
BUT THE GREEN HORNET? MAAAAAN-- WHEN I WAS A KID? HE SOUNDED SO ***BAD-ASS!*** THE NAME ALONE WAS ***TITS.***
I ALWAYS IMAGINED THE GUY TO BE A KINDA GIANT, SATANIC ***WASP*** OR SOMETHING-- ***SWOOPING*** DOWN FROM THE SKY TO CAPTURE BAD GUYS.
THEN I GREW UP.
THE NEW GUY MAY HAVE CHANGED COLORS, BUT NOT SPECIES. GREEN HORNET, BLACK HORNET-- EITHER WAY, IT'S JUST SOME GUY IN A MASK.

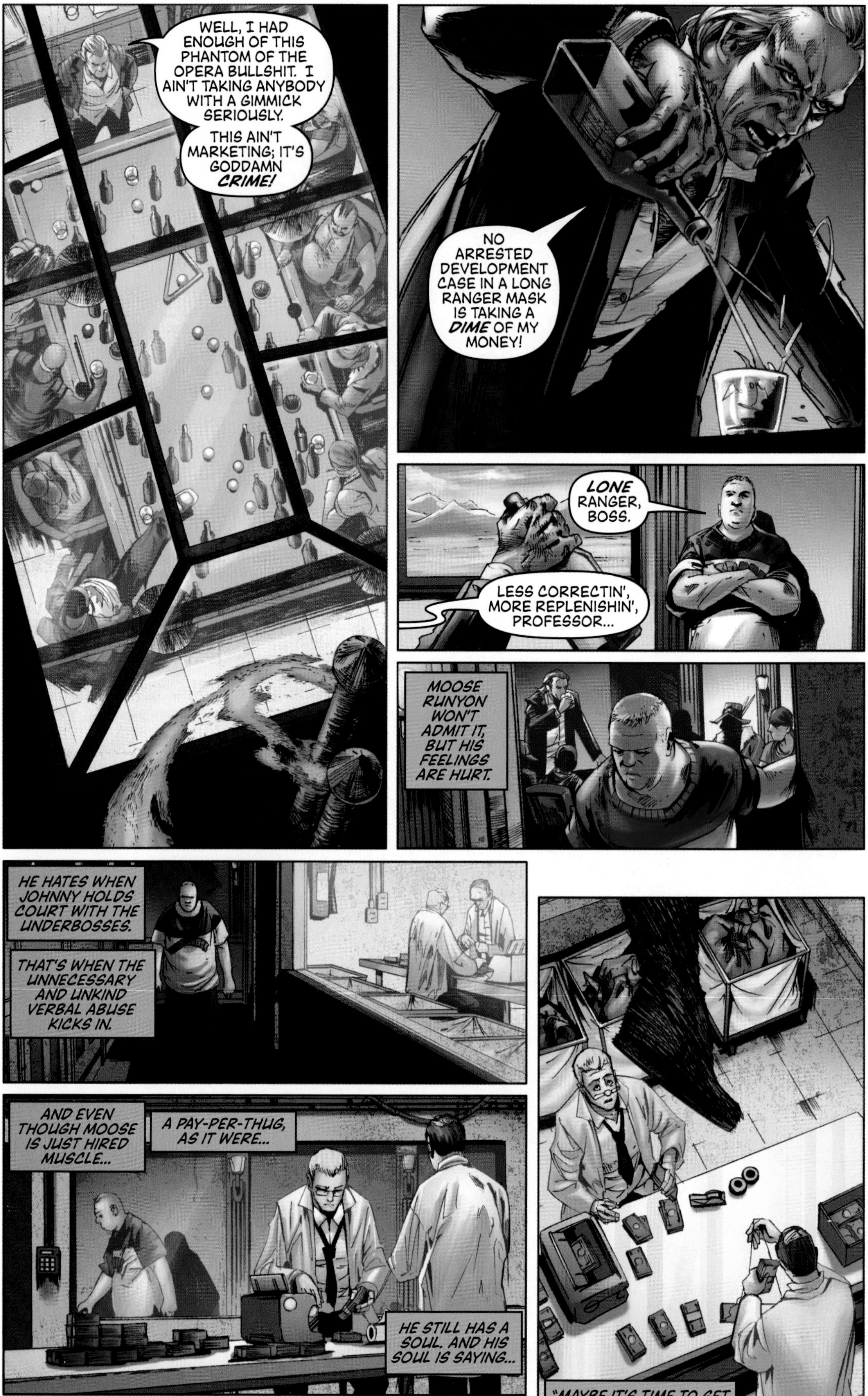

WELL, I HAD ENOUGH OF THIS PHANTOM OF THE OPERA BULLSHIT. I AIN'T TAKING ANYBODY WITH A GIMMICK SERIOUSLY.
THIS AIN'T MARKETING; IT'S GODDAMN *CRIME!*
NO ARRESTED DEVELOPMENT CASE IN A LONG RANGER MASK IS TAKING A *DIME* OF MY MONEY!
LONE RANGER, BOSS.
LESS CORRECTIN', MORE REPLENISHIN', PROFESSOR...
MOOSE RUNYON WON'T ADMIT IT, BUT HIS FEELINGS ARE HURT.
HE HATES WHEN JOHNNY HOLDS COURT WITH THE UNDERBOSSES.
THAT'S WHEN THE UNNECESSARY AND UNKIND VERBAL ABUSE KICKS IN.
AND EVEN THOUGH MOOSE IS JUST HIRED MUSCLE...
A PAY-PER-THUG, AS IT WERE...
HE STILL HAS A SOUL. AND HIS SOUL IS SAYING...
"MAYBE IT'S TIME TO GET OUT OF THIS LOUSY BUSINESS..."

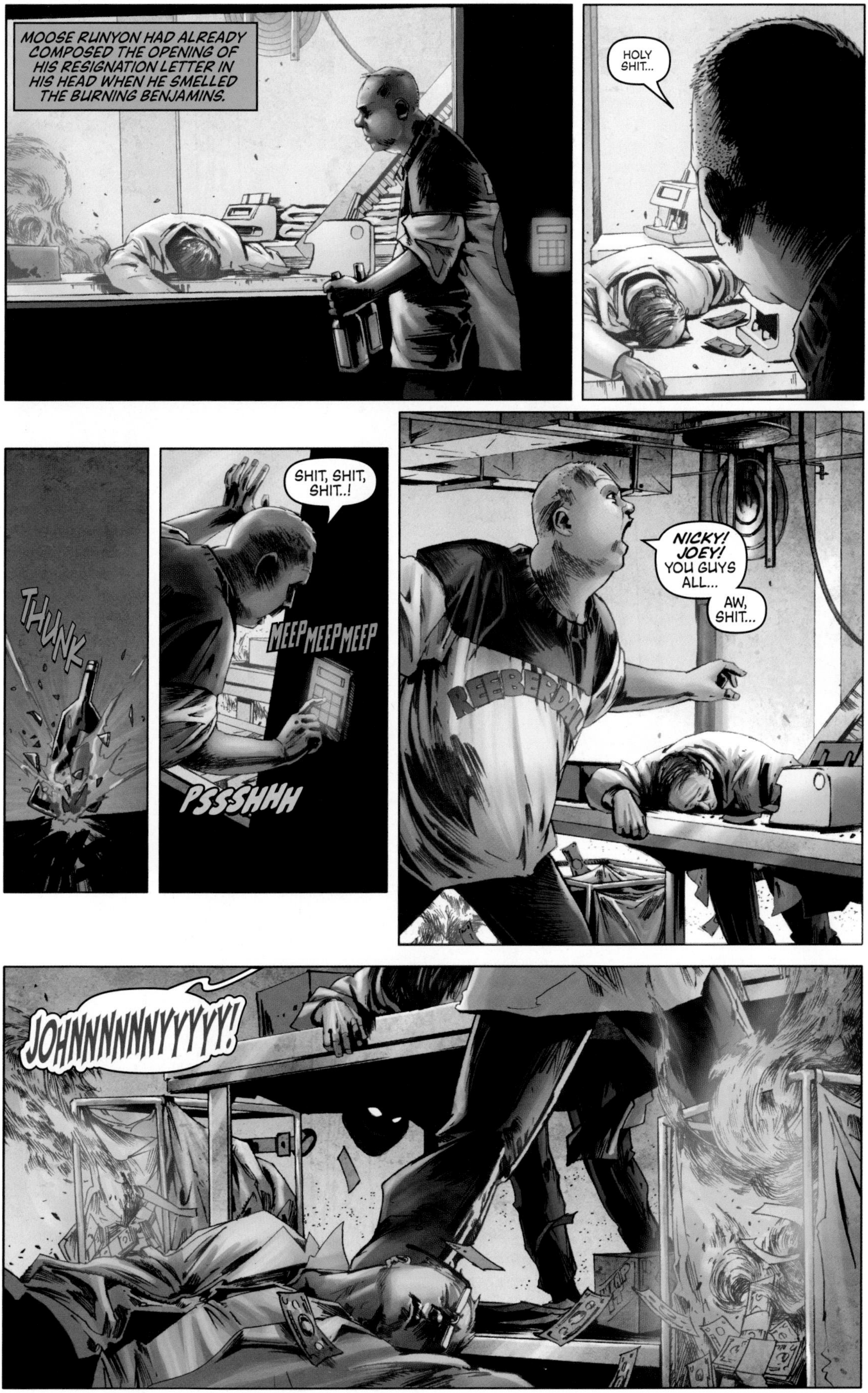
MOOSE RUNYON HAD ALREADY COMPOSED THE OPENING OF HIS RESIGNATION LETTER IN HIS HEAD WHEN HE SMELLED THE BURNING BENJAMINS.
HOLY SHIT...
THUNK
SHIT, SHIT, SHIT..!
MEEP MEEP MEEP
PSSSHHH
NICKY! JOEY! YOU GUYS ALL...
AW, SHIT...
JOHNNNNNNYYYY!

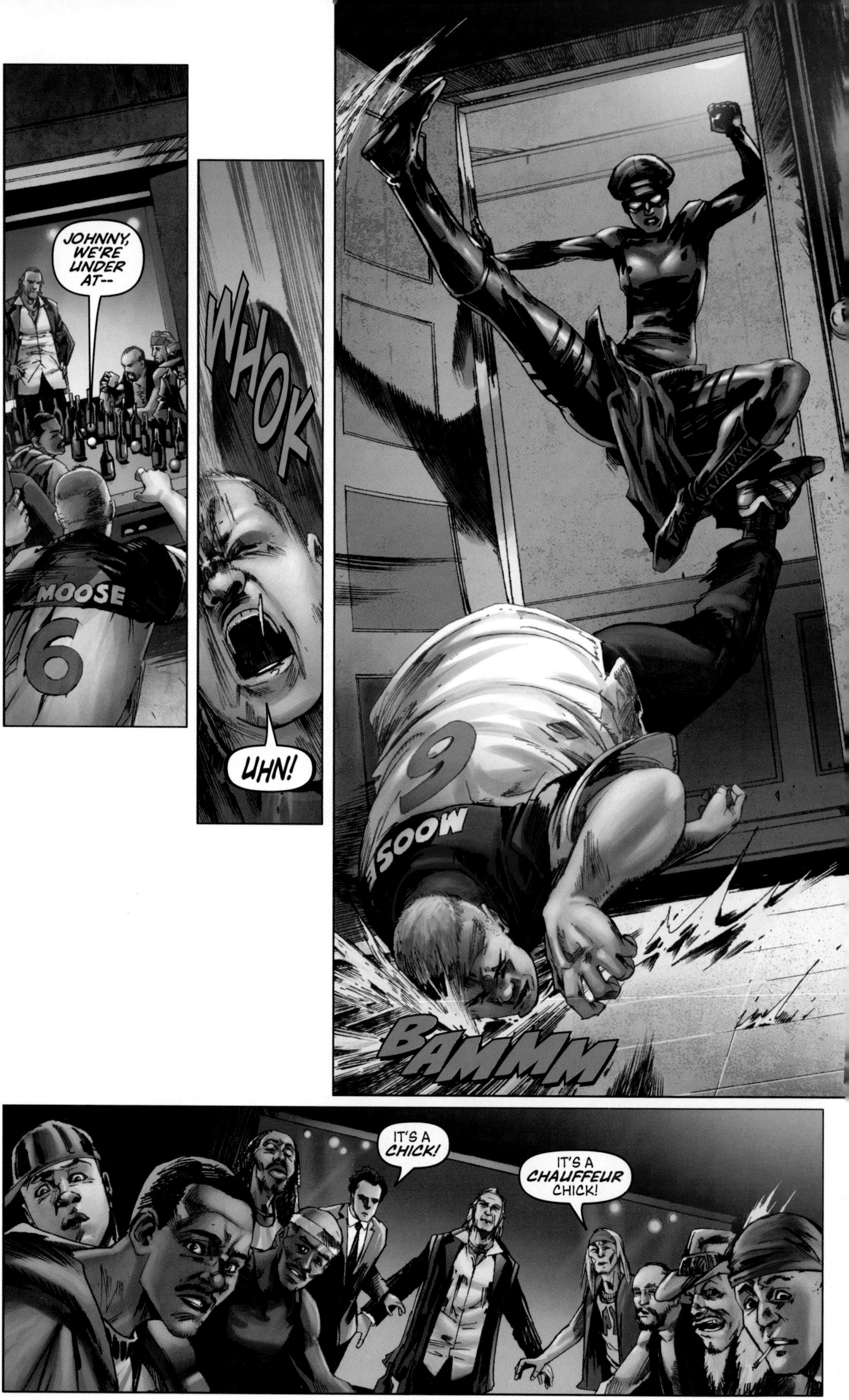
JOHNNY, WE'RE UNDER AT--
MOOSE
6
WHOK
UHN!
MOOSE
6
BAMMM
IT'S A CHICK!
IT'S A CHAUFFEUR CHICK!

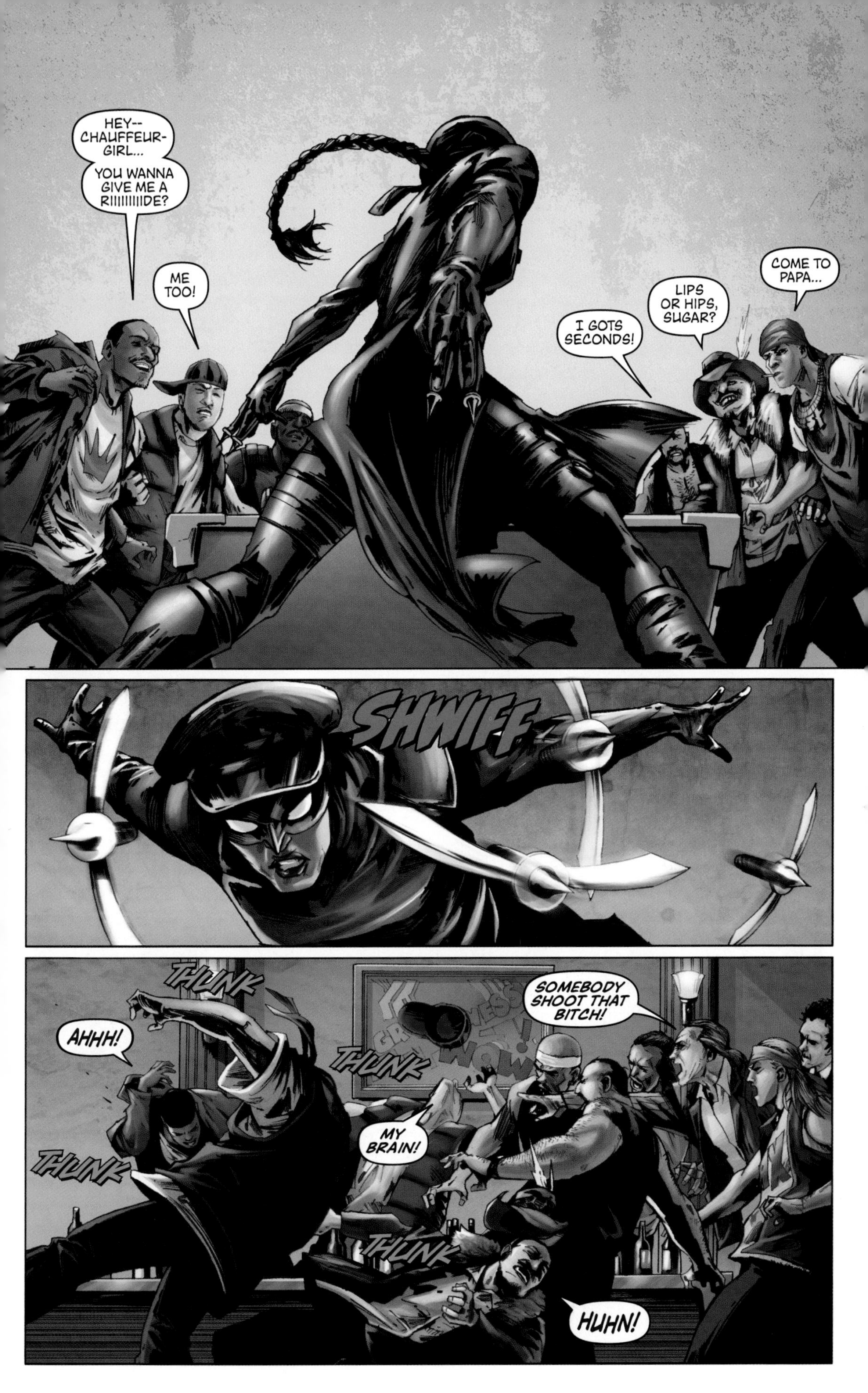
HEY-- CHAUFFEUR-GIRL...
YOU WANNA GIVE ME A RIIIIIIIIDE?
ME TOO!
I GOTS SECONDS!
LIPS OR HIPS, SUGAR?
COME TO PAPA...
SHWIFF
THUNK
AHHH!
THUNK
SOMEBODY SHOOT THAT BITCH!
THUNK
MY BRAIN!
THUNK
HUHN!

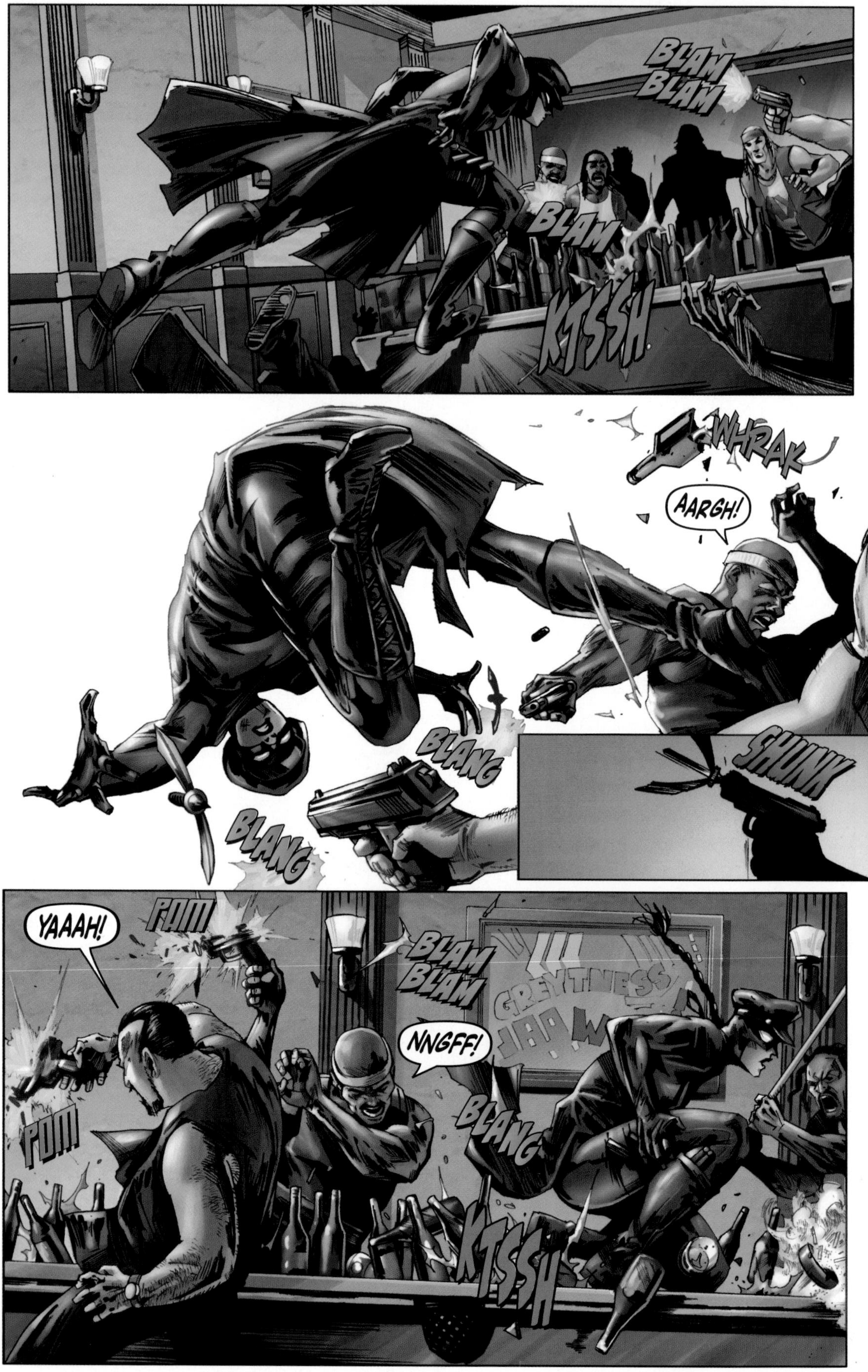
BLAM
BLAM
BLAM
KTSSH
WHRAK
AARGH!
BLANG
BLANG
SHUNK
YAAAH!
POM
BLAM
BLAM
POM
NNGFF!
GREYTNESS
BLANG
KTSSH

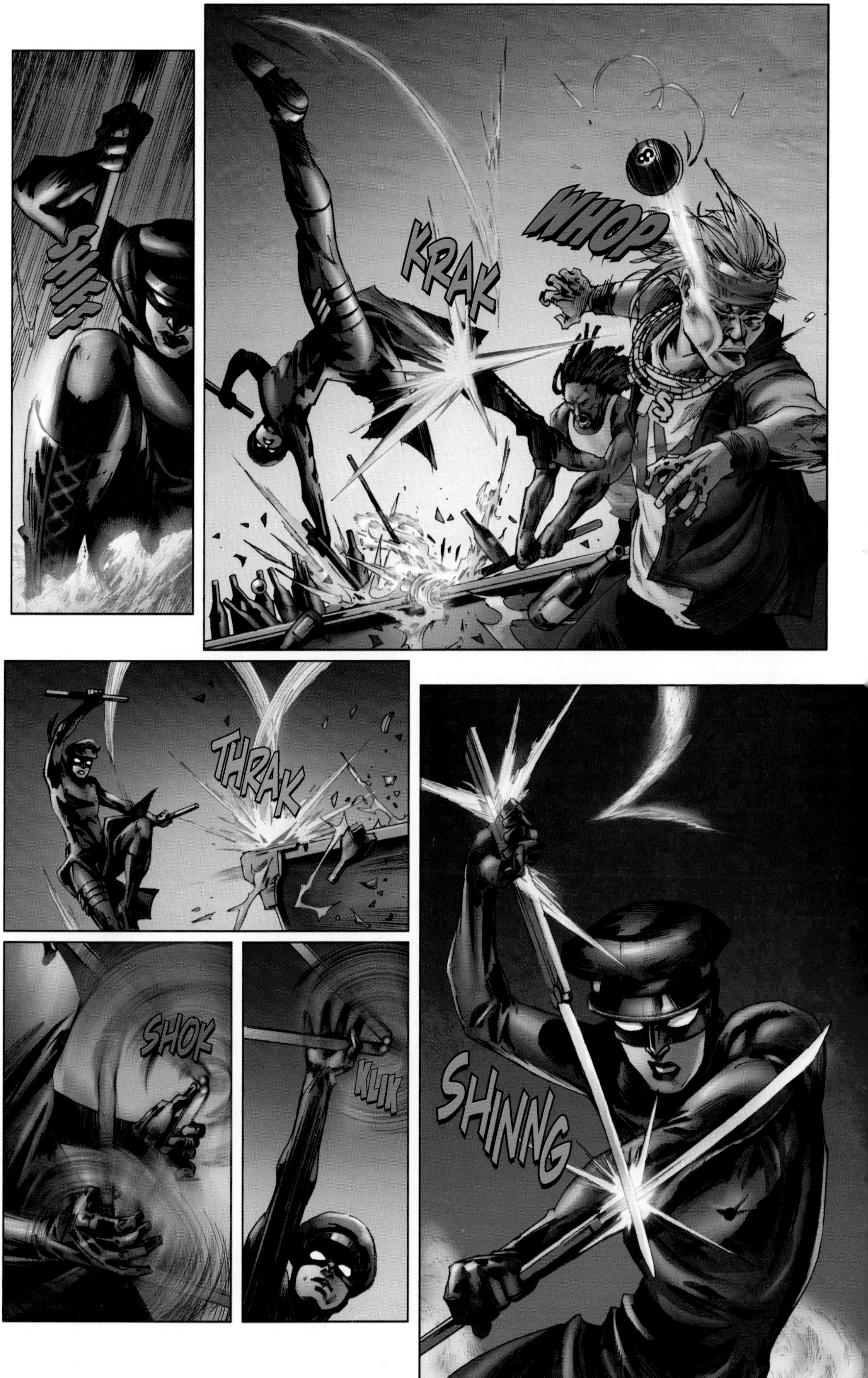
SHIFF
KRAK
WHOP
THRAK
SHOK
KLIK
SHINNG

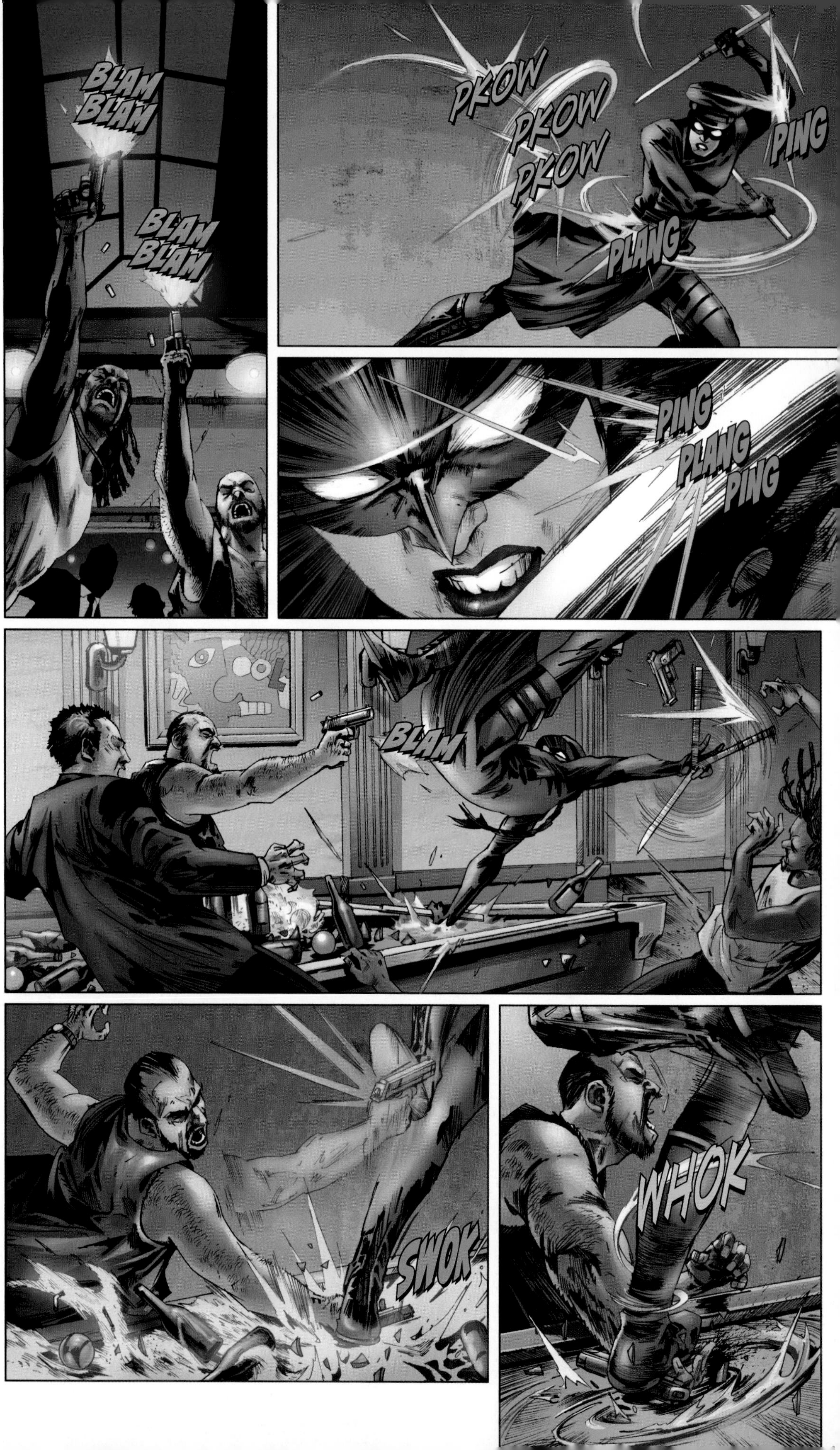
BLAM
BLAM
BLAM
BLAM
PKOW
PKOW
PKOW
PING
PLANG
PING
PLANG
PING
BLAM
SWOK
WHOK

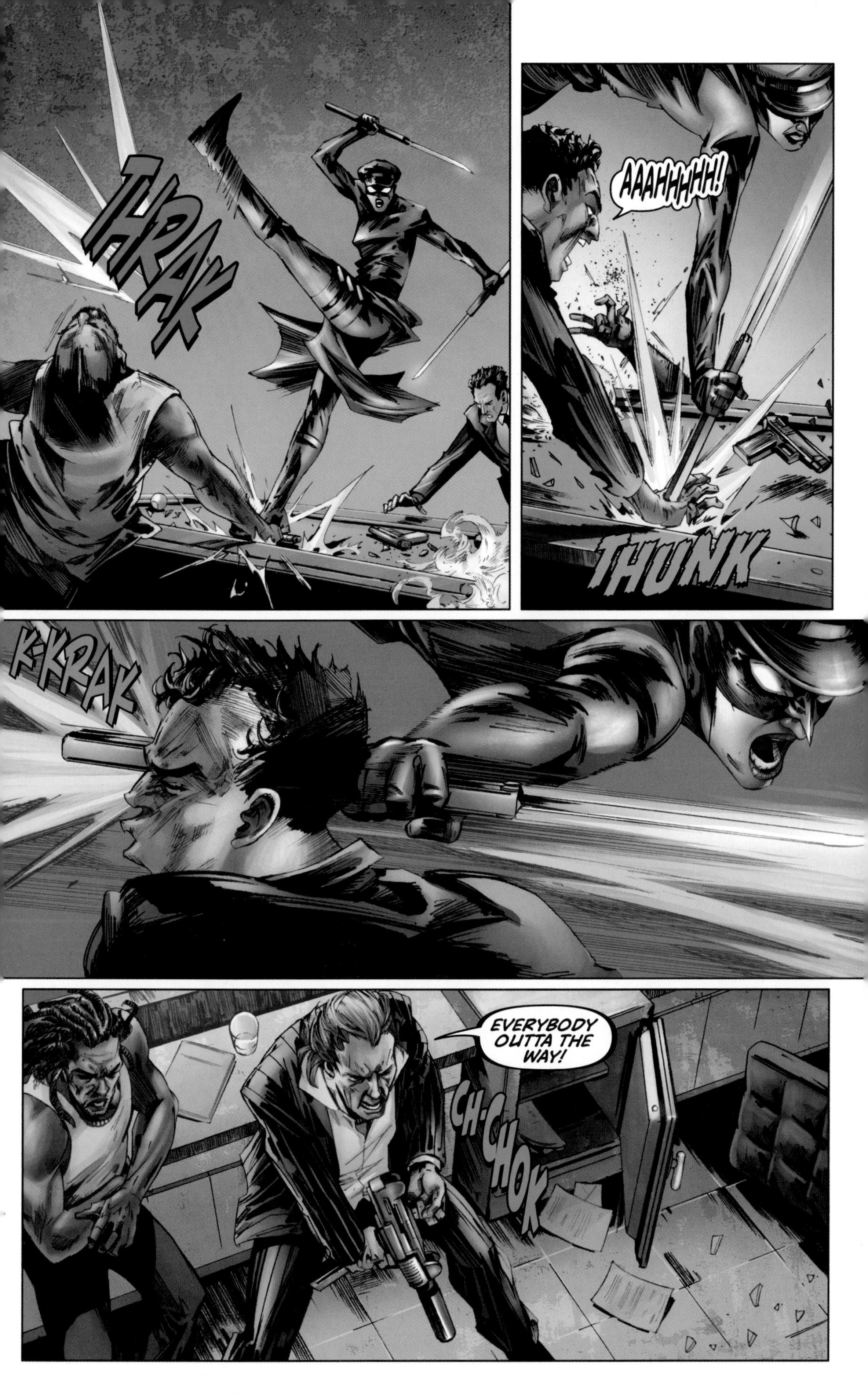
THRAK
AAAHHHHH!
THUNK
K-KRAK
EVERYBODY OUTTA THE WAY!
CH-CHOK

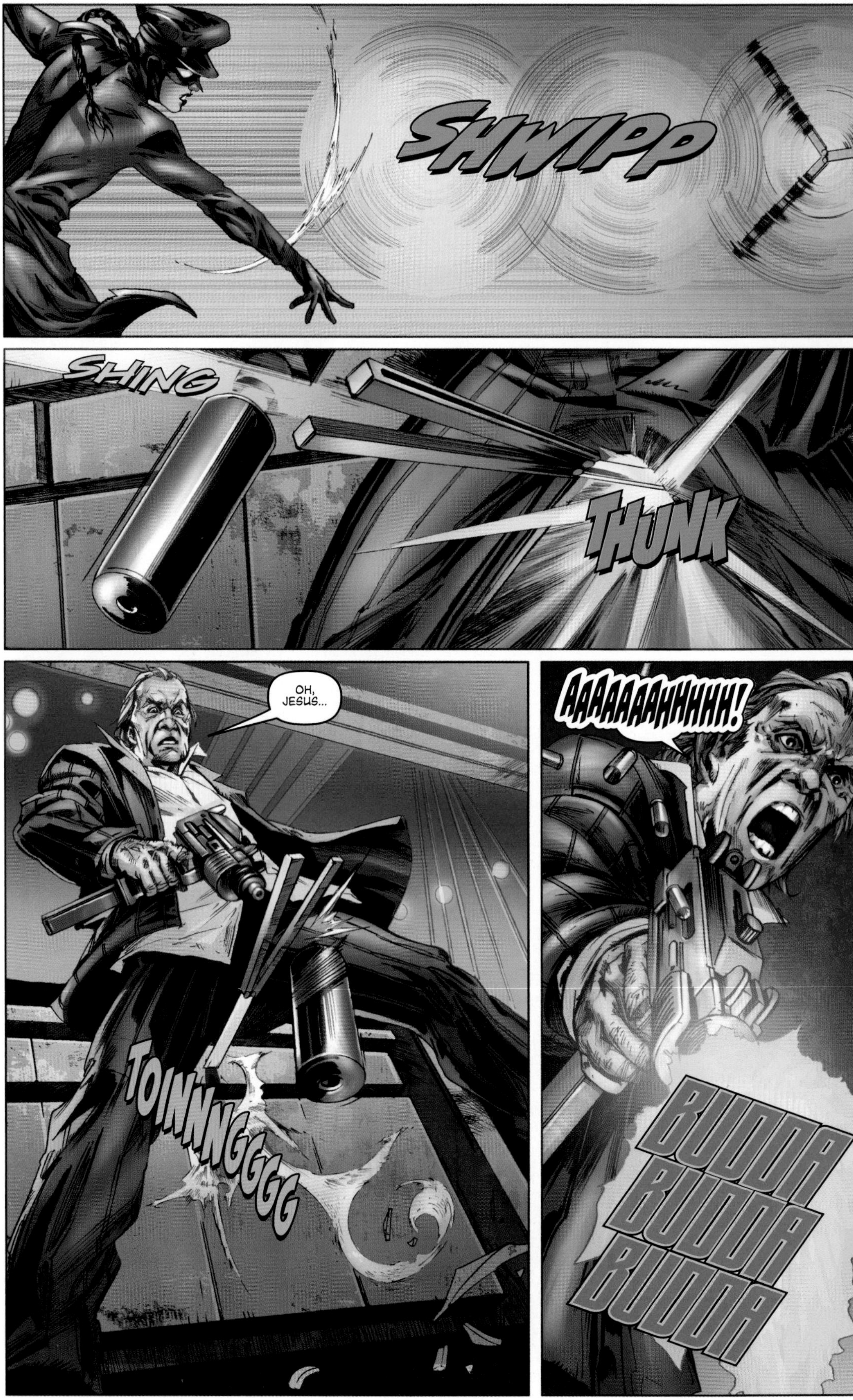
SHWIPP
SHING
THUNK
OH, JESUS...
TOINNNGGGG
AAAAAAAHHHHH!
BUDDA BUDDA BUDDA

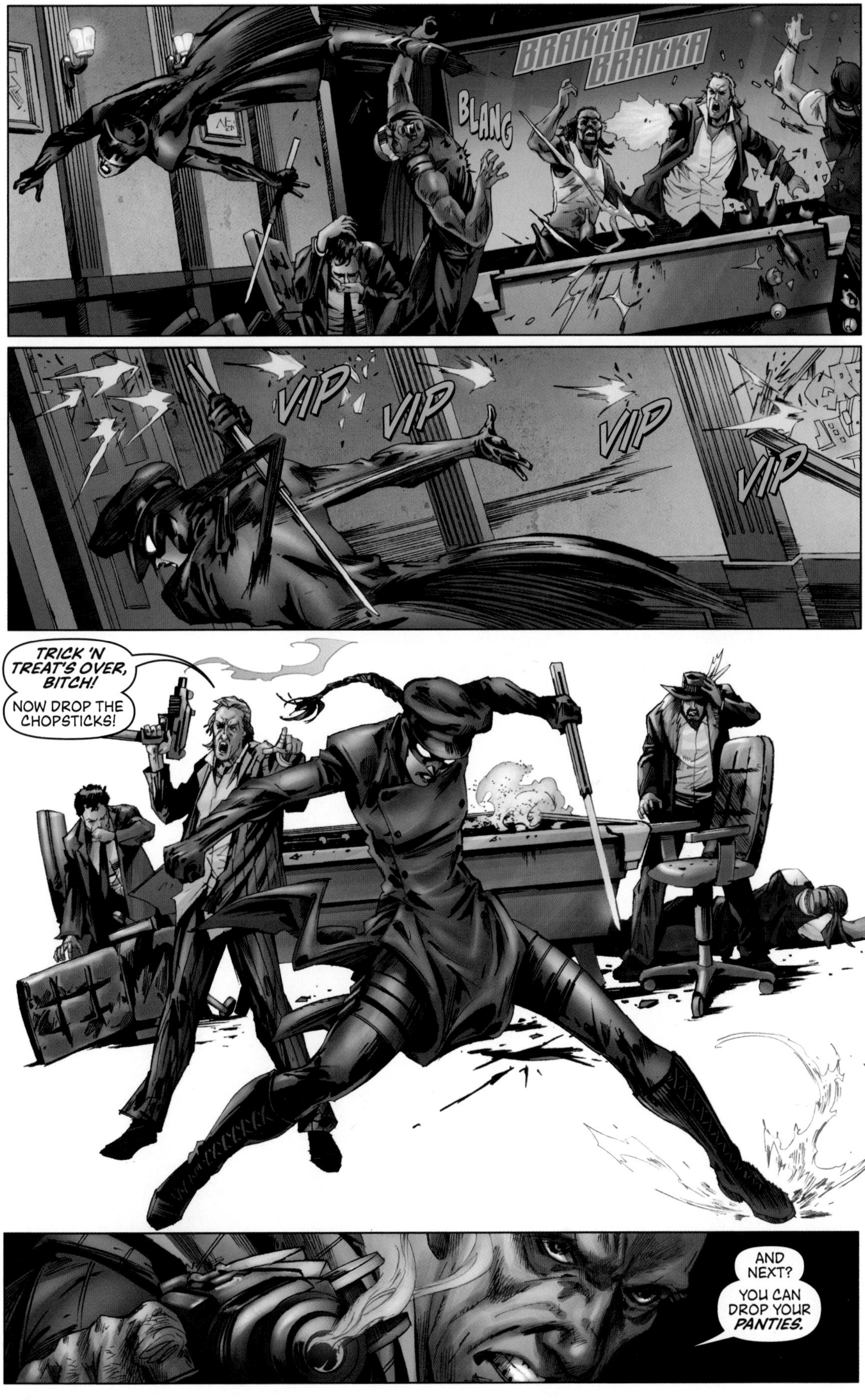
BRAKKA BRAKKA
BLANG
VIP
VIP
VIP
VIP
TRICK 'N TREAT'S OVER, BITCH!
NOW DROP THE CHOPSTICKS!
AND NEXT?
YOU CAN DROP YOUR PANTIES.

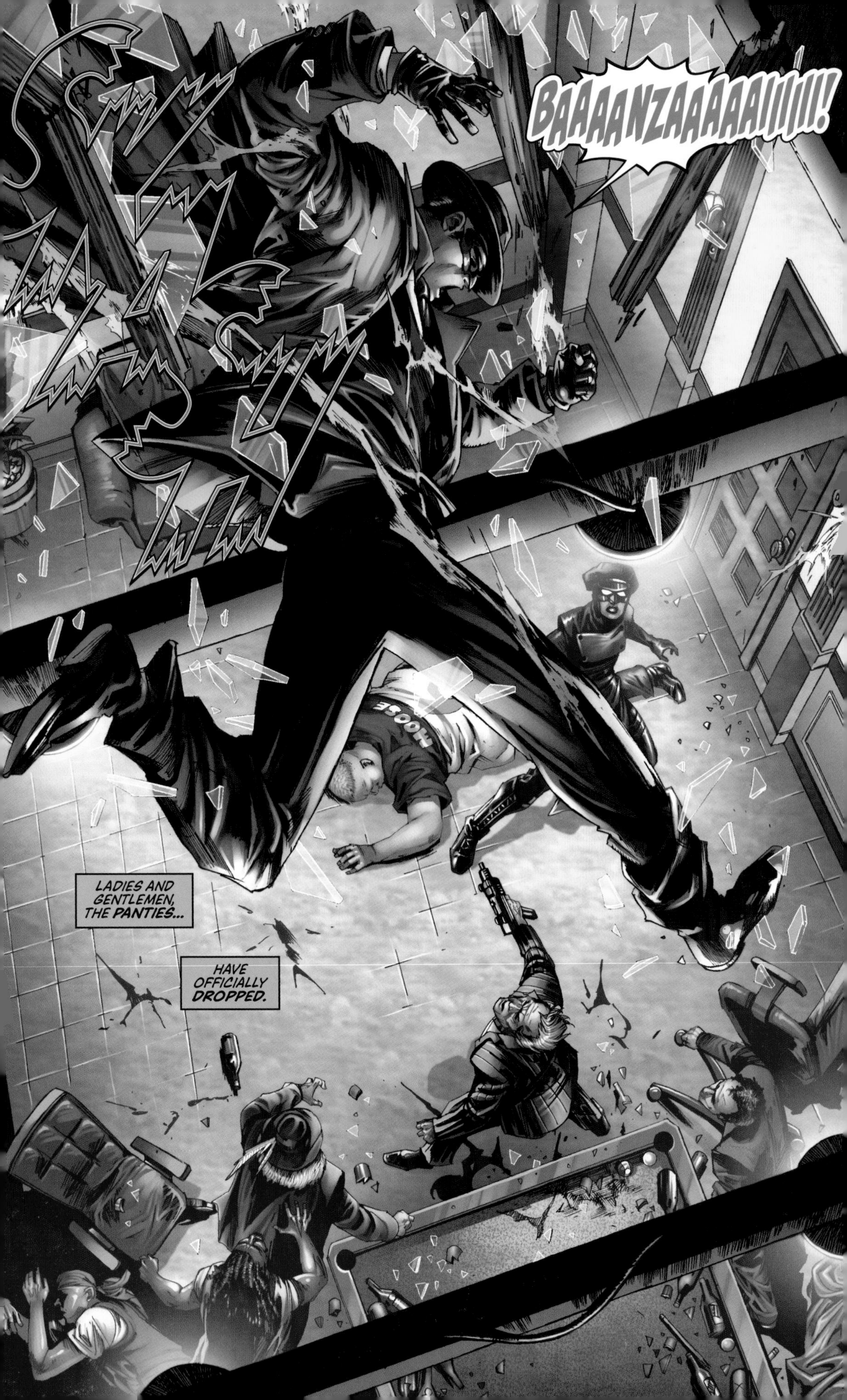
BAAAANZAAAAAI!!!!!!!!
MOOSE
LADIES AND GENTLEMEN, THE PANTIES...
HAVE OFFICIALLY DROPPED.

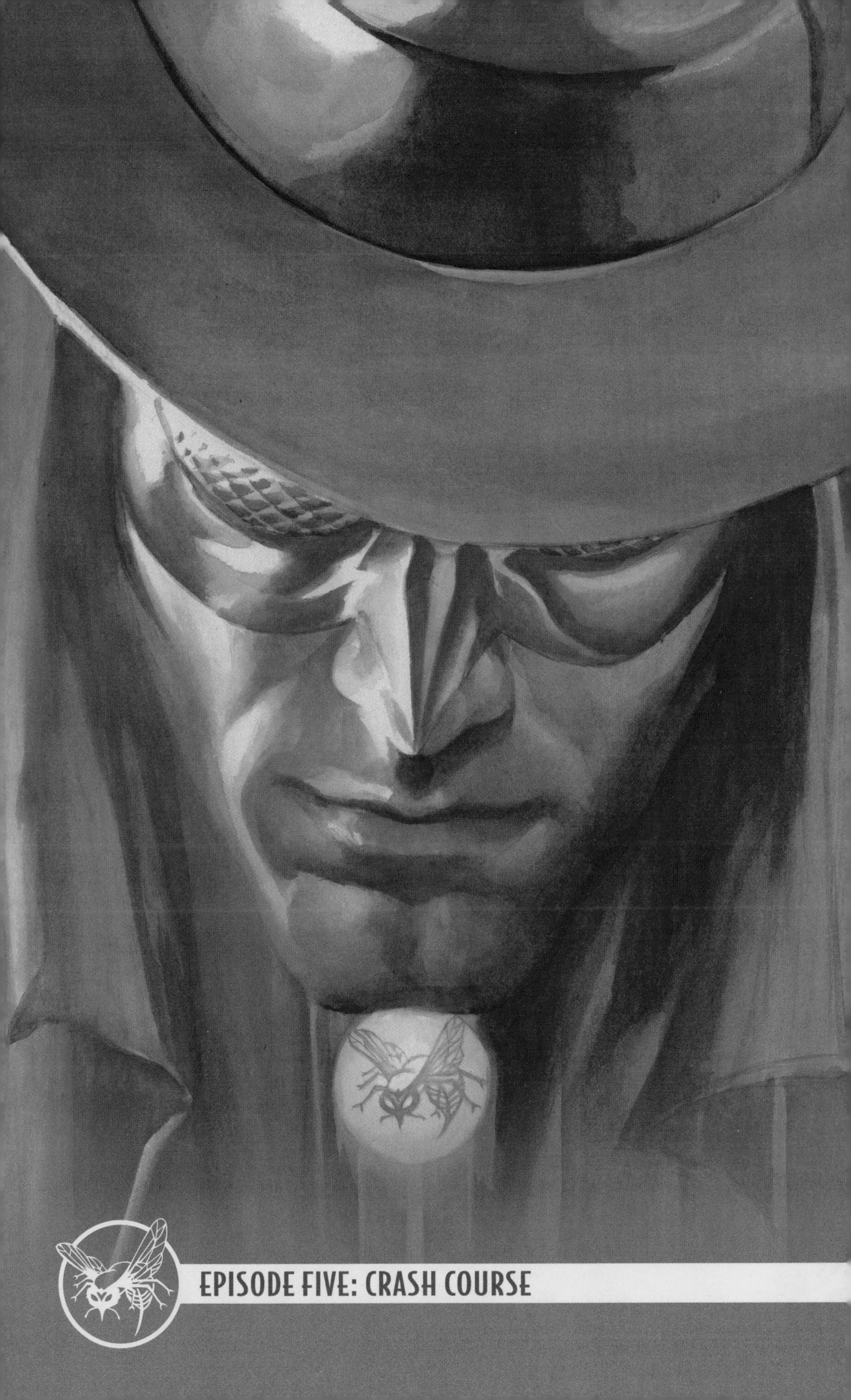

EPISODE FIVE: CRASH COURSE

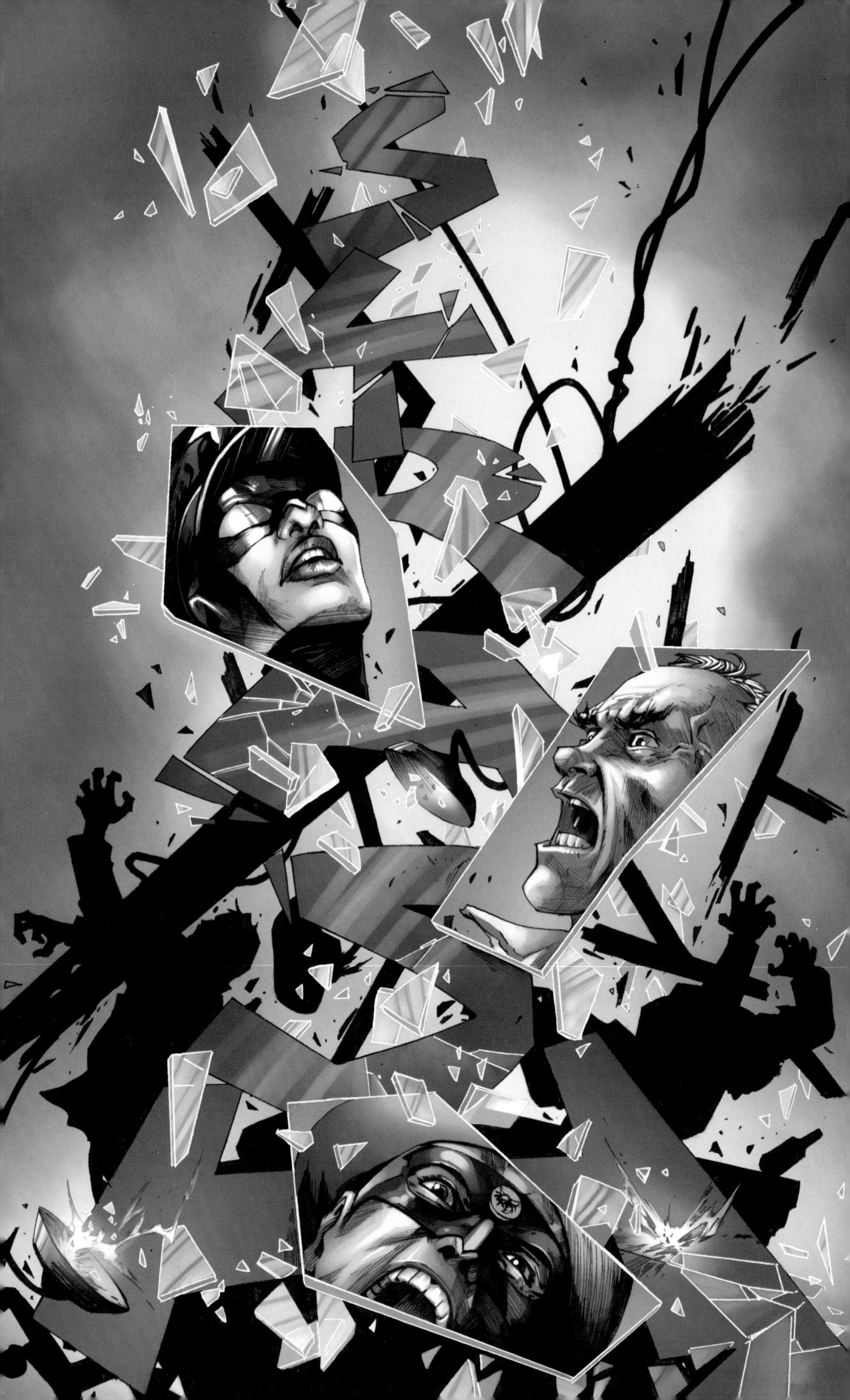

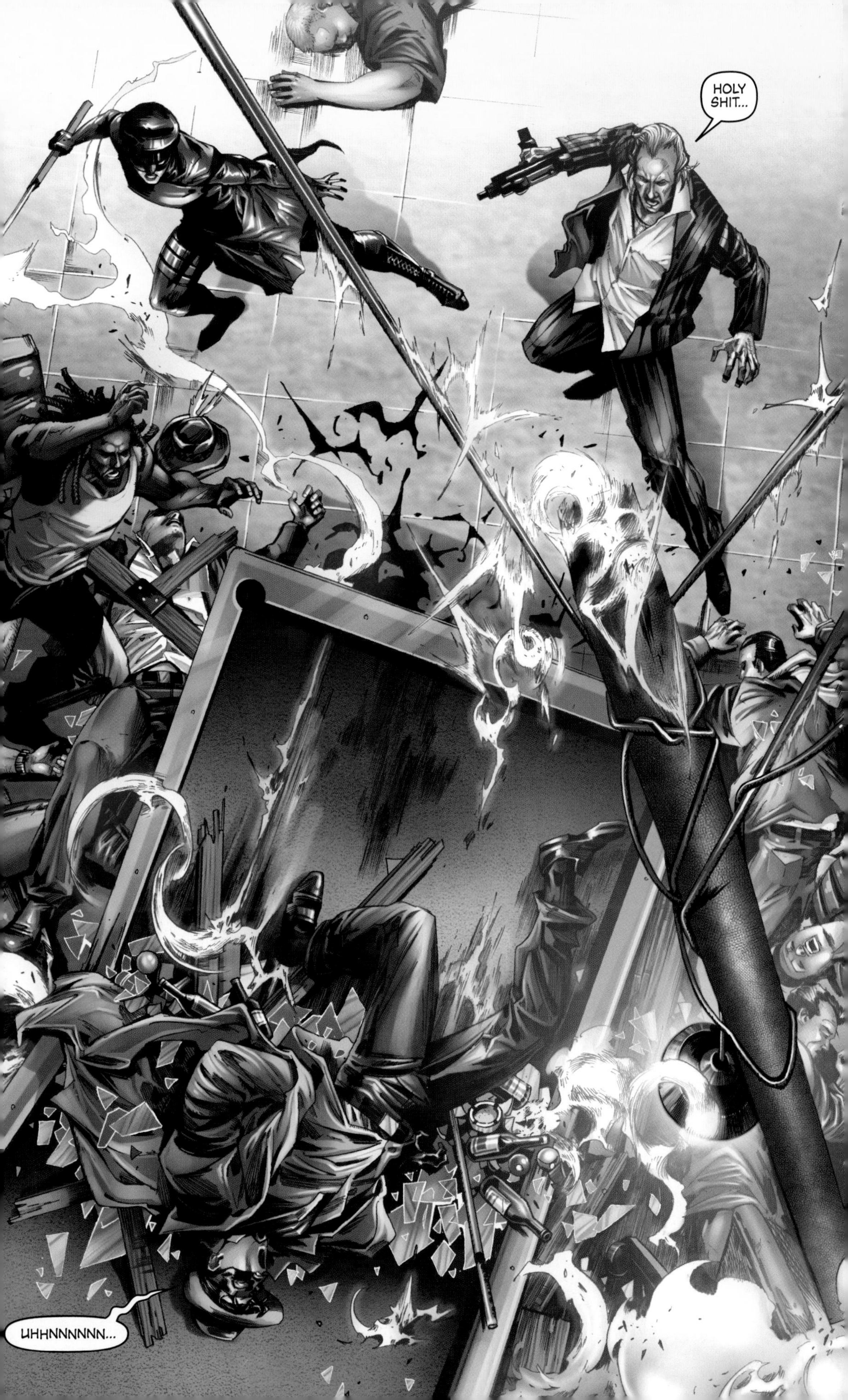
HOLY SHIT...
UHHNNNNNN...

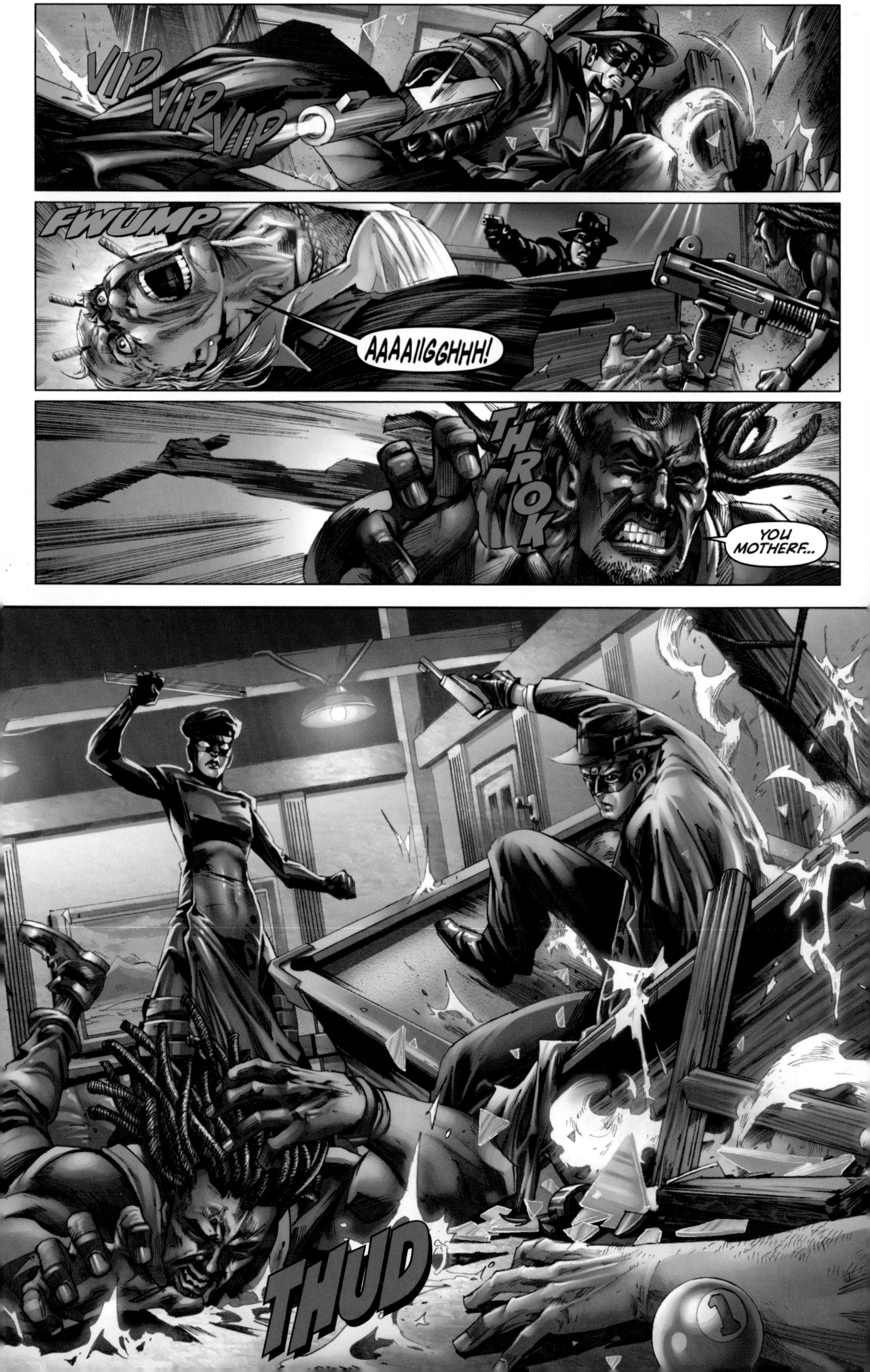
VIP VIP VIP
FWUMP
AAAAIIGGHHH!
THROK
YOU MOTHERF...
THUD

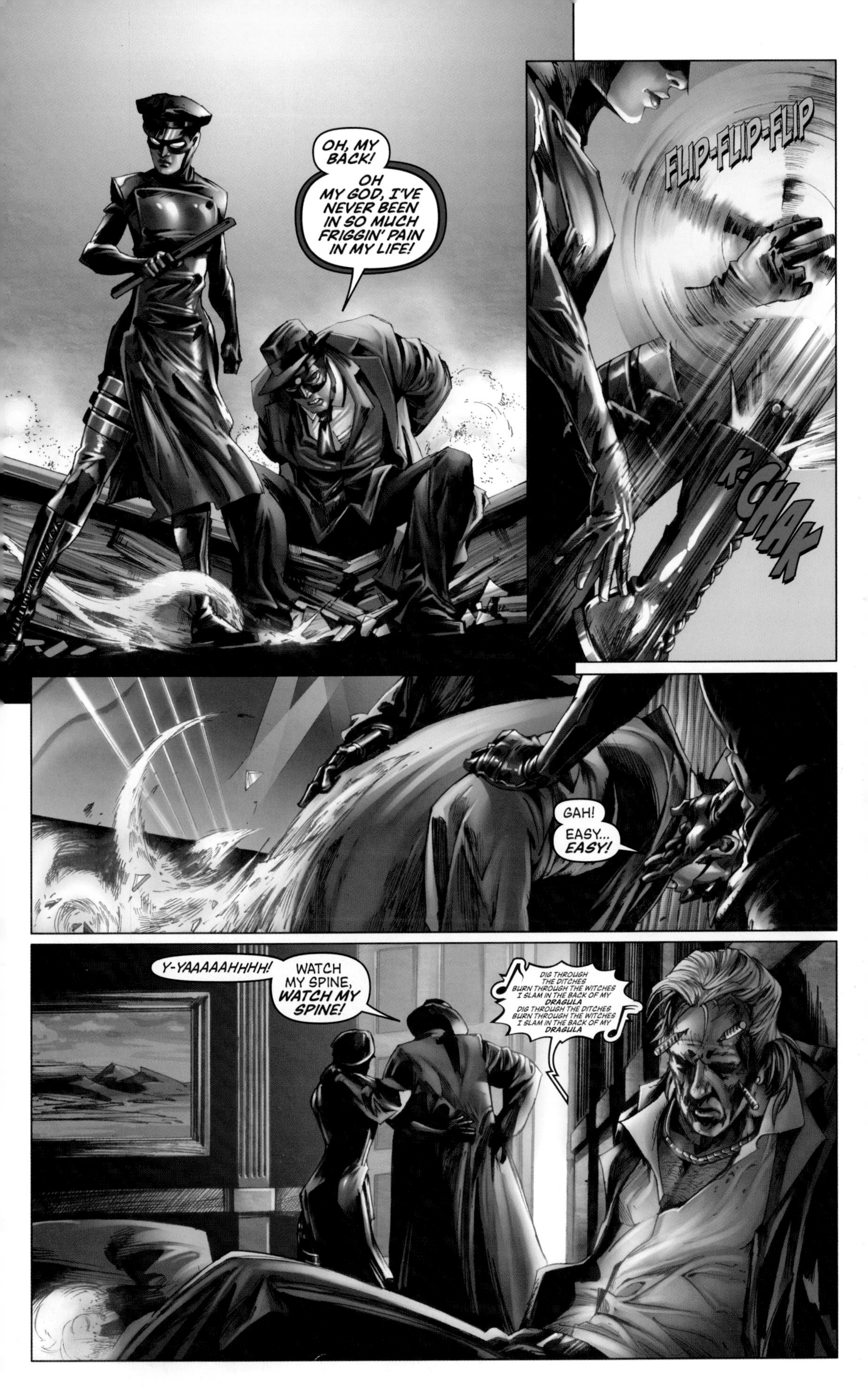
OH, MY BACK!
OH MY GOD, I'VE NEVER BEEN IN SO MUCH FRIGGIN' PAIN IN MY LIFE!
FLIP-FLIP-FLIP
K-CHAK
GAH!
EASY... EASY!
Y-YAAAAAHHHH!
WATCH MY SPINE, WATCH MY SPINE!
DIG THROUGH THE DITCHES
BURN THROUGH THE WITCHES
I SLAM IN THE BACK OF MY DRAGULA
DIG THROUGH THE DITCHES
BURN THROUGH THE WITCHES
I SLAM IN THE BACK OF MY DRAGULA

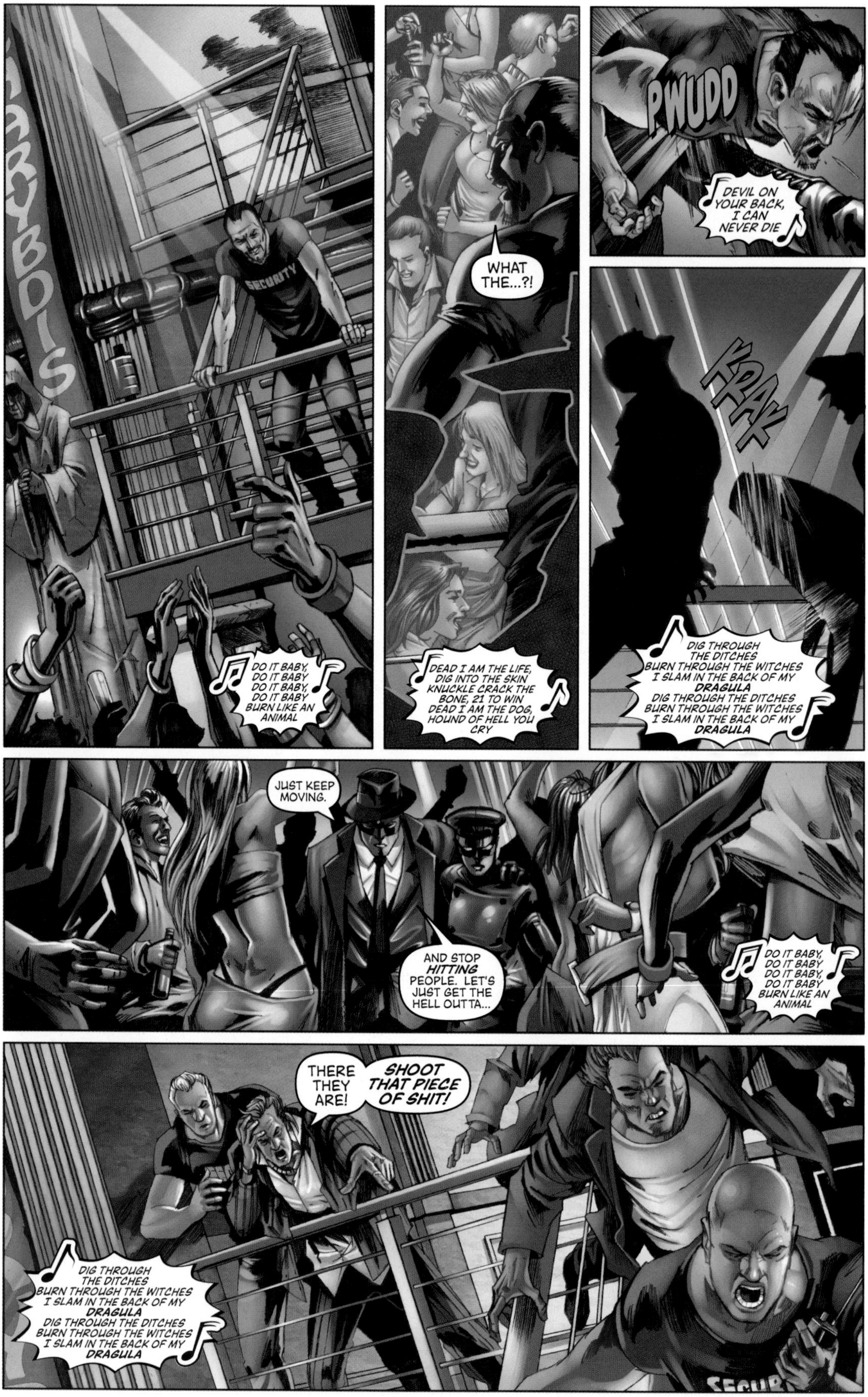
DO IT BABY, DO IT BABY DO IT BABY, DO IT BABY BURN LIKE AN ANIMAL
WHAT THE...?!
DEAD I AM THE LIFE, DIG INTO THE SKIN KNUCKLE CRACK THE BONE, 21 TO WIN DEAD I AM THE DOG, HOUND OF HELL YOU CRY
PWUDD
DEVIL ON YOUR BACK, I CAN NEVER DIE
KRAK
DIG THROUGH THE DITCHES BURN THROUGH THE WITCHES I SLAM IN THE BACK OF MY DRAGULA DIG THROUGH THE DITCHES BURN THROUGH THE WITCHES I SLAM IN THE BACK OF MY DRAGULA
JUST KEEP MOVING.
AND STOP HITTING PEOPLE. LET'S JUST GET THE HELL OUTTA...
DO IT BABY, DO IT BABY DO IT BABY, DO IT BABY BURN LIKE AN ANIMAL
THERE THEY ARE!
SHOOT THAT PIECE OF SHIT!
DIG THROUGH THE DITCHES BURN THROUGH THE WITCHES I SLAM IN THE BACK OF MY DRAGULA DIG THROUGH THE DITCHES BURN THROUGH THE WITCHES I SLAM IN THE BACK OF MY DRAGULA

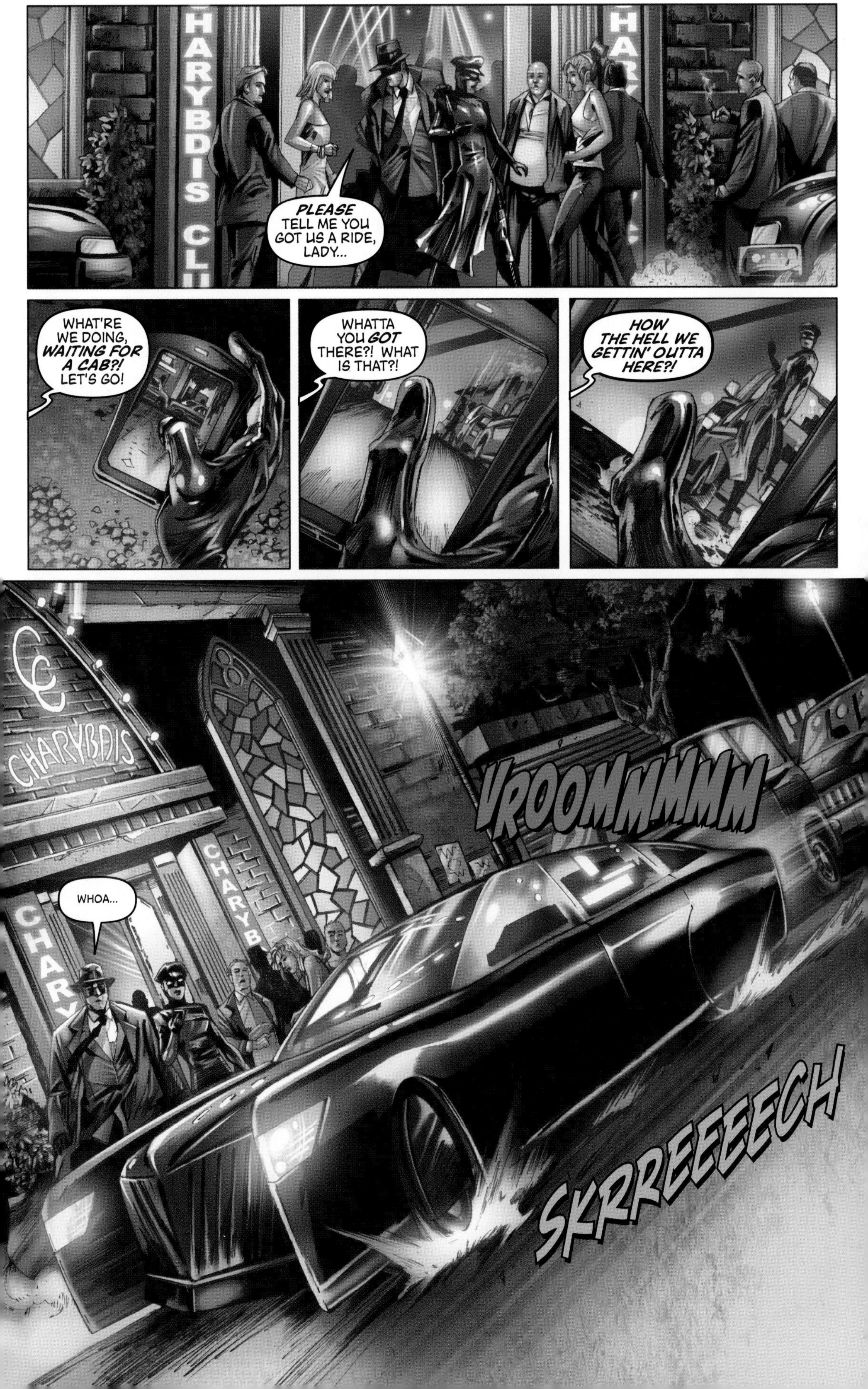
CHARYBDIS CLU
PLEASE TELL ME YOU GOT US A RIDE, LADY...
WHAT'RE WE DOING, WAITING FOR A CAB?! LET'S GO!
WHATTA YOU GOT THERE?! WHAT IS THAT?!
HOW THE HELL WE GETTIN' OUTTA HERE?!
CHARYBDIS
WHOA...
VROOMMMMM
SKRREEEEECH

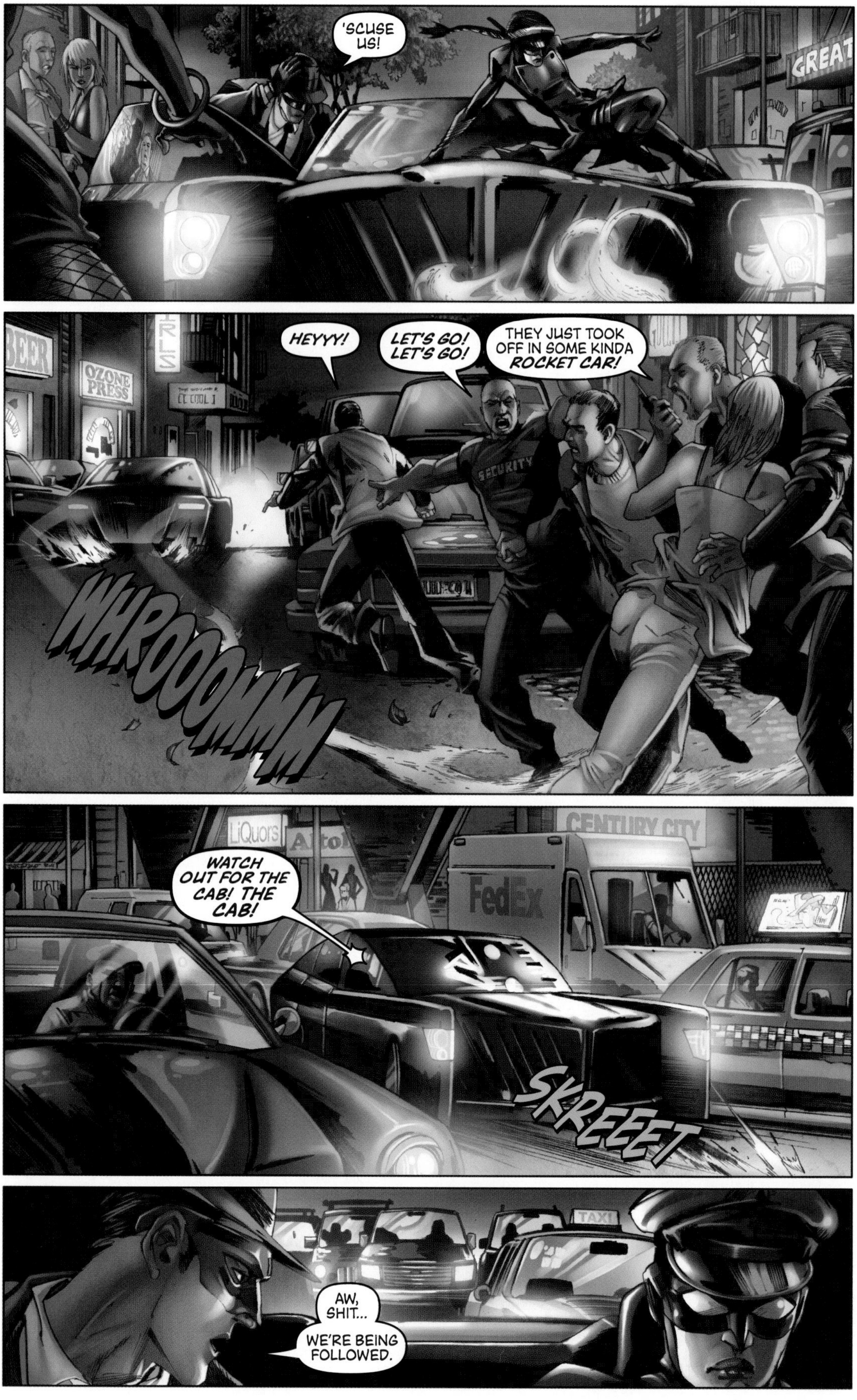
'SCUSE US!
GREAT
BEER
OZONE PRESS
HEYYY!
LET'S GO! LET'S GO!
THEY JUST TOOK OFF IN SOME KINDA ROCKET CAR!
SECURITY
WHROOOMMM
LiQuors
CENTURY CITY
FedEx
WATCH OUT FOR THE CAB! THE CAB!
SKREEET
TAXI
AW, SHIT...
WE'RE BEING FOLLOWED.

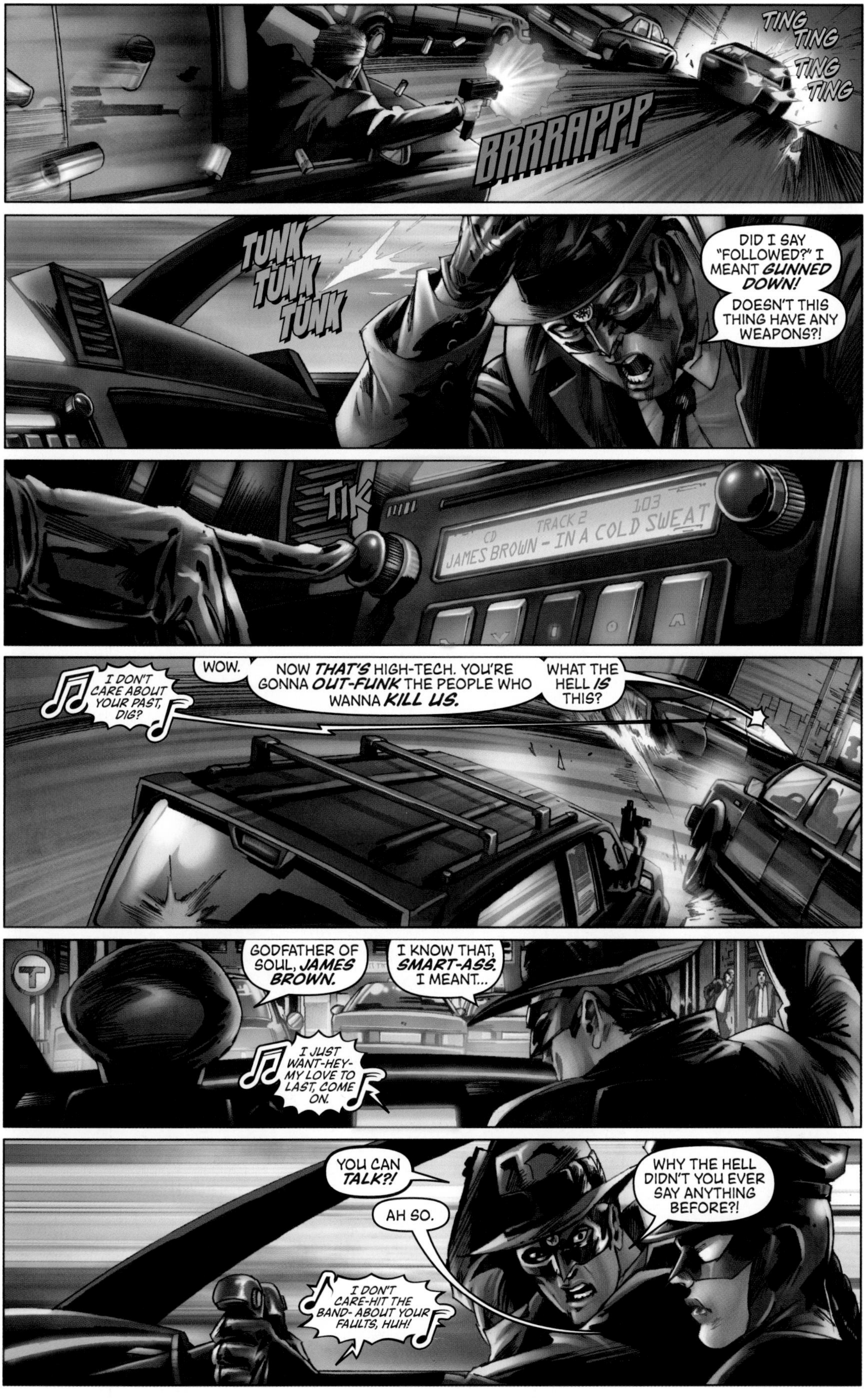

TING TING TING TING
BRRRAPPP
TUNK TUNK TUNK
DID I SAY "FOLLOWED?" I MEANT GUNNED DOWN!
DOESN'T THIS THING HAVE ANY WEAPONS?!
TIK
CD TRACK 2 103
JAMES BROWN - IN A COLD SWEAT
I DON'T CARE ABOUT YOUR PAST, DIG?
WOW.
NOW THAT'S HIGH-TECH. YOU'RE GONNA OUT-FUNK THE PEOPLE WHO WANNA KILL US.
WHAT THE HELL IS THIS?
GODFATHER OF SOUL, JAMES BROWN.
I KNOW THAT, SMART-ASS. I MEANT...
I JUST WANT-HEY-MY LOVE TO LAST, COME ON.
YOU CAN TALK?!
WHY THE HELL DIDN'T YOU EVER SAY ANYTHING BEFORE?!
AH SO.
I DON'T CARE-HIT THE BAND- ABOUT YOUR FAULTS, HUH!

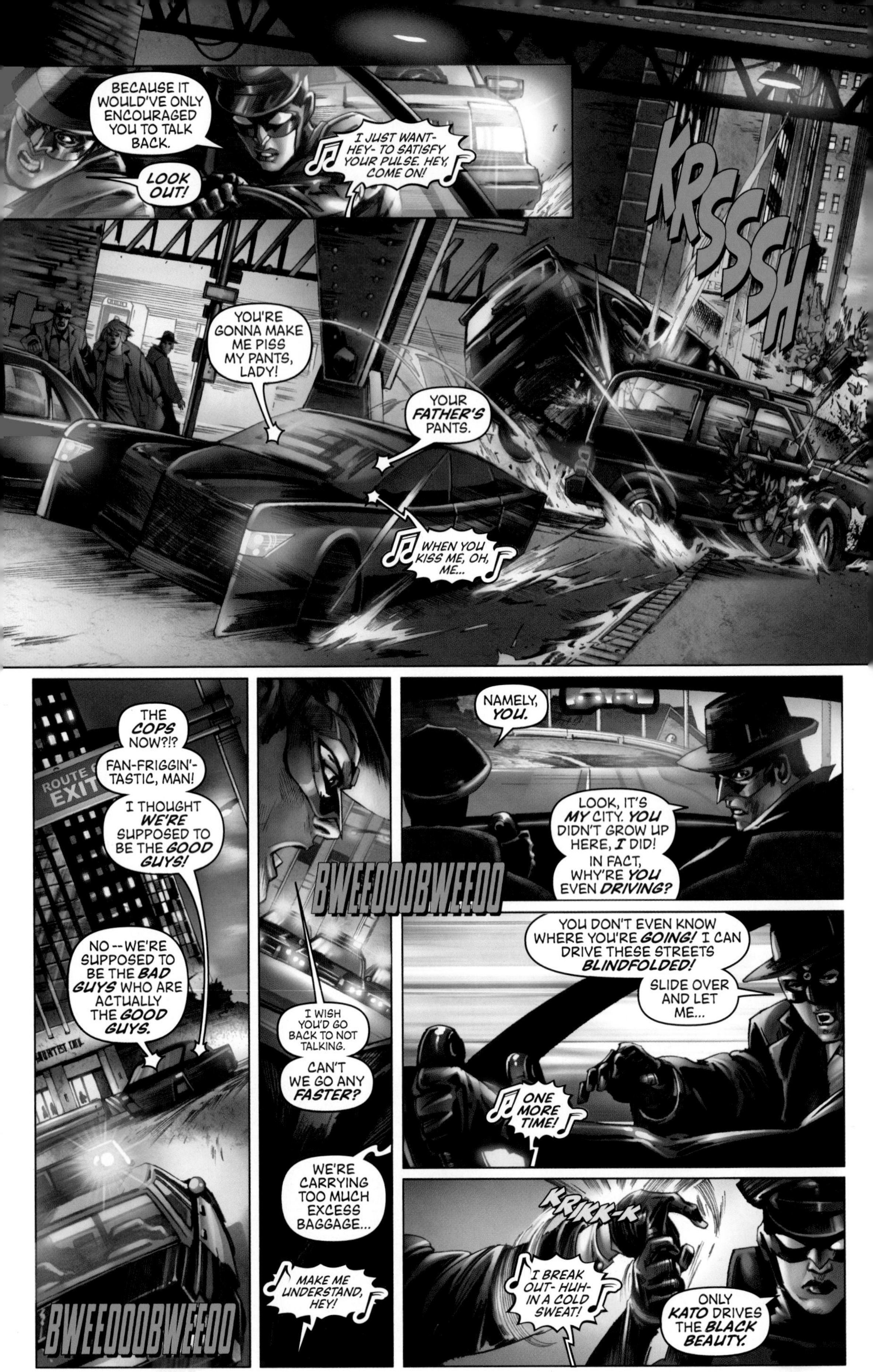
BECAUSE IT WOULD'VE ONLY ENCOURAGED YOU TO TALK BACK.
LOOK OUT!
I JUST WANT- HEY- TO SATISFY YOUR PULSE. HEY, COME ON!
KRSSSH
YOU'RE GONNA MAKE ME PISS MY PANTS, LADY!
YOUR FATHER'S PANTS.
WHEN YOU KISS ME, OH, ME...
THE COPS NOW?!?
FAN-FRIGGIN'-TASTIC, MAN!
I THOUGHT WE'RE SUPPOSED TO BE THE GOOD GUYS!
NO --WE'RE SUPPOSED TO BE THE BAD GUYS WHO ARE ACTUALLY THE GOOD GUYS.
ROUTE EXIT
BWEEOOOBWEEOO
BWEEOOOBWEEOO
I WISH YOU'D GO BACK TO NOT TALKING.
CAN'T WE GO ANY FASTER?
WE'RE CARRYING TOO MUCH EXCESS BAGGAGE...
MAKE ME UNDERSTAND, HEY!
NAMELY, YOU.
LOOK, IT'S MY CITY. YOU DIDN'T GROW UP HERE, I DID!
IN FACT, WHY'RE YOU EVEN DRIVING?
YOU DON'T EVEN KNOW WHERE YOU'RE GOING! I CAN DRIVE THESE STREETS BLINDFOLDED!
SLIDE OVER AND LET ME...
ONE MORE TIME!
KRIKK-K
I BREAK OUT- HUH- IN A COLD SWEAT!
ONLY KATO DRIVES THE BLACK BEAUTY.

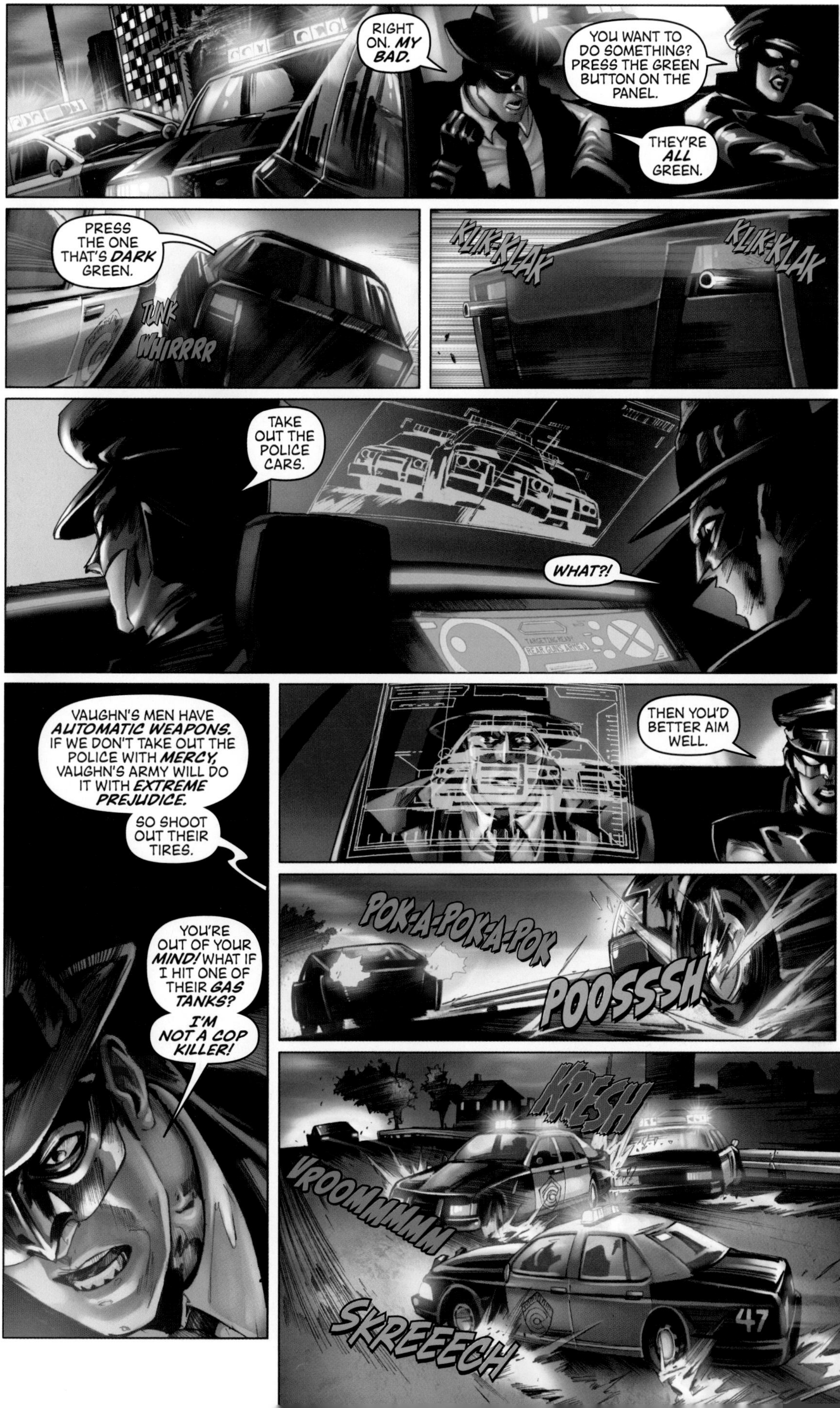
RIGHT ON. MY BAD.
YOU WANT TO DO SOMETHING? PRESS THE GREEN BUTTON ON THE PANEL.
THEY'RE ALL GREEN.
PRESS THE ONE THAT'S DARK GREEN.
TUNK
WHIRRRR
KLIK-KLAK
KLIK-KLAK
TAKE OUT THE POLICE CARS.
WHAT?!
VAUGHN'S MEN HAVE AUTOMATIC WEAPONS. IF WE DON'T TAKE OUT THE POLICE WITH MERCY, VAUGHN'S ARMY WILL DO IT WITH EXTREME PREJUDICE.
SO SHOOT OUT THEIR TIRES.
YOU'RE OUT OF YOUR MIND! WHAT IF I HIT ONE OF THEIR GAS TANKS?
I'M NOT A COP KILLER!
THEN YOU'D BETTER AIM WELL.
POK-A-POK-A-POK
POOSSSH
KRESH
VROOMMMMMM
SKREEECH

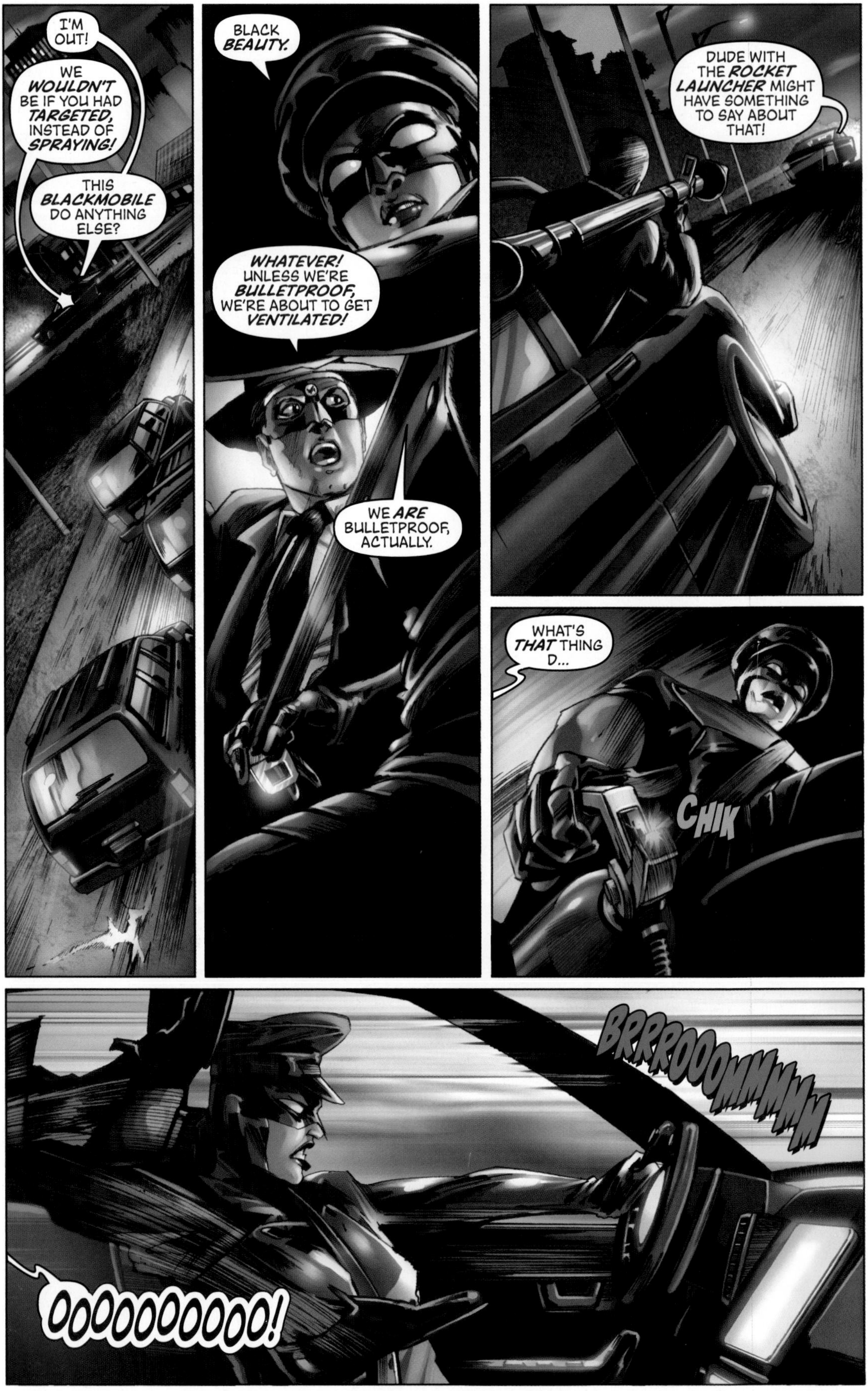
I'M OUT!
WE WOULDN'T BE IF YOU HAD TARGETED, INSTEAD OF SPRAYING!
THIS BLACKMOBILE DO ANYTHING ELSE?
BLACK BEAUTY.
WHATEVER! UNLESS WE'RE BULLETPROOF, WE'RE ABOUT TO GET VENTILATED!
WE ARE BULLETPROOF, ACTUALLY.
DUDE WITH THE ROCKET LAUNCHER MIGHT HAVE SOMETHING TO SAY ABOUT THAT!
WHAT'S THAT THING D...
CHIK
BRRROOOMMMMM
OOOOOOOOOO!

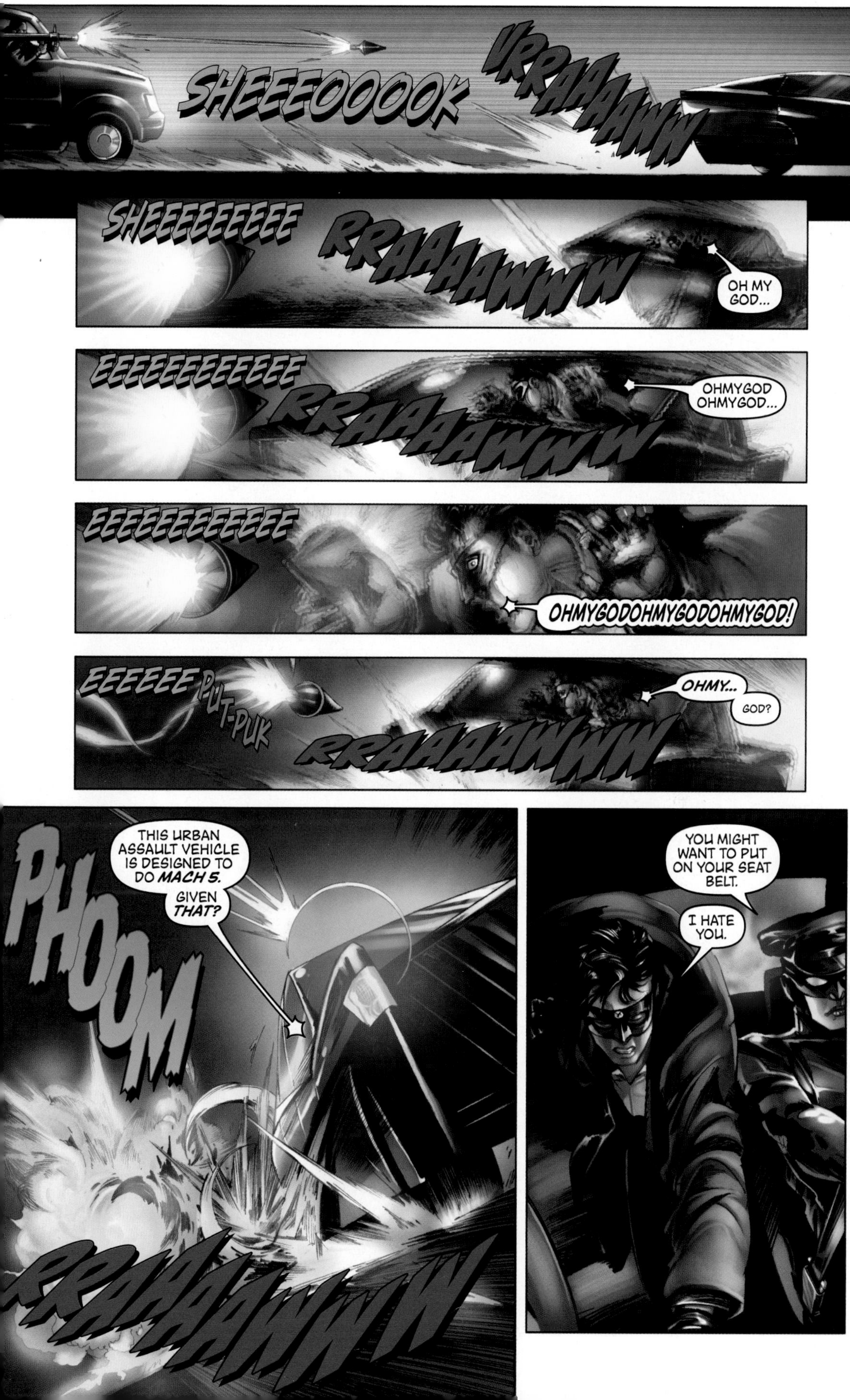
SHEEEOOOOK
URRAAAAWW
SHEEEEEEEEEE
RRAAAAAWWW
OH MY GOD...
EEEEEEEEEEEE
RRAAAAAWWW
OHMYGOD OHMYGOD...
EEEEEEEEEEEE
OHMYGODOHMYGODOHMYGOD!
EEEEEE
PUT-PUK
RRAAAAAWWW
OHMY...
GOD?
PHOOM
THIS URBAN ASSAULT VEHICLE IS DESIGNED TO DO *MACH 5.*
GIVEN *THAT?*
RRAAAAAWWW
YOU MIGHT WANT TO PUT ON YOUR SEAT BELT.
I HATE YOU.

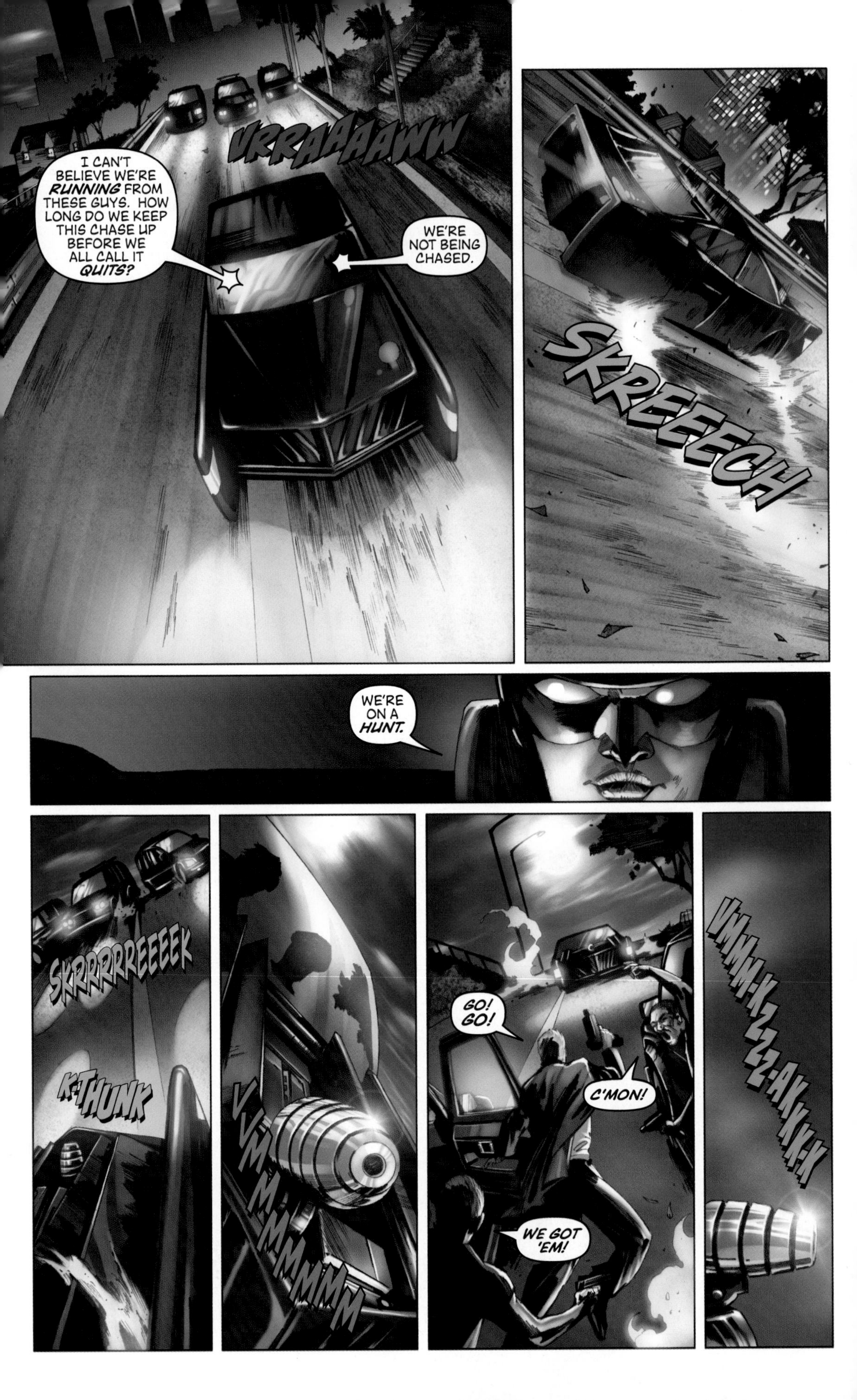
VRRAAAAAWW
I CAN'T BELIEVE WE'RE RUNNING FROM THESE GUYS. HOW LONG DO WE KEEP THIS CHASE UP BEFORE WE ALL CALL IT QUITS?
WE'RE NOT BEING CHASED.
SKREEECH
WE'RE ON A HUNT.
SKRRRRREEEEK
K-THUNK
VVMMMMMMMM
GO! GO!
C'MON!
WE GOT 'EM!
VMMM-KZZ-AKKK-K

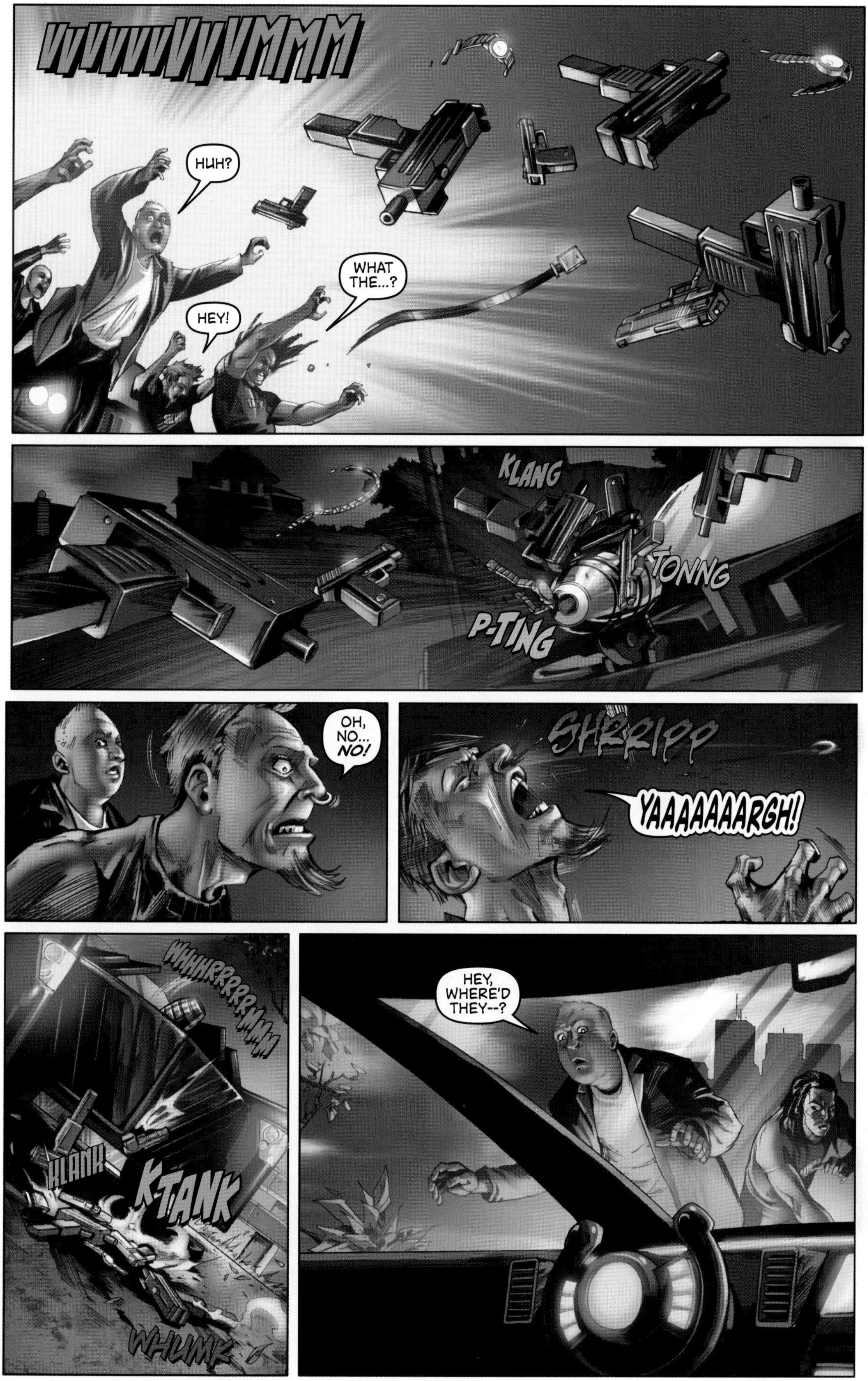
VVVVVVVVVMMMM
HUH?
HEY!
WHAT THE...?
KLANG
TONNG
P-TING
OH, NO... NO!
SHRRIPP
YAAAAAAARGH!
WHHHRRRRRMMM
KLANK
KTANK
WHUMK
HEY, WHERE'D THEY--?

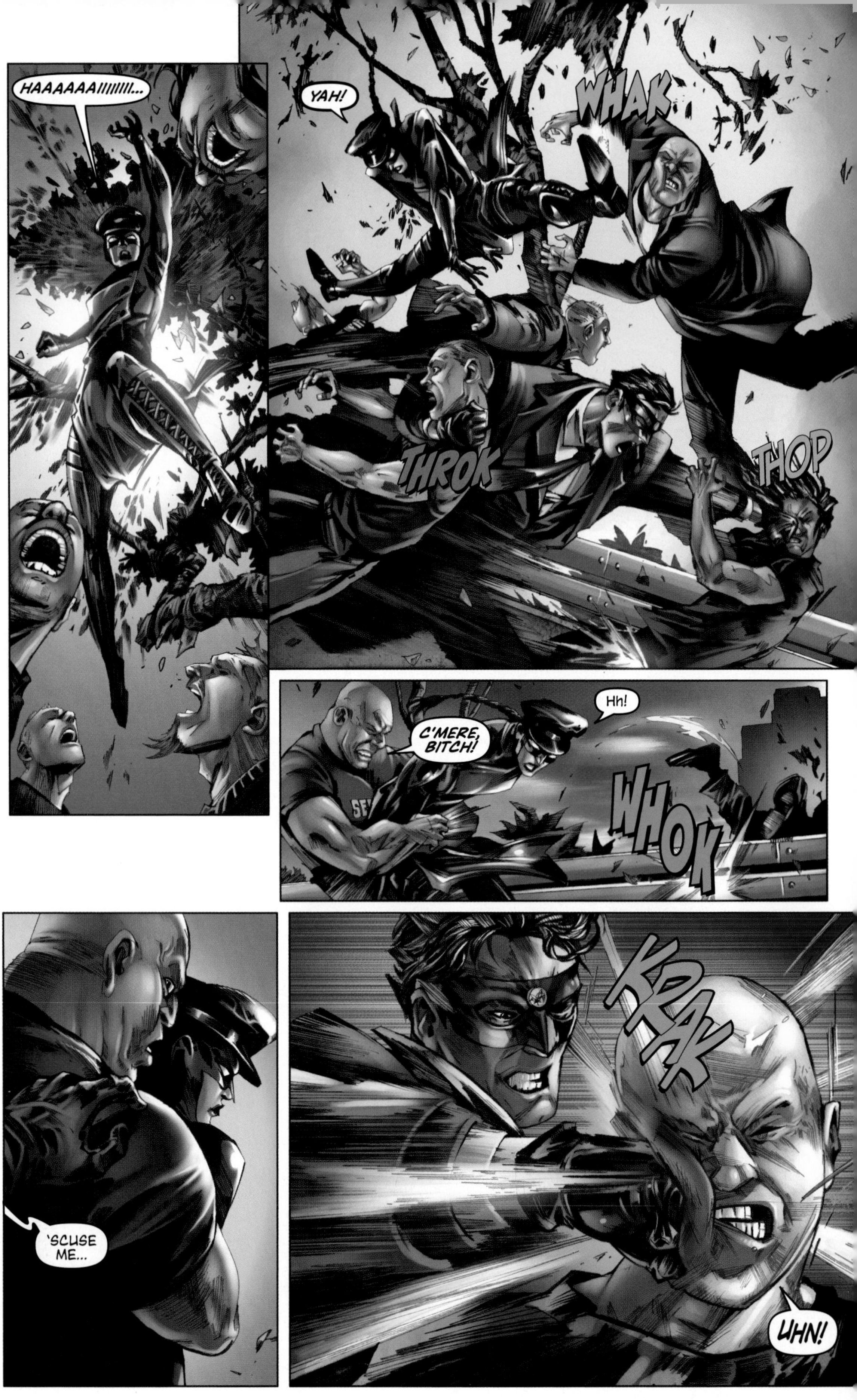
HAAAAAAIIIIIIII...
YAH!
WHAK
THROK
THOP
C'MERE, BITCH!
Hh!
WHOK
'SCUSE ME...
KRAK
UHN!

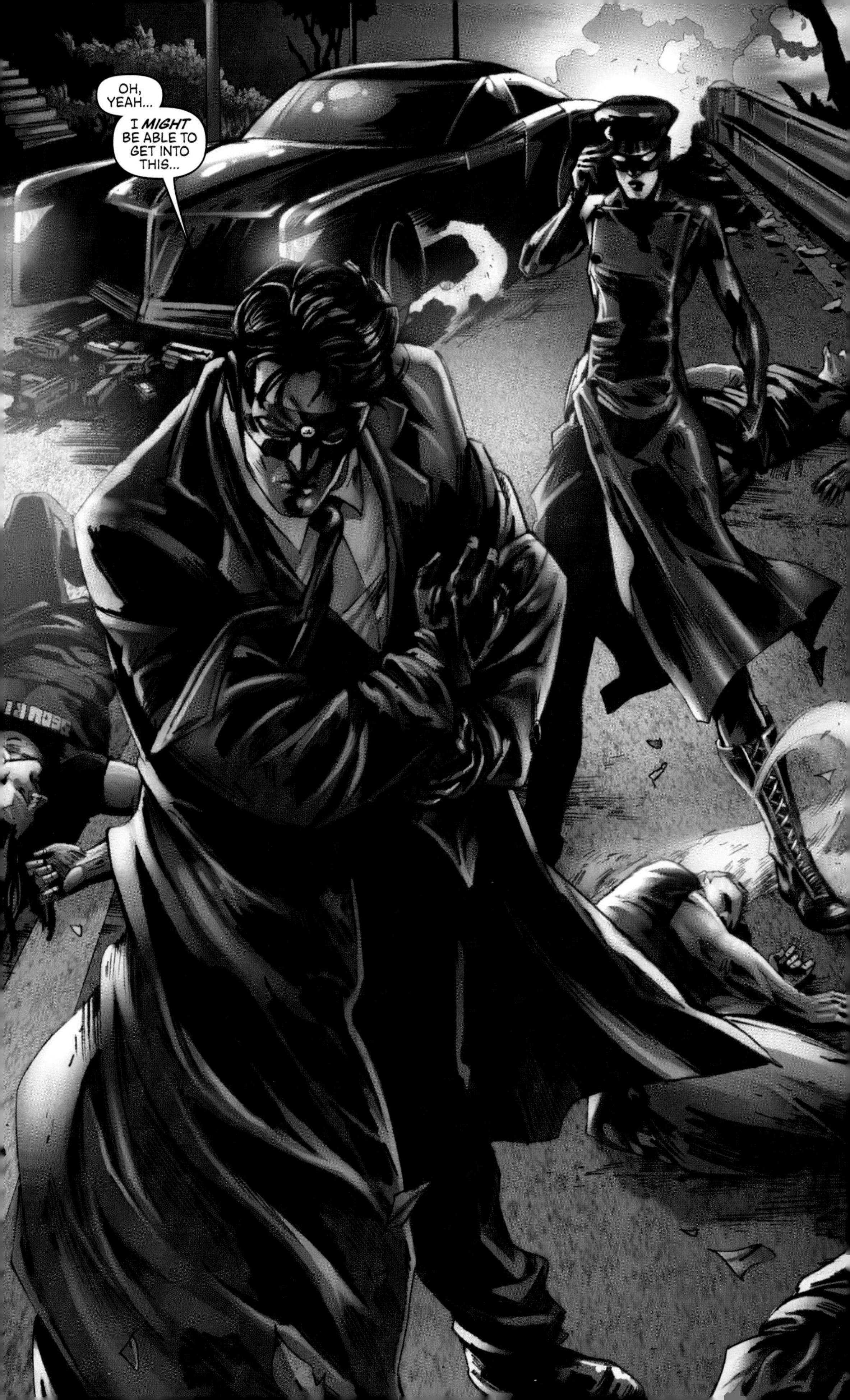
OH, YEAH...
I MIGHT BE ABLE TO GET INTO THIS...

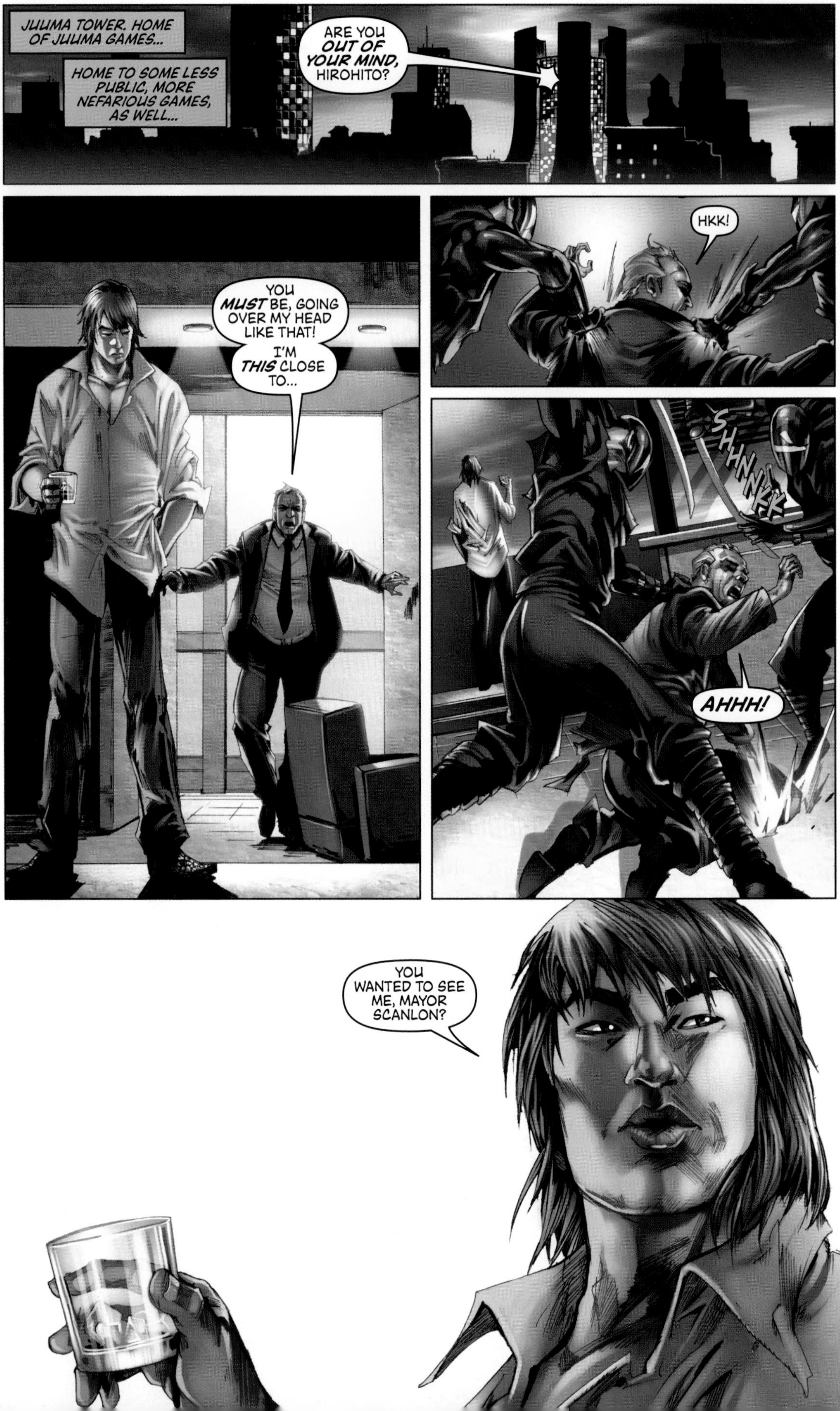
JUUMA TOWER. HOME OF JUUMA GAMES...
HOME TO SOME LESS PUBLIC, MORE NEFARIOUS GAMES, AS WELL...
ARE YOU OUT OF YOUR MIND, HIROHITO?
YOU MUST BE, GOING OVER MY HEAD LIKE THAT!
I'M THIS CLOSE TO...
HKK!
SHHHNNKK
AHHH!
YOU WANTED TO SEE ME, MAYOR SCANLON?

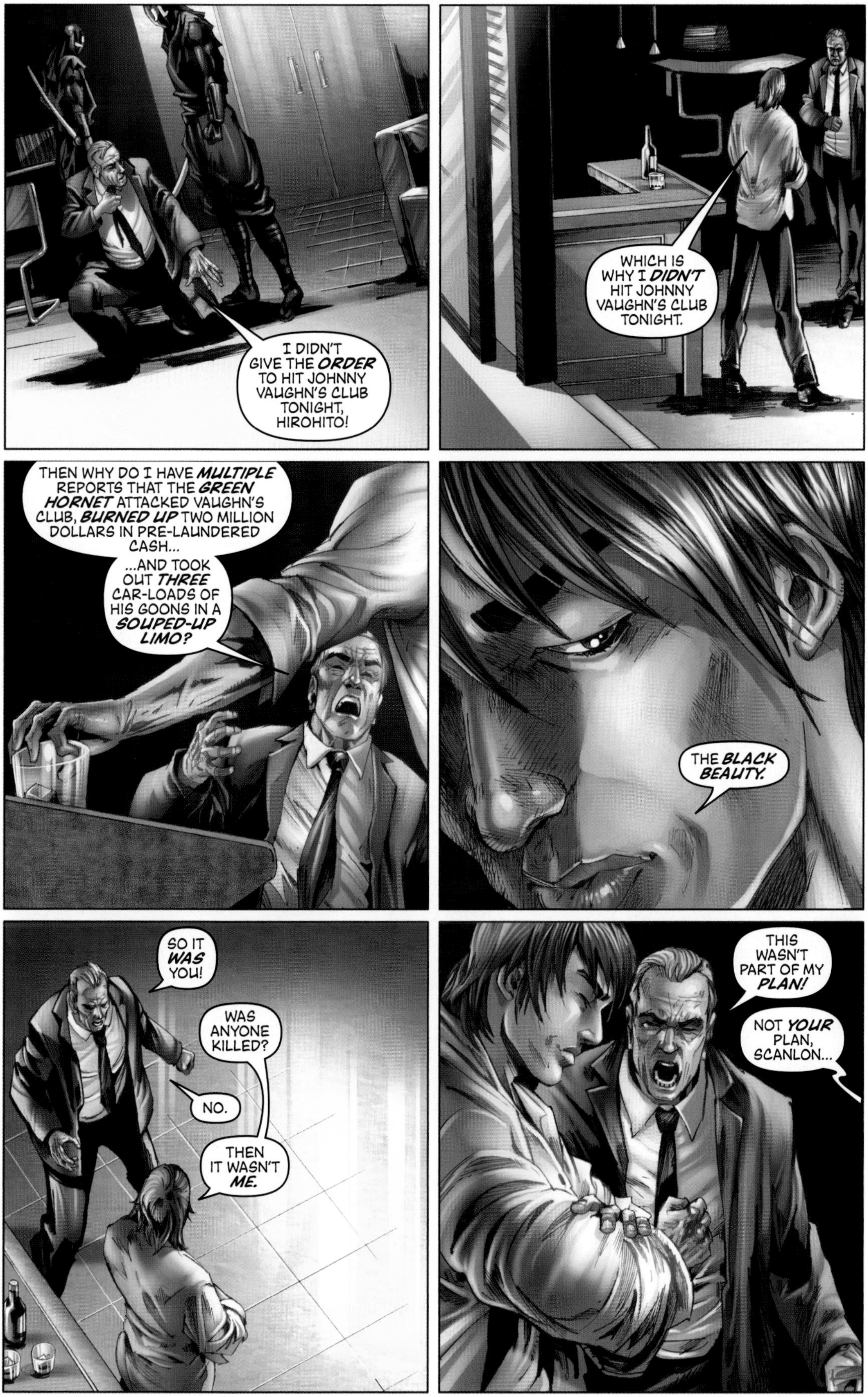
I DIDN'T GIVE THE ORDER TO HIT JOHNNY VAUGHN'S CLUB TONIGHT, HIROHITO!
WHICH IS WHY I DIDN'T HIT JOHNNY VAUGHN'S CLUB TONIGHT.
THEN WHY DO I HAVE MULTIPLE REPORTS THAT THE GREEN HORNET ATTACKED VAUGHN'S CLUB, BURNED UP TWO MILLION DOLLARS IN PRE-LAUNDERED CASH...
...AND TOOK OUT THREE CAR-LOADS OF HIS GOONS IN A SOUPED-UP LIMO?
THE BLACK BEAUTY.
SO IT WAS YOU!
WAS ANYONE KILLED?
NO.
THEN IT WASN'T ME.
THIS WASN'T PART OF MY PLAN!
NOT YOUR PLAN, SCANLON...

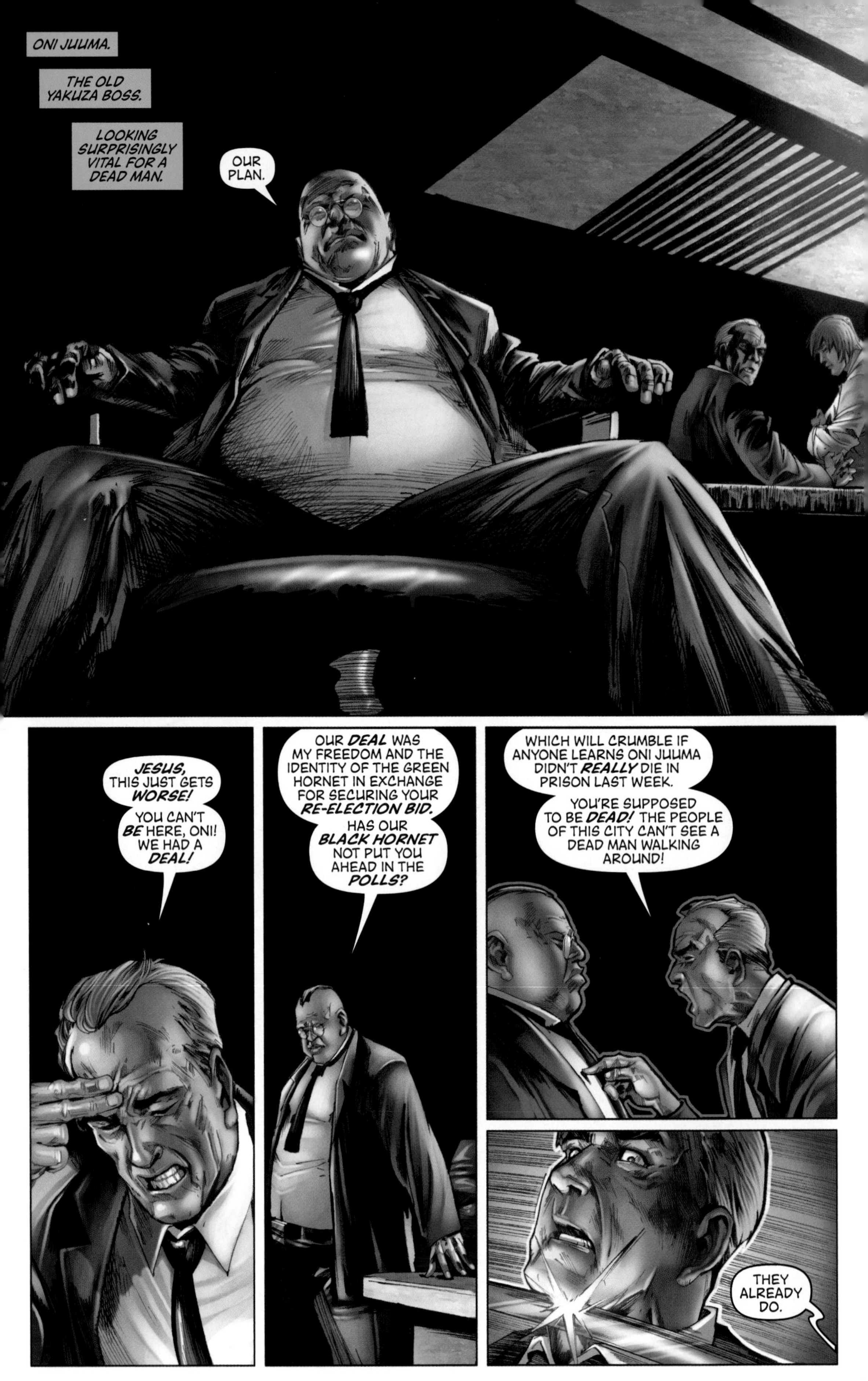
ONI JUUMA.
THE OLD YAKUZA BOSS.
LOOKING SURPRISINGLY VITAL FOR A DEAD MAN.
OUR PLAN.
JESUS, THIS JUST GETS WORSE!
YOU CAN'T BE HERE, ONI! WE HAD A DEAL!
OUR DEAL WAS MY FREEDOM AND THE IDENTITY OF THE GREEN HORNET IN EXCHANGE FOR SECURING YOUR RE-ELECTION BID.
HAS OUR BLACK HORNET NOT PUT YOU AHEAD IN THE POLLS?
WHICH WILL CRUMBLE IF ANYONE LEARNS ONI JUUMA DIDN'T REALLY DIE IN PRISON LAST WEEK.
YOU'RE SUPPOSED TO BE DEAD! THE PEOPLE OF THIS CITY CAN'T SEE A DEAD MAN WALKING AROUND!
THEY ALREADY DO.

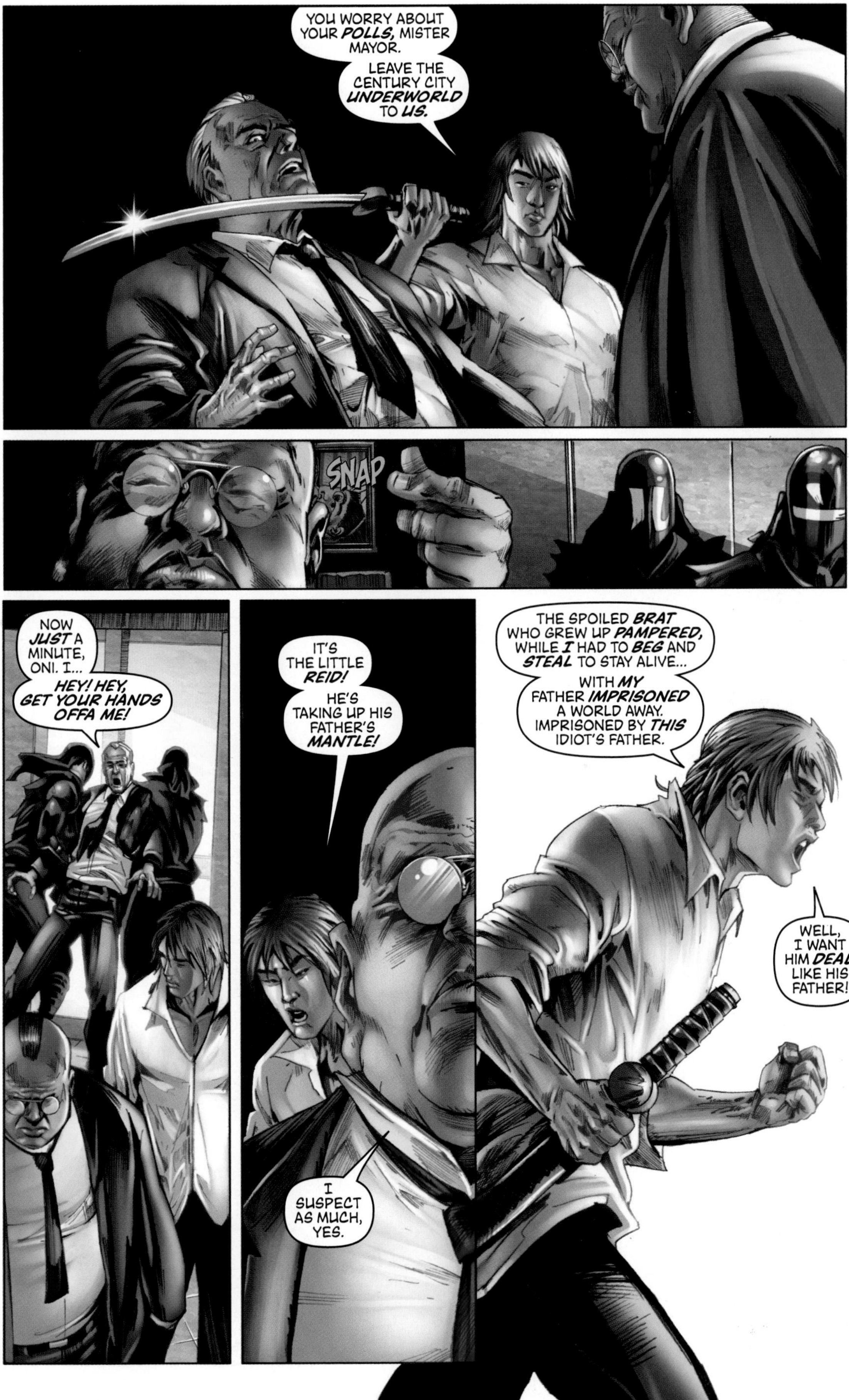
YOU WORRY ABOUT YOUR POLLS, MISTER MAYOR.
LEAVE THE CENTURY CITY UNDERWORLD TO US.
SNAP
NOW JUST A MINUTE, ONI. I...
HEY! HEY, GET YOUR HANDS OFFA ME!
IT'S THE LITTLE REID!
HE'S TAKING UP HIS FATHER'S MANTLE!
I SUSPECT AS MUCH, YES.
THE SPOILED BRAT WHO GREW UP PAMPERED, WHILE I HAD TO BEG AND STEAL TO STAY ALIVE...
WITH MY FATHER IMPRISONED A WORLD AWAY. IMPRISONED BY THIS IDIOT'S FATHER.
WELL, I WANT HIM DEAD LIKE HIS FATHER!

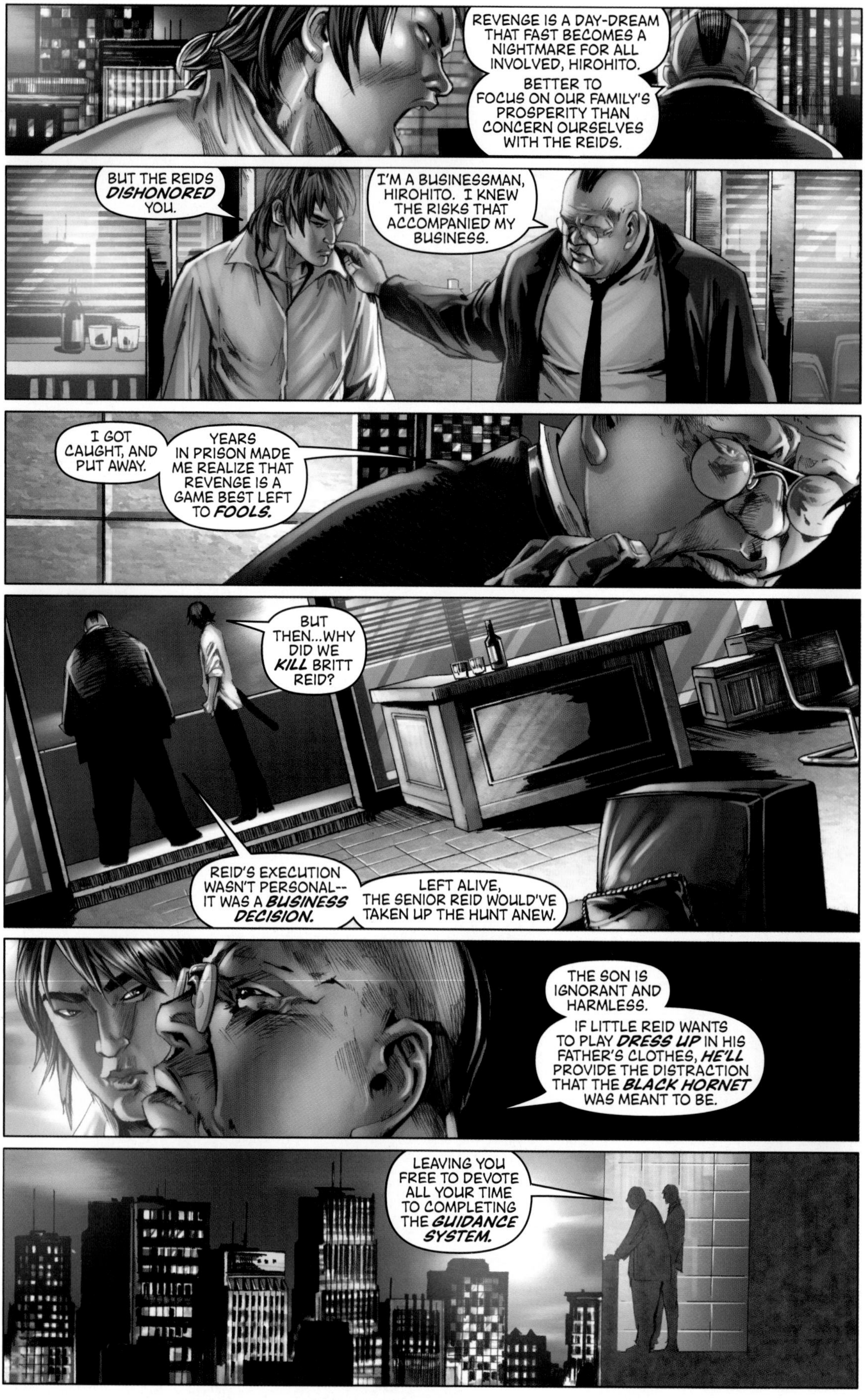
REVENGE IS A DAY-DREAM THAT FAST BECOMES A NIGHTMARE FOR ALL INVOLVED, HIROHITO.
BETTER TO FOCUS ON OUR FAMILY'S PROSPERITY THAN CONCERN OURSELVES WITH THE REIDS.
BUT THE REIDS *DISHONORED* YOU.
I'M A BUSINESSMAN, HIROHITO. I KNEW THE RISKS THAT ACCOMPANIED MY BUSINESS.
I GOT CAUGHT, AND PUT AWAY.
YEARS IN PRISON MADE ME REALIZE THAT REVENGE IS A GAME BEST LEFT TO *FOOLS.*
BUT THEN...WHY DID WE *KILL* BRITT REID?
REID'S EXECUTION WASN'T PERSONAL-- IT WAS A *BUSINESS DECISION.*
LEFT ALIVE, THE SENIOR REID WOULD'VE TAKEN UP THE HUNT ANEW.
THE SON IS IGNORANT AND HARMLESS.
IF LITTLE REID WANTS TO PLAY *DRESS UP* IN HIS FATHER'S CLOTHES, *HE'LL* PROVIDE THE DISTRACTION THAT THE *BLACK HORNET* WAS MEANT TO BE.
LEAVING YOU FREE TO DEVOTE ALL YOUR TIME TO COMPLETING THE *GUIDANCE SYSTEM.*

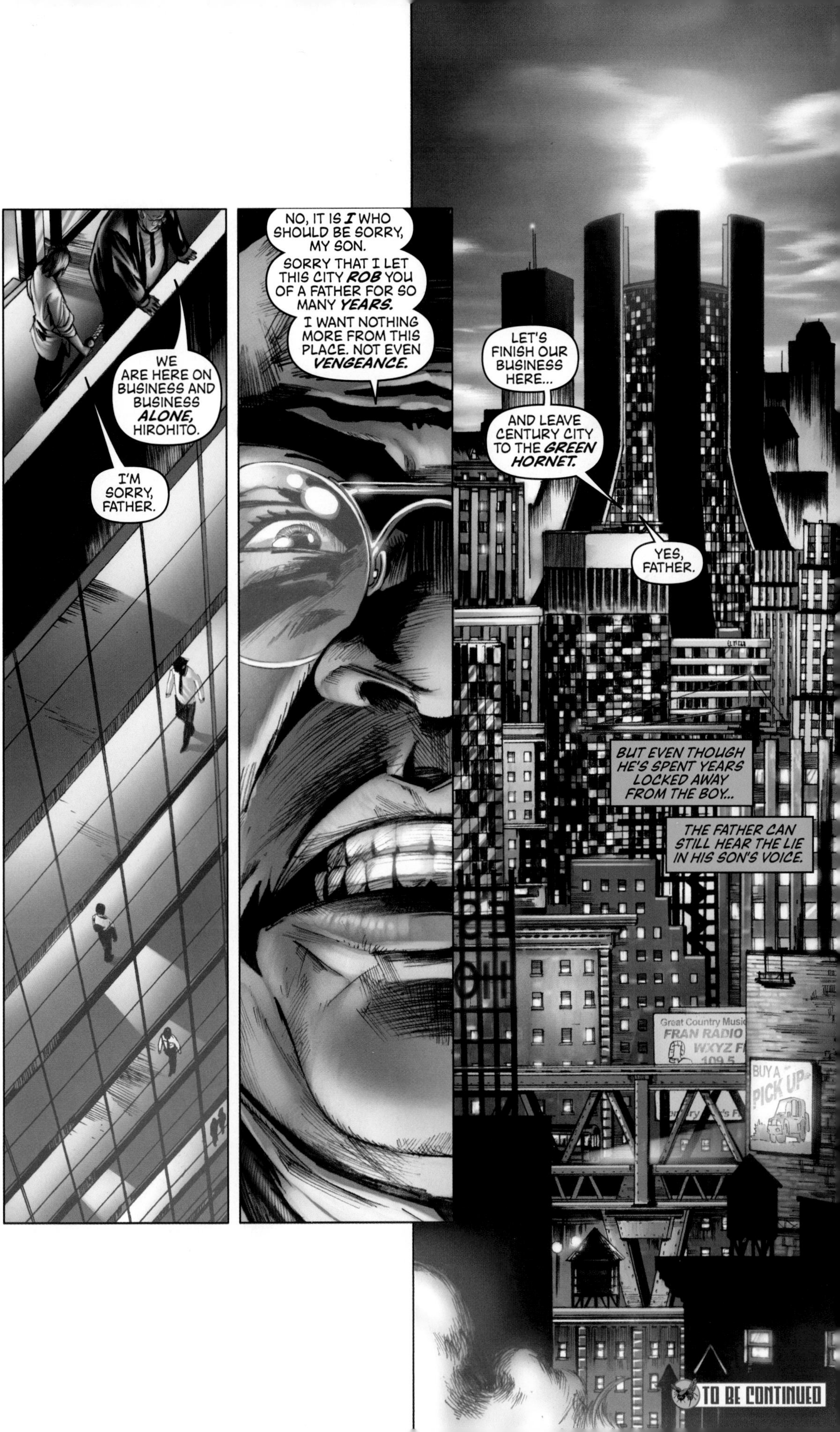
WE ARE HERE ON BUSINESS AND BUSINESS ALONE, HIROHITO.
I'M SORRY, FATHER.
NO, IT IS I WHO SHOULD BE SORRY, MY SON.
SORRY THAT I LET THIS CITY ROB YOU OF A FATHER FOR SO MANY YEARS.
I WANT NOTHING MORE FROM THIS PLACE. NOT EVEN VENGEANCE.
LET'S FINISH OUR BUSINESS HERE...
AND LEAVE CENTURY CITY TO THE GREEN HORNET.
YES, FATHER.
BUT EVEN THOUGH HE'S SPENT YEARS LOCKED AWAY FROM THE BOY...
THE FATHER CAN STILL HEAR THE LIE IN HIS SON'S VOICE.
Great Country Music
FRAN RADIO
WXYZ F
109.5
BUY A PICK UP
TO BE CONTINUED

Cover to issue #1 by ALEX ROSS

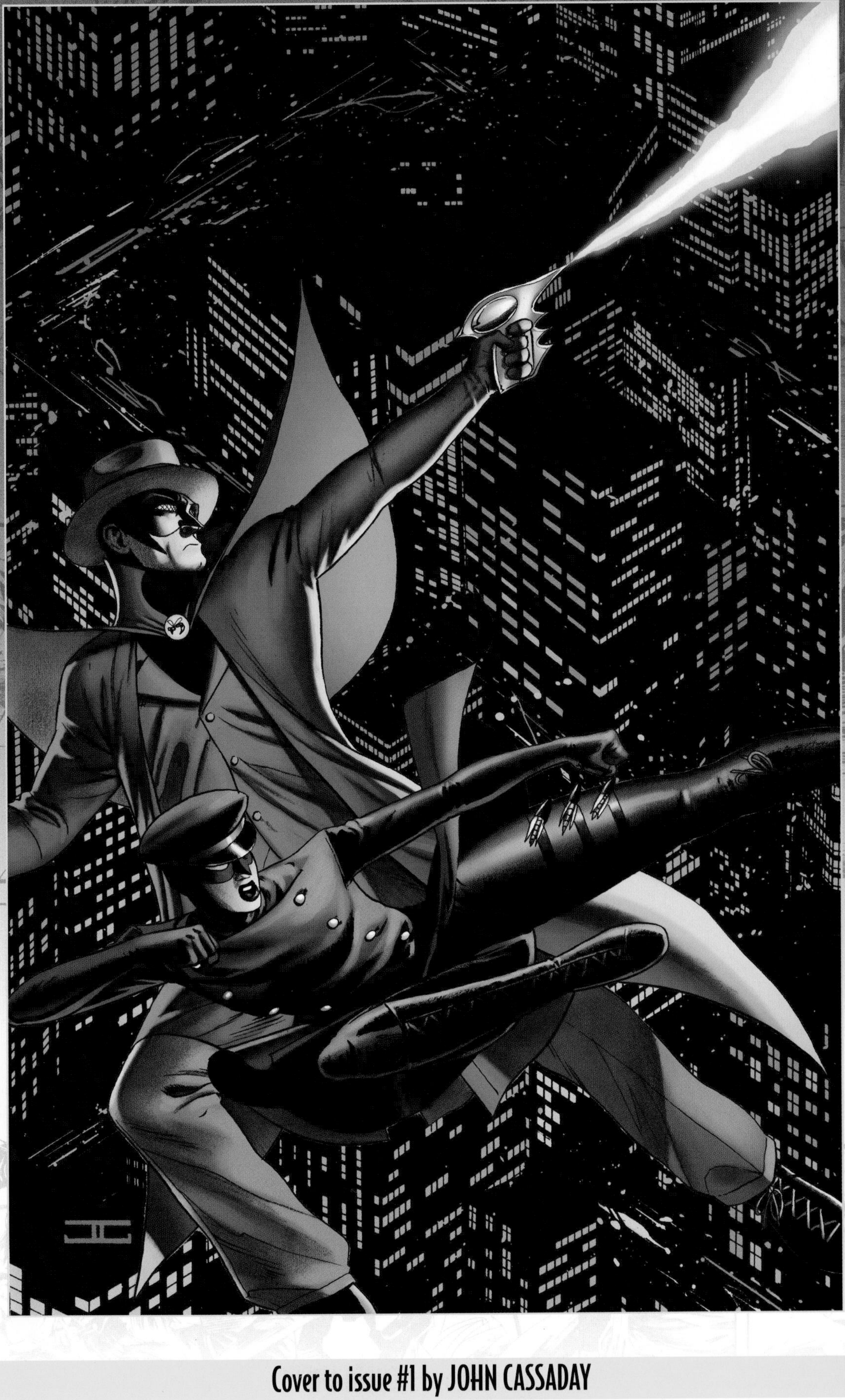

Cover to issue #1 by JOHN CASSADAY

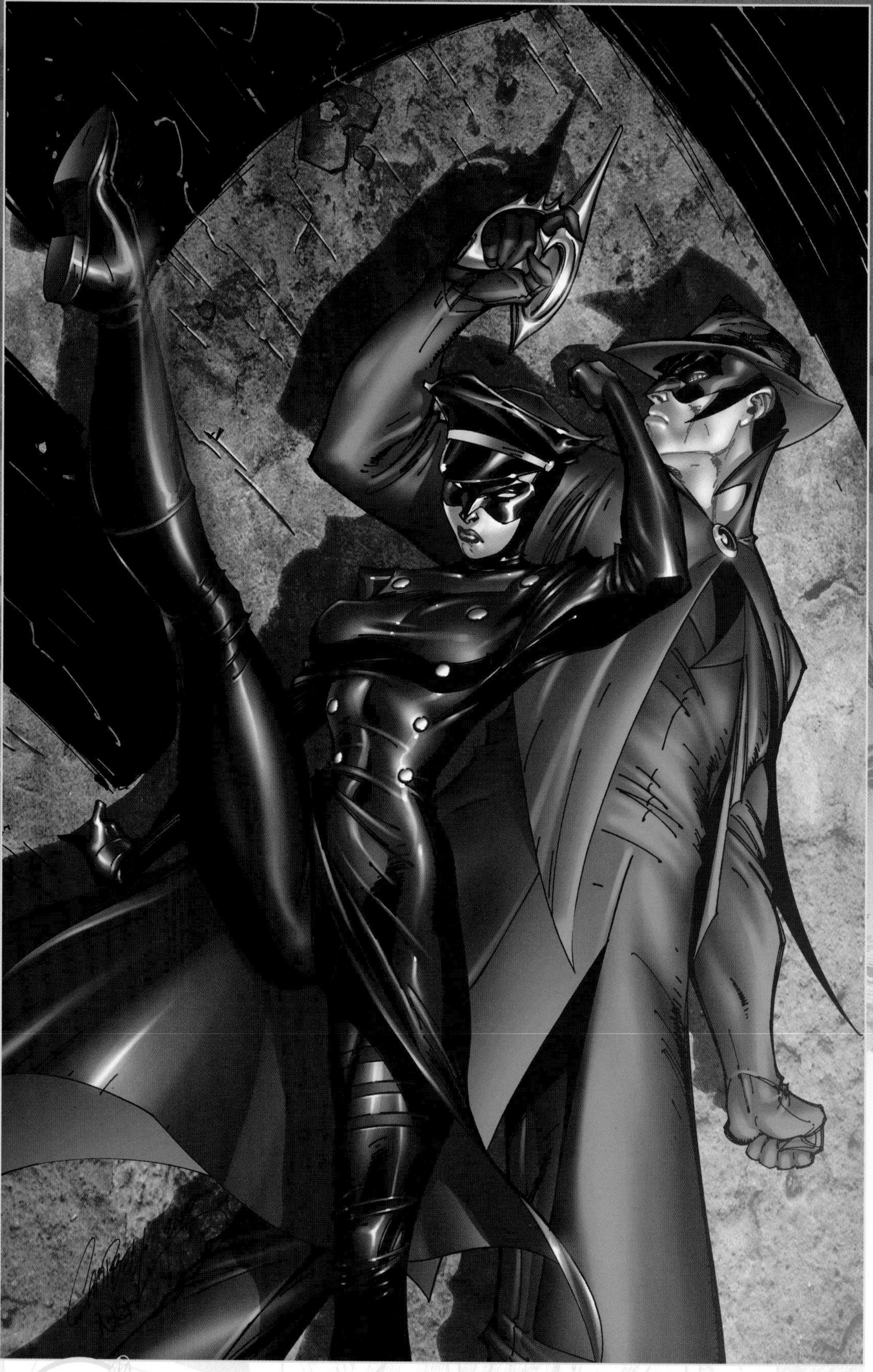

Cover to issue #1 by J. SCOTT CAMPBELL

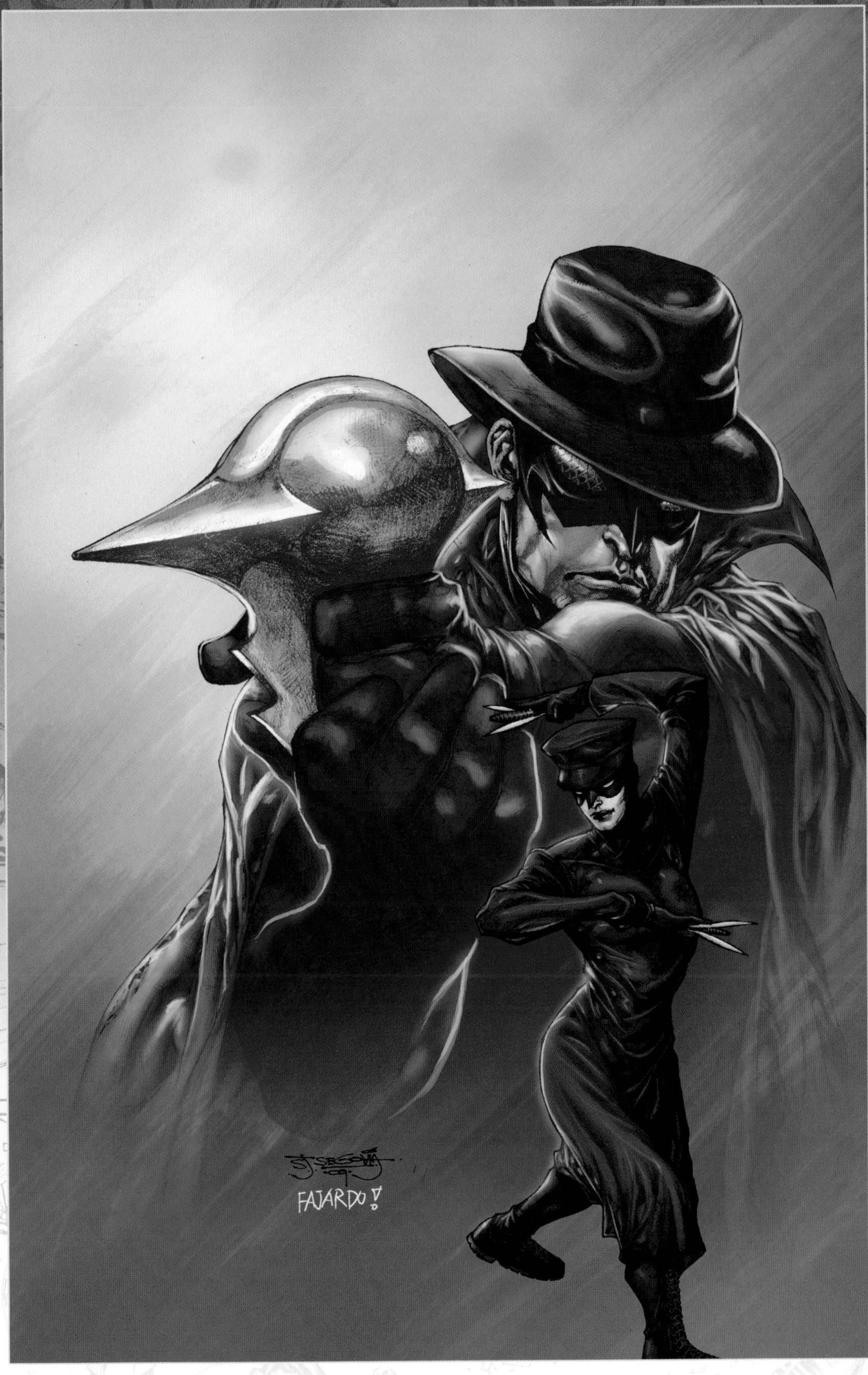
FAJARDO

Cover to issue #1 by STEPHEN SEGOVIA

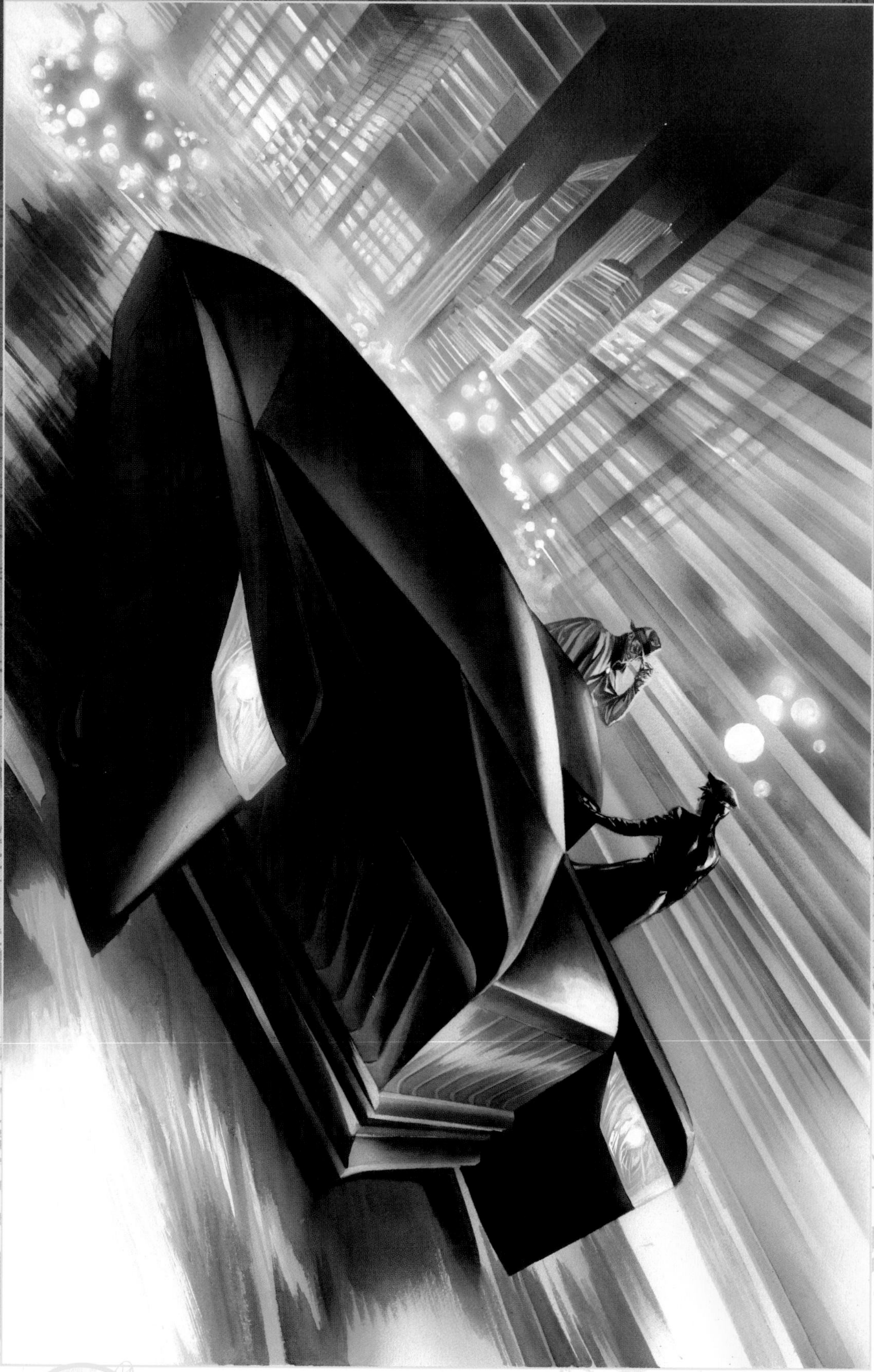

Cover to issue #2 by ALEX ROSS

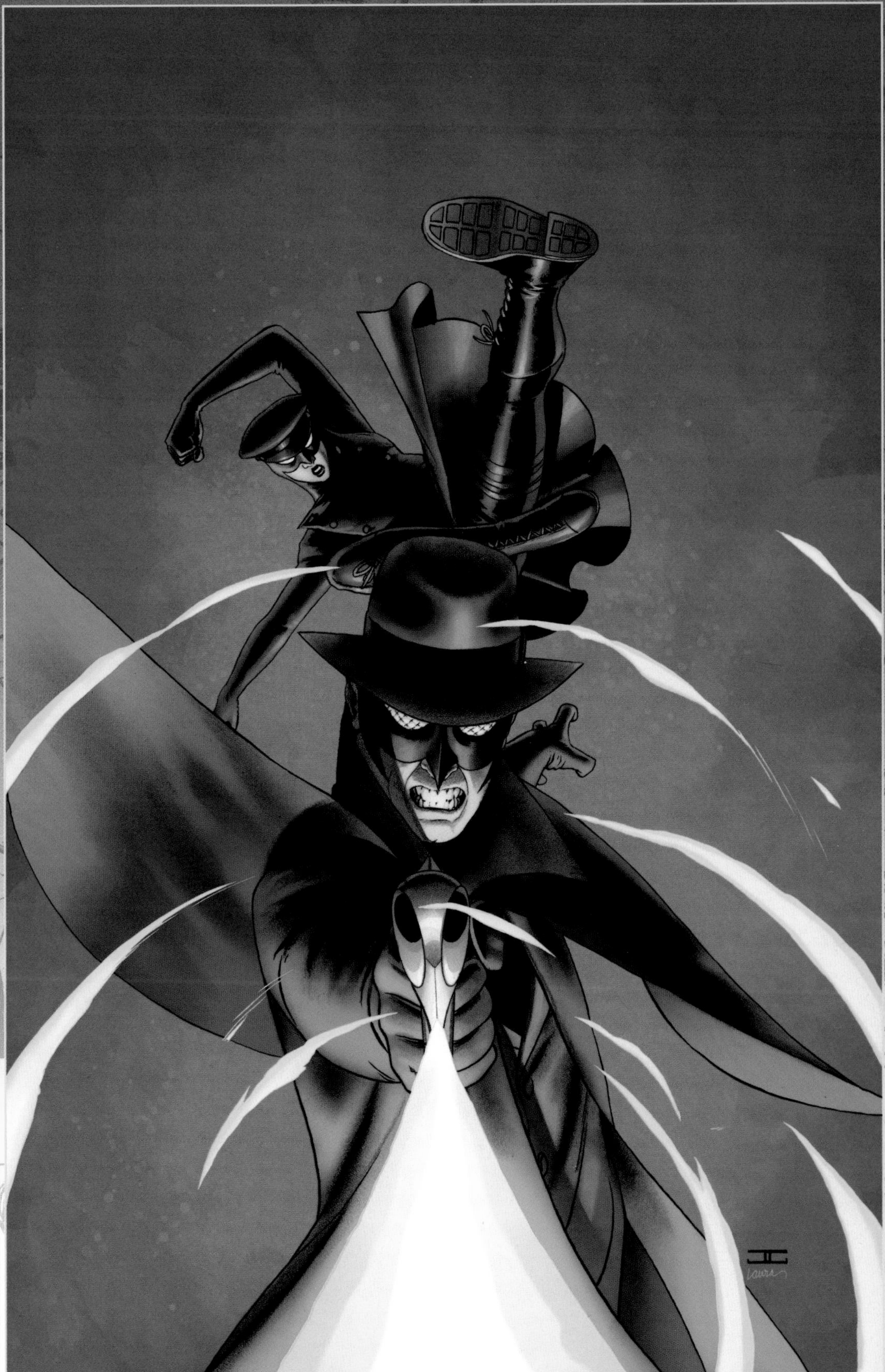

Cover to issue #2 by JOHN CASSADAY

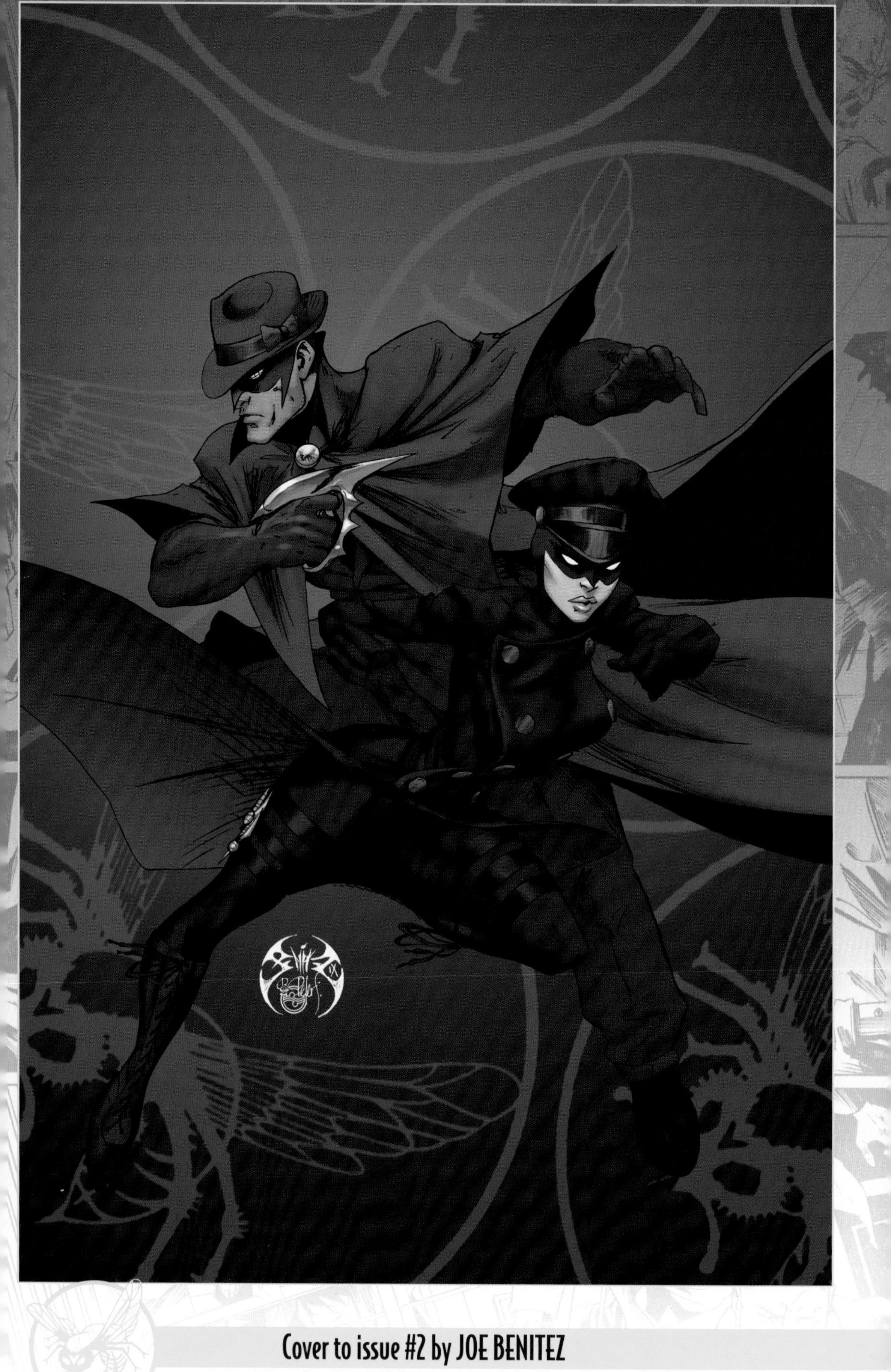

Cover to issue #2 by JOE BENITEZ

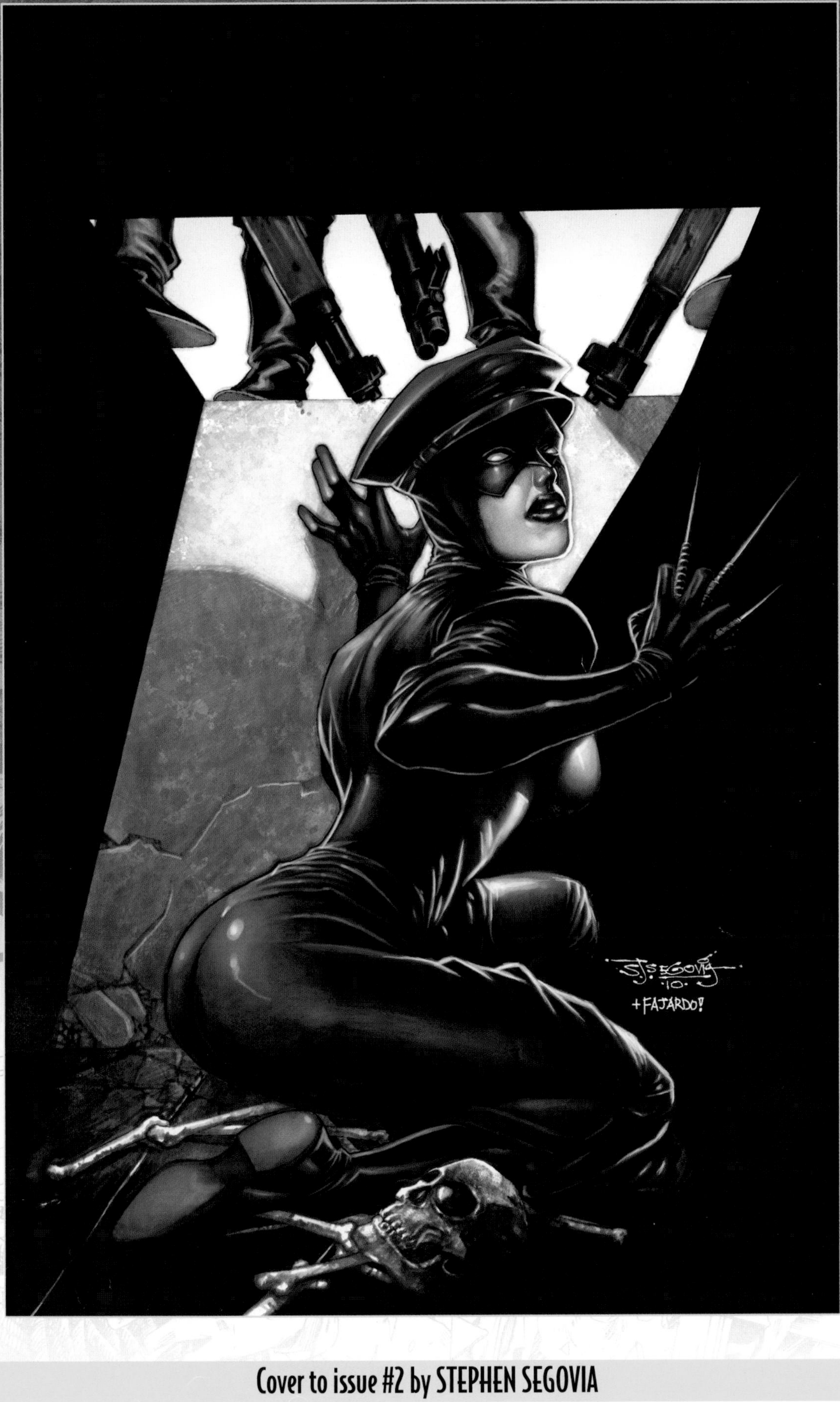
S.J. SEGOVIA
·10·
+FAJARDO!

Cover to issue #2 by STEPHEN SEGOVIA

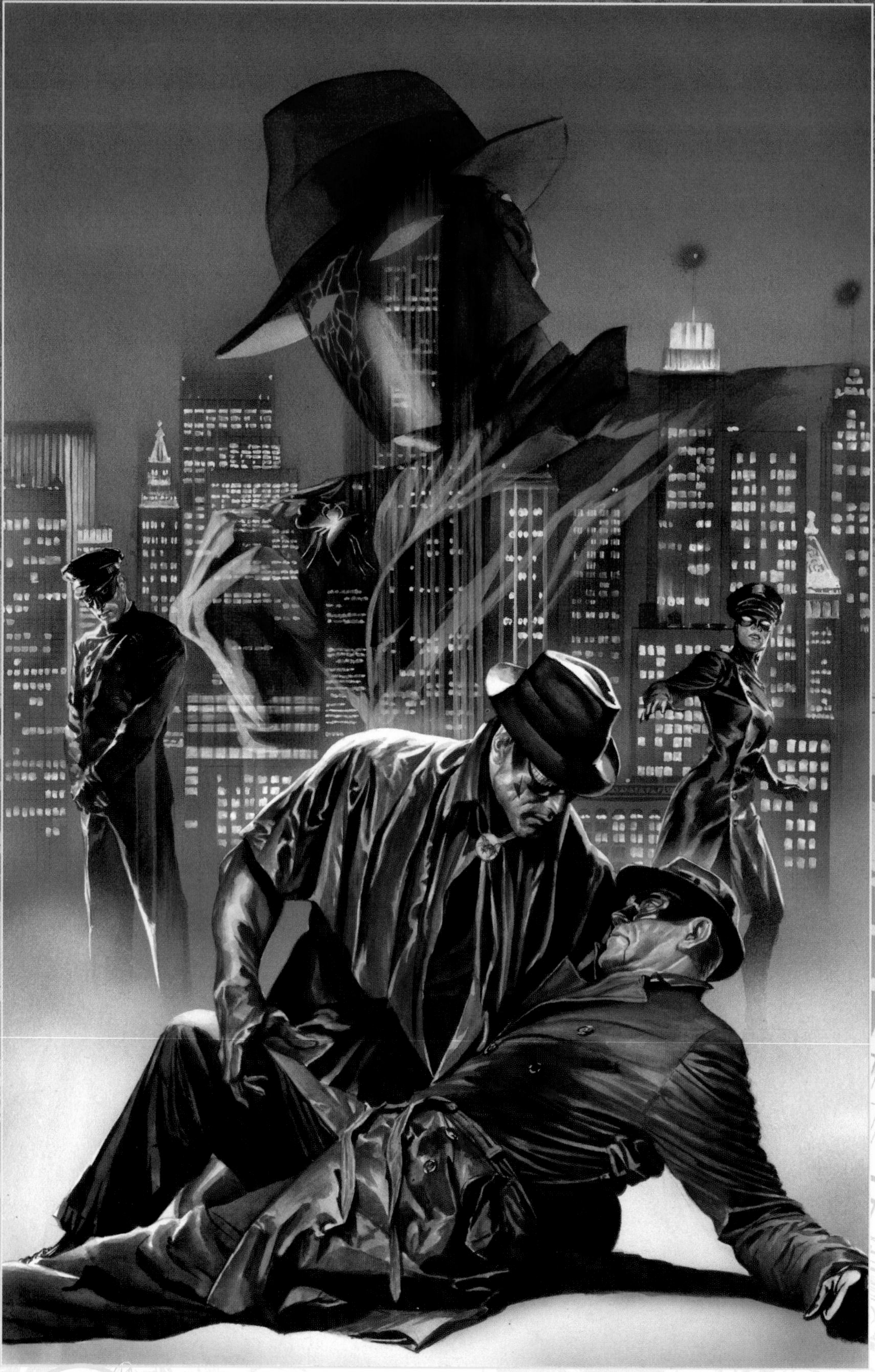

Cover to issue #3 by ALEX ROSS

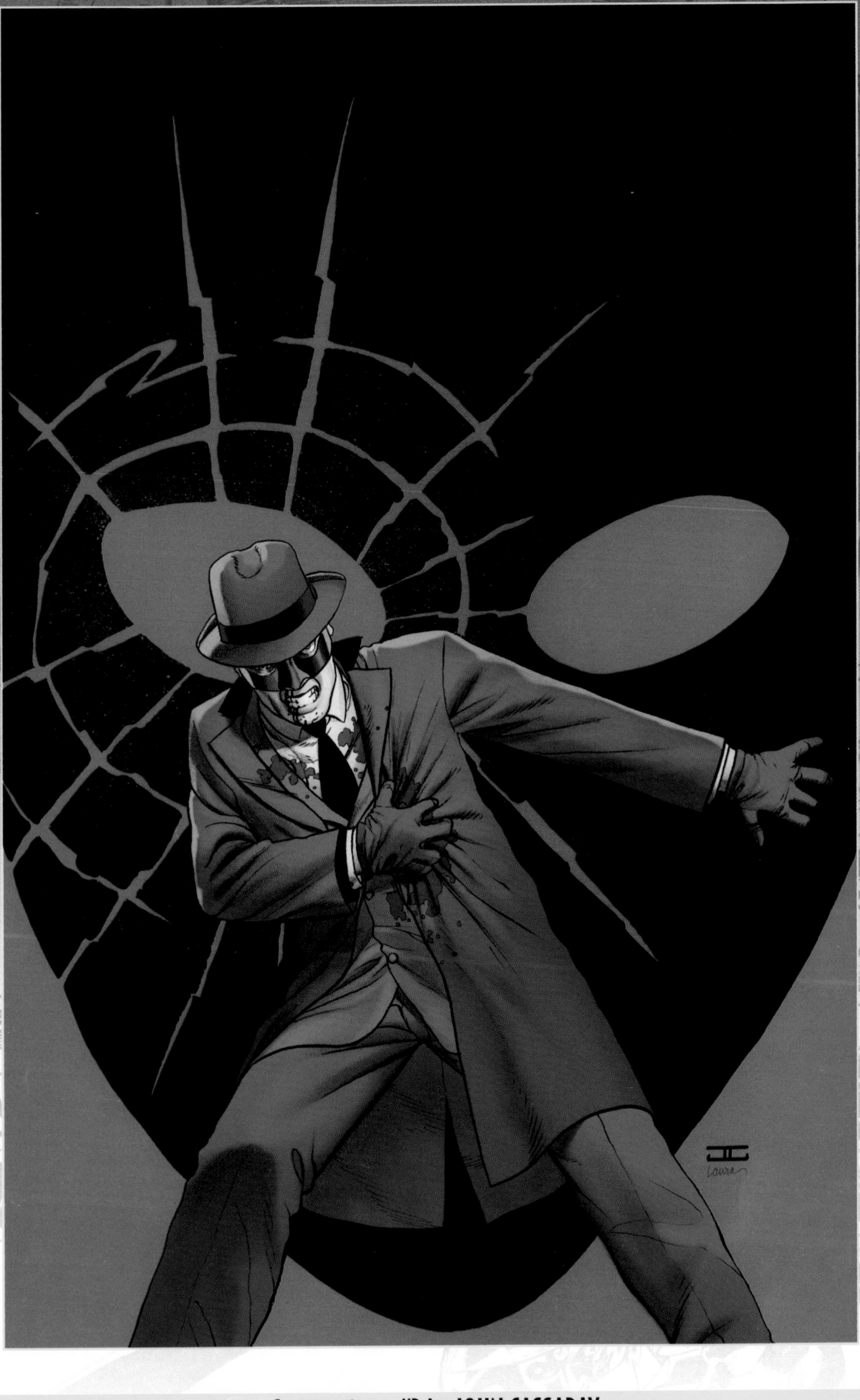

Cover to issue #3 by JOHN CASSADAY

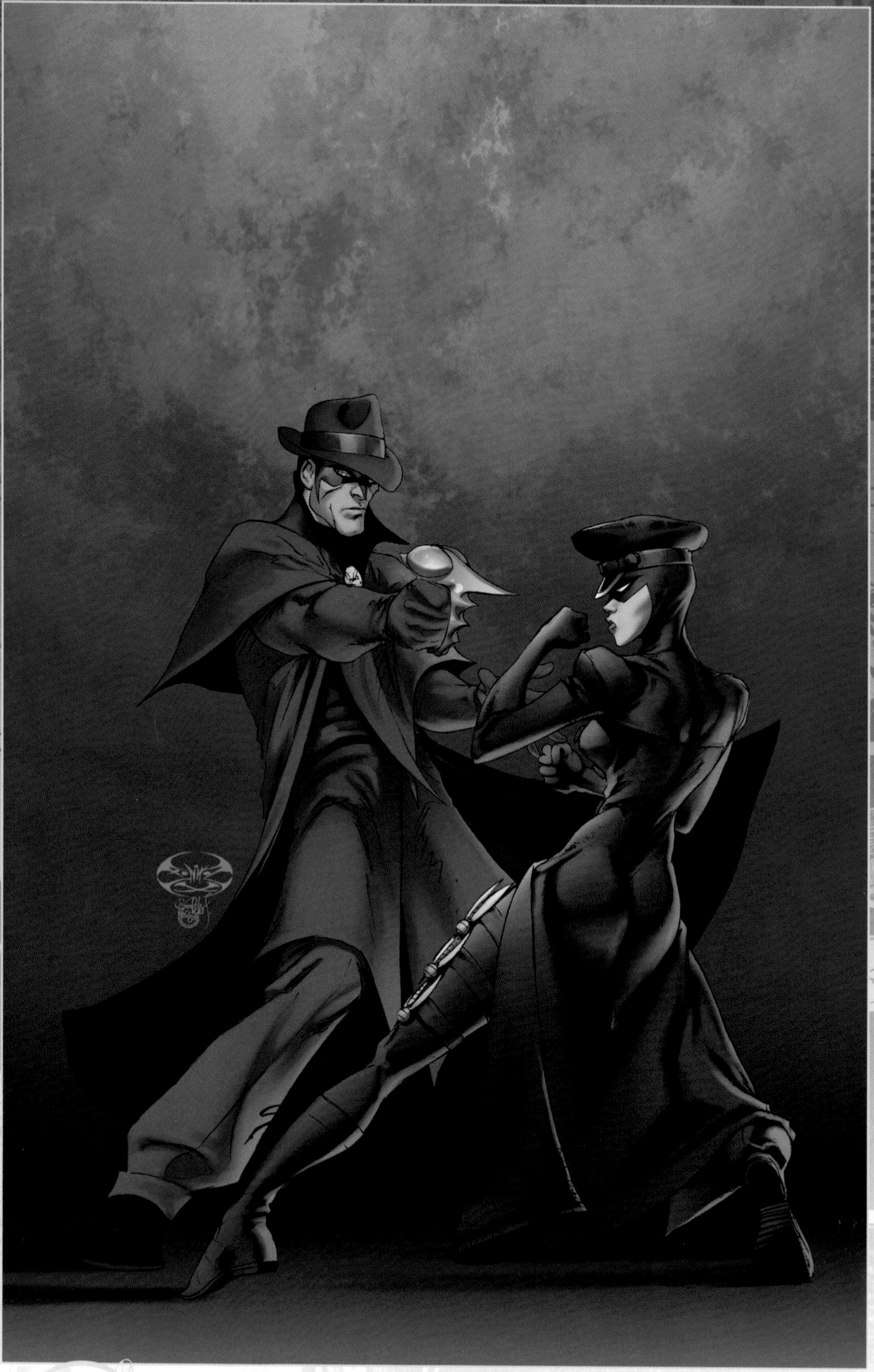

Cover to issue #3 by JOE BENITEZ

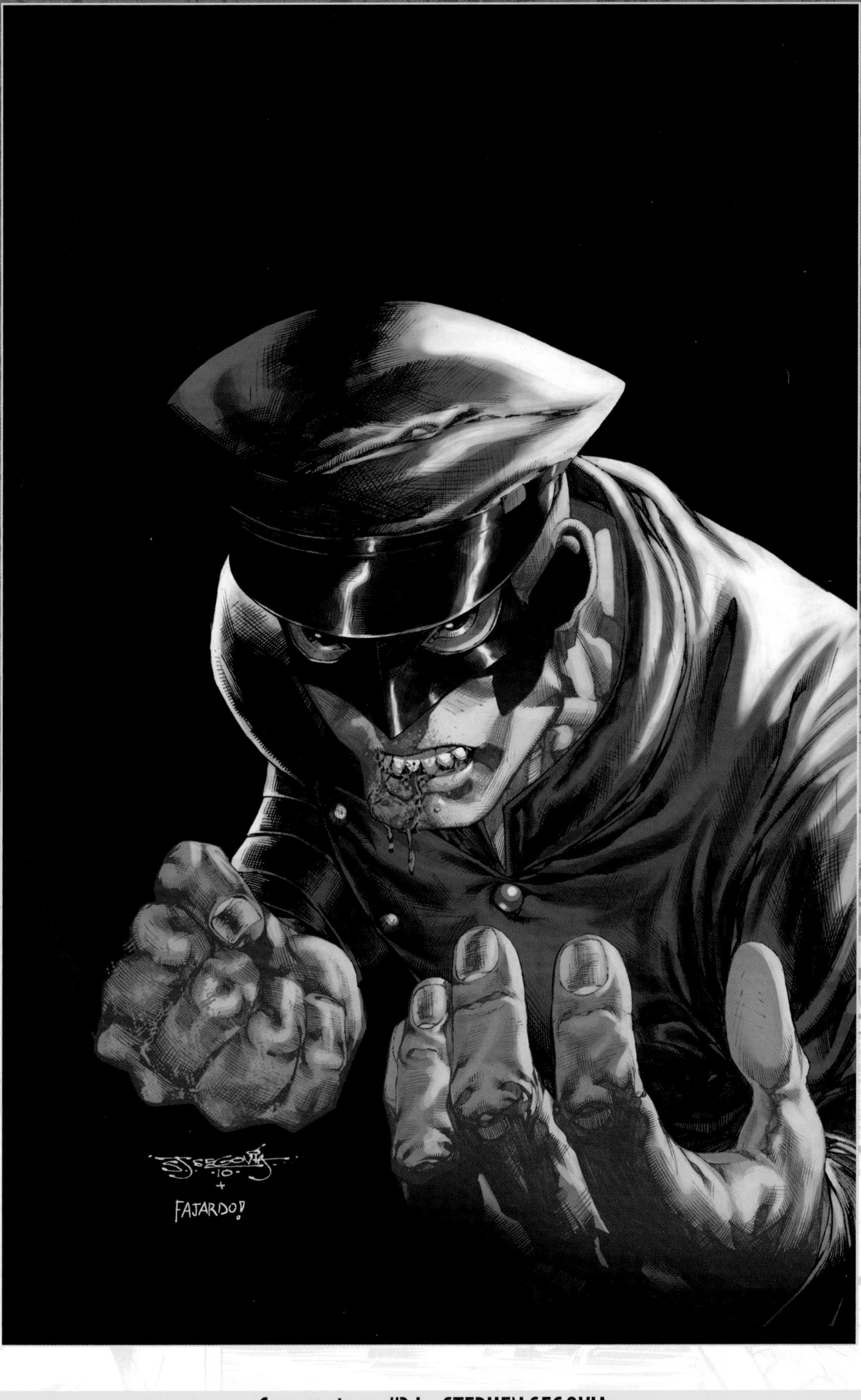
S. SEGOVIA
·10·
+
FAJARDO!

Cover to issue #3 by STEPHEN SEGOVIA

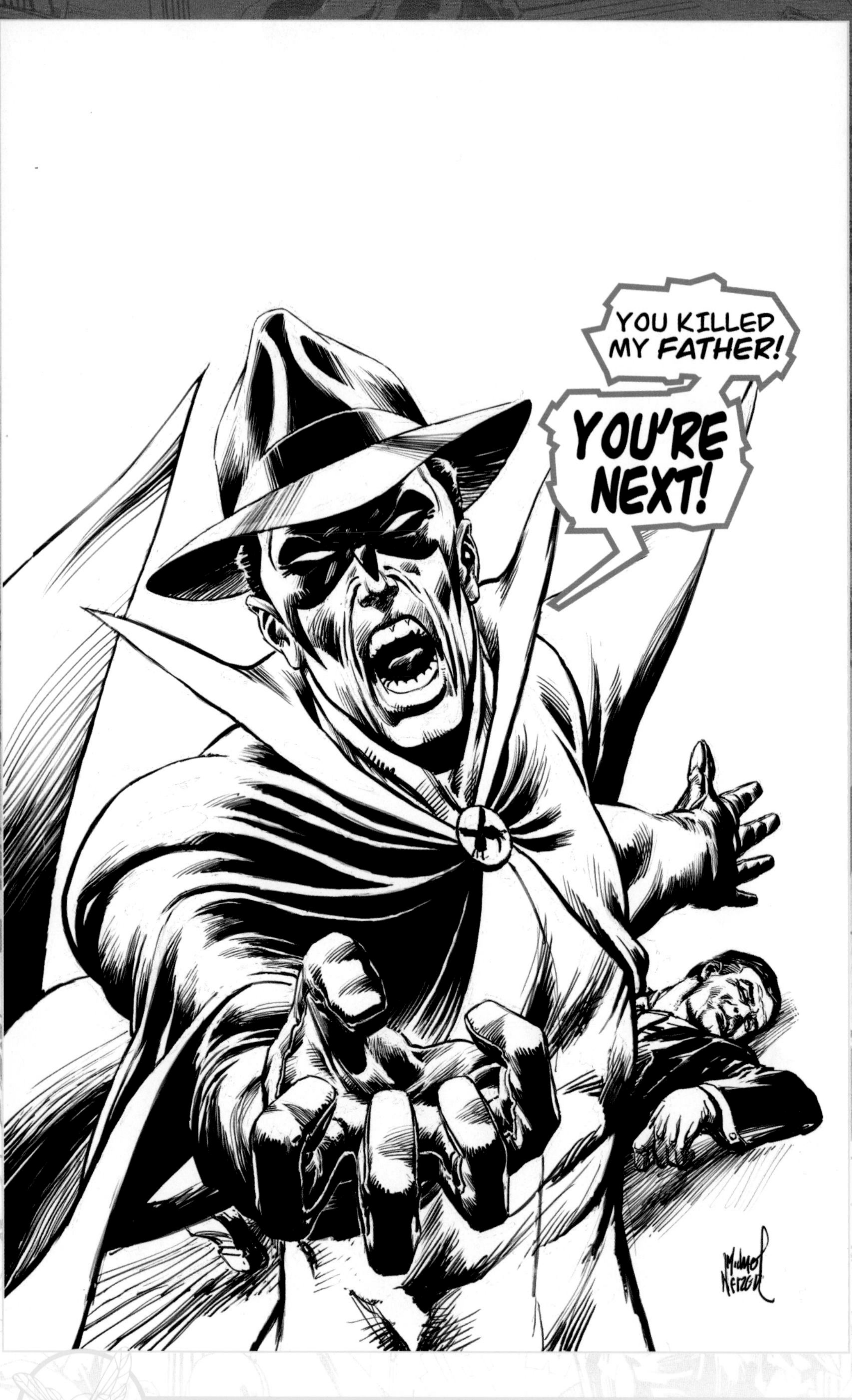
YOU KILLED MY FATHER!
YOU'RE NEXT!
Michael Netzer

"Actual Death Cover" to issue #3 by MICHAEL NETZER

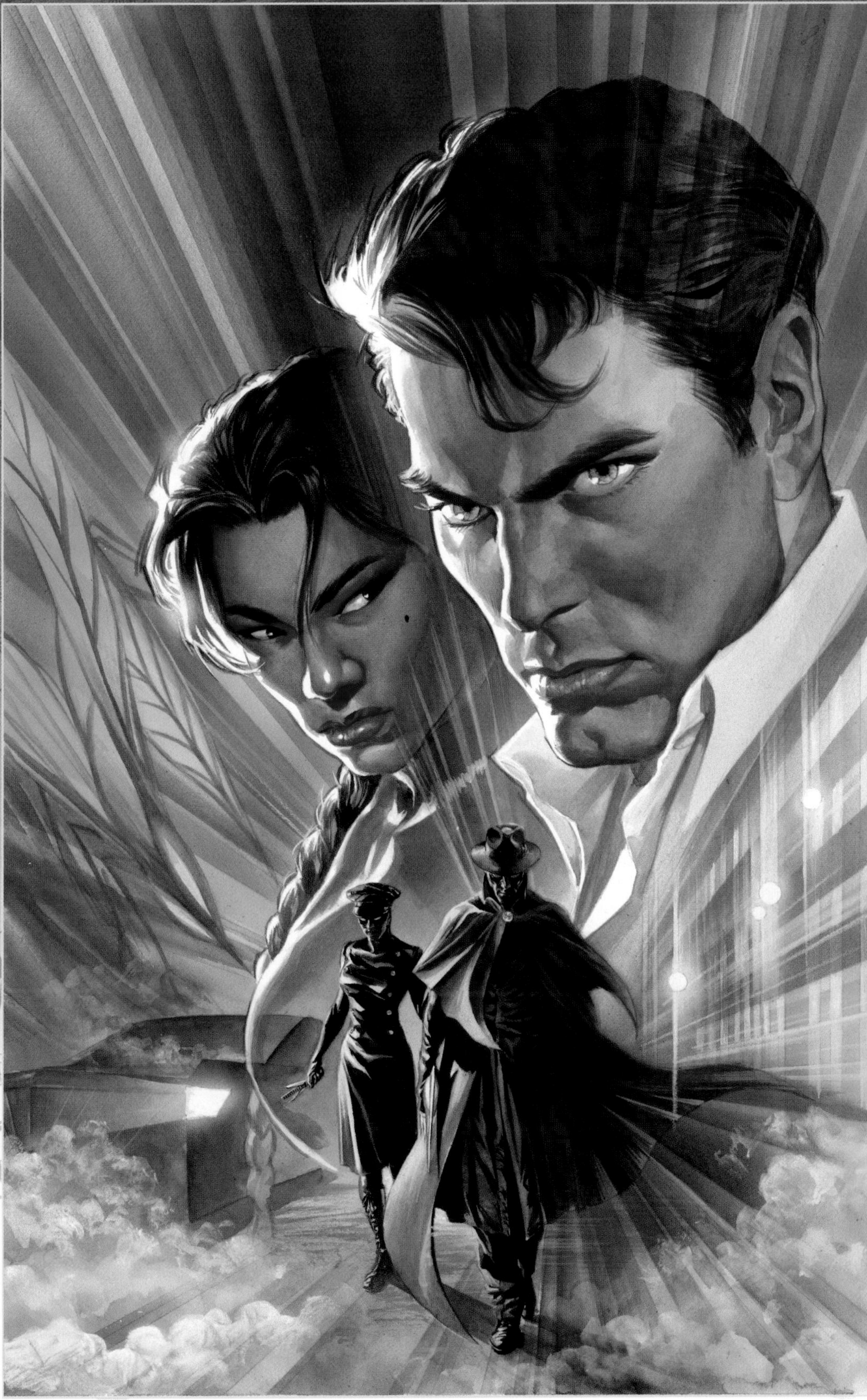

Cover to issue #4 by ALEX ROSS

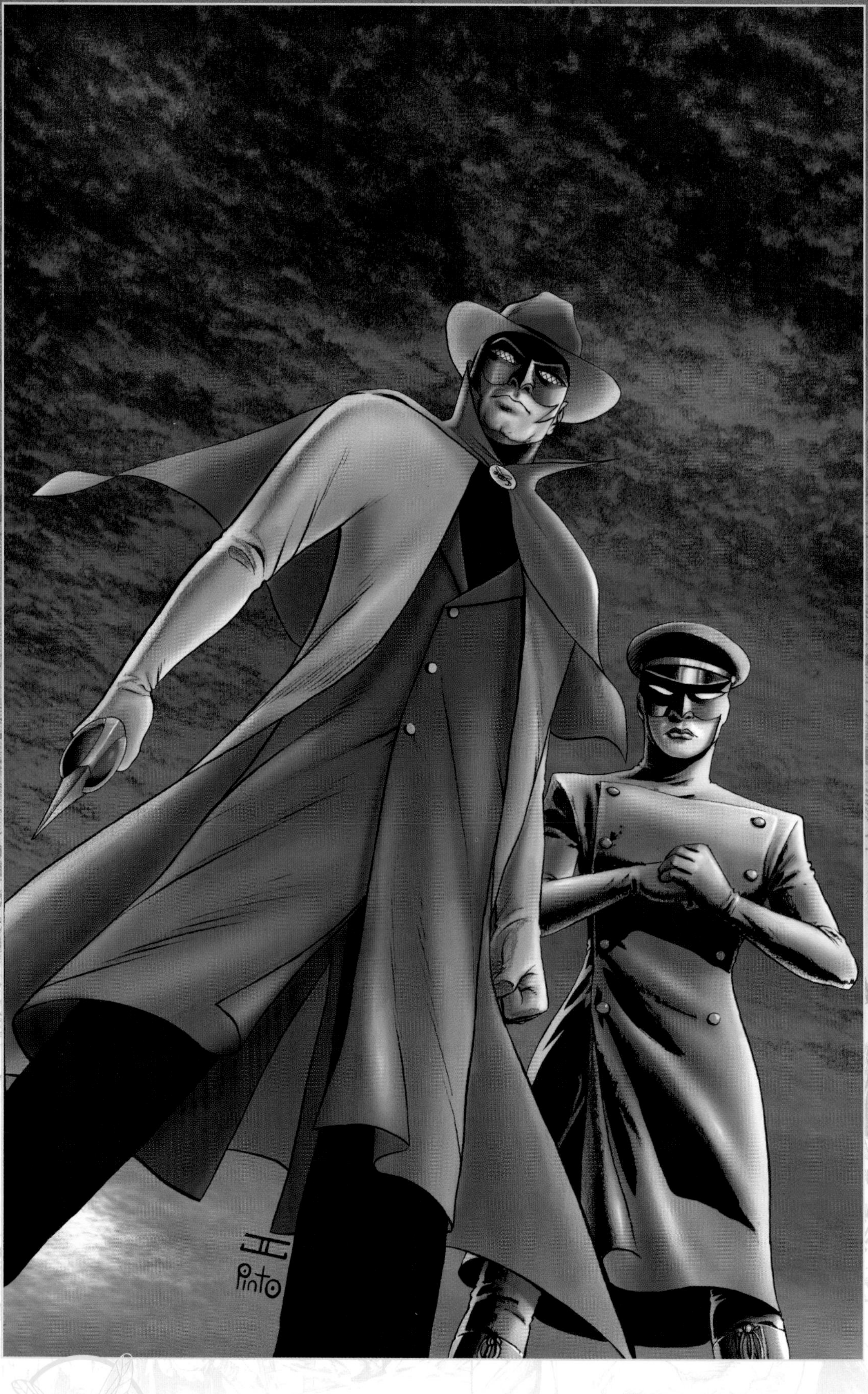
Pinto

Cover to issue #4 by JOHN CASSADAY

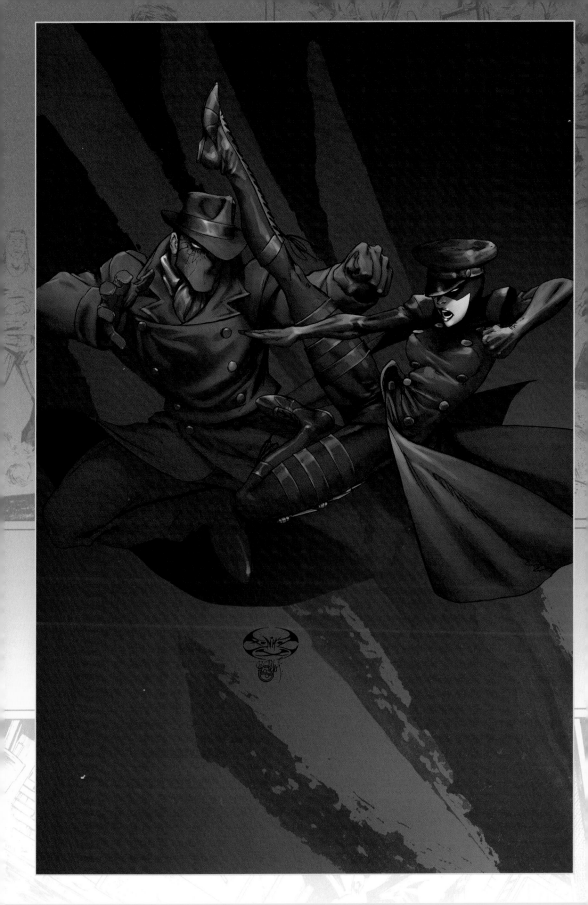

Cover to issue #4 by JOE BENITEZ

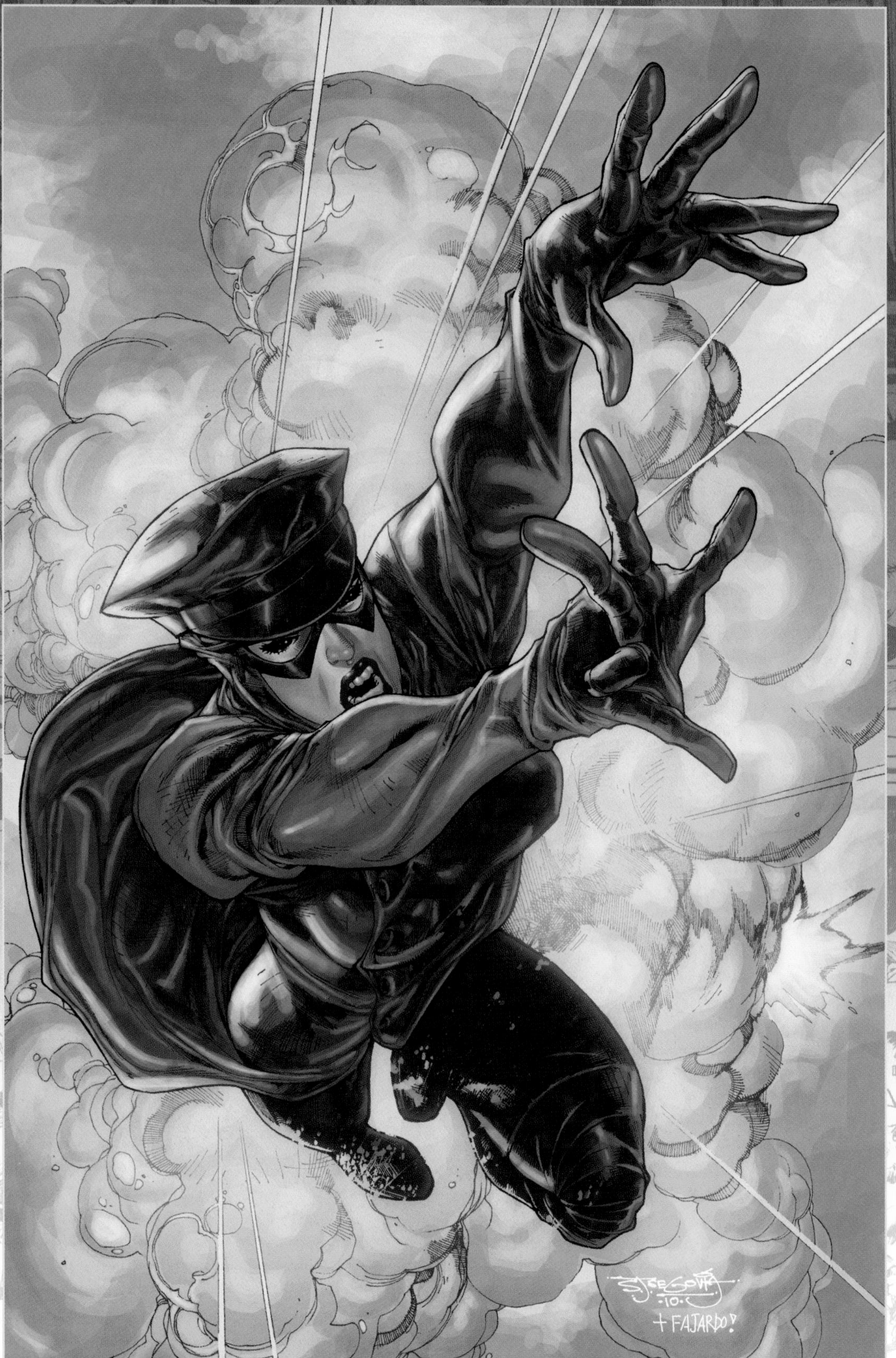
S JOE SEGOVIA
·10·
+ FAJARDO!

Cover to issue #4 by STEPHEN SEGOVIA

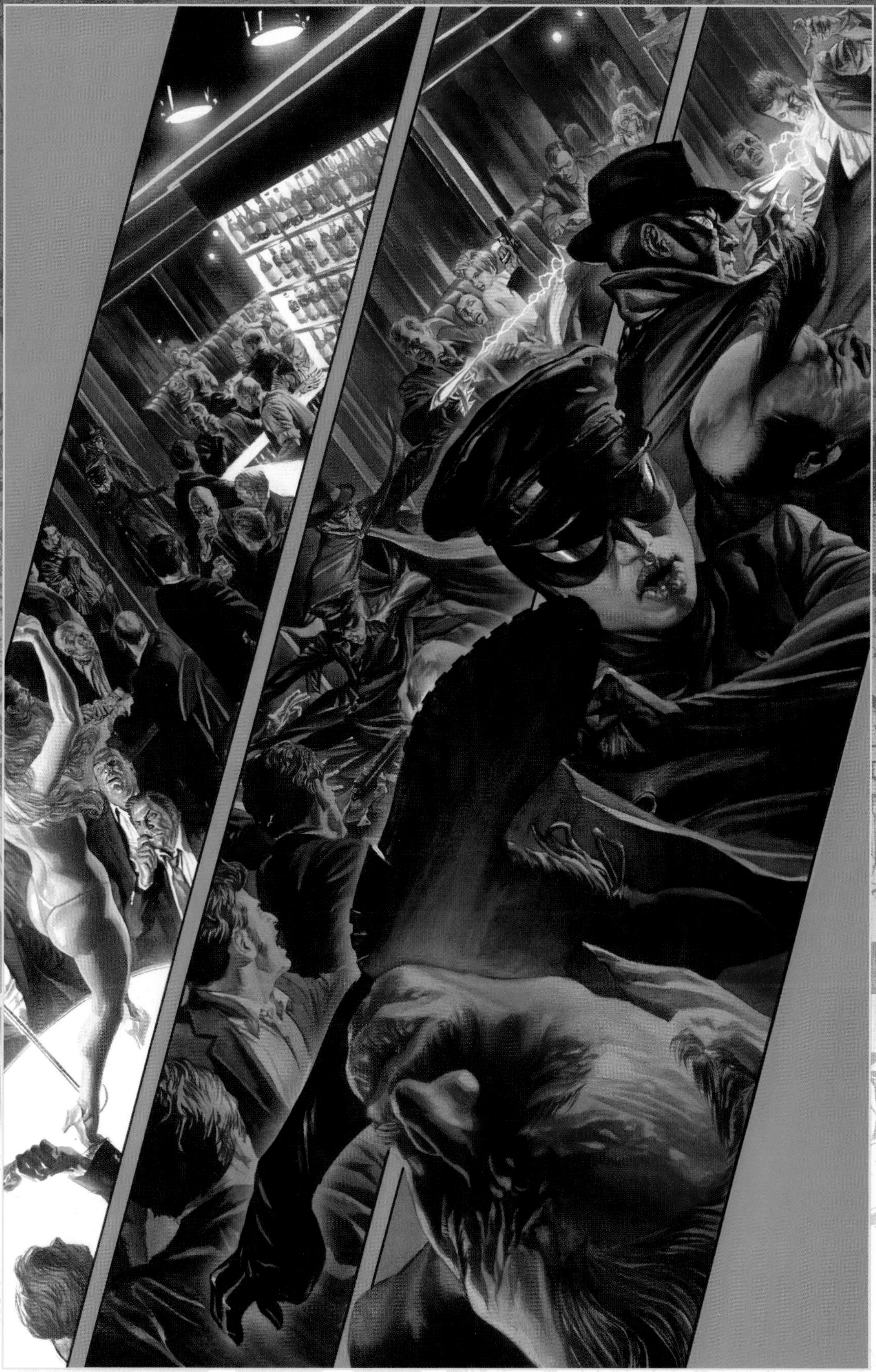

Cover to issue #5 by ALEX ROSS

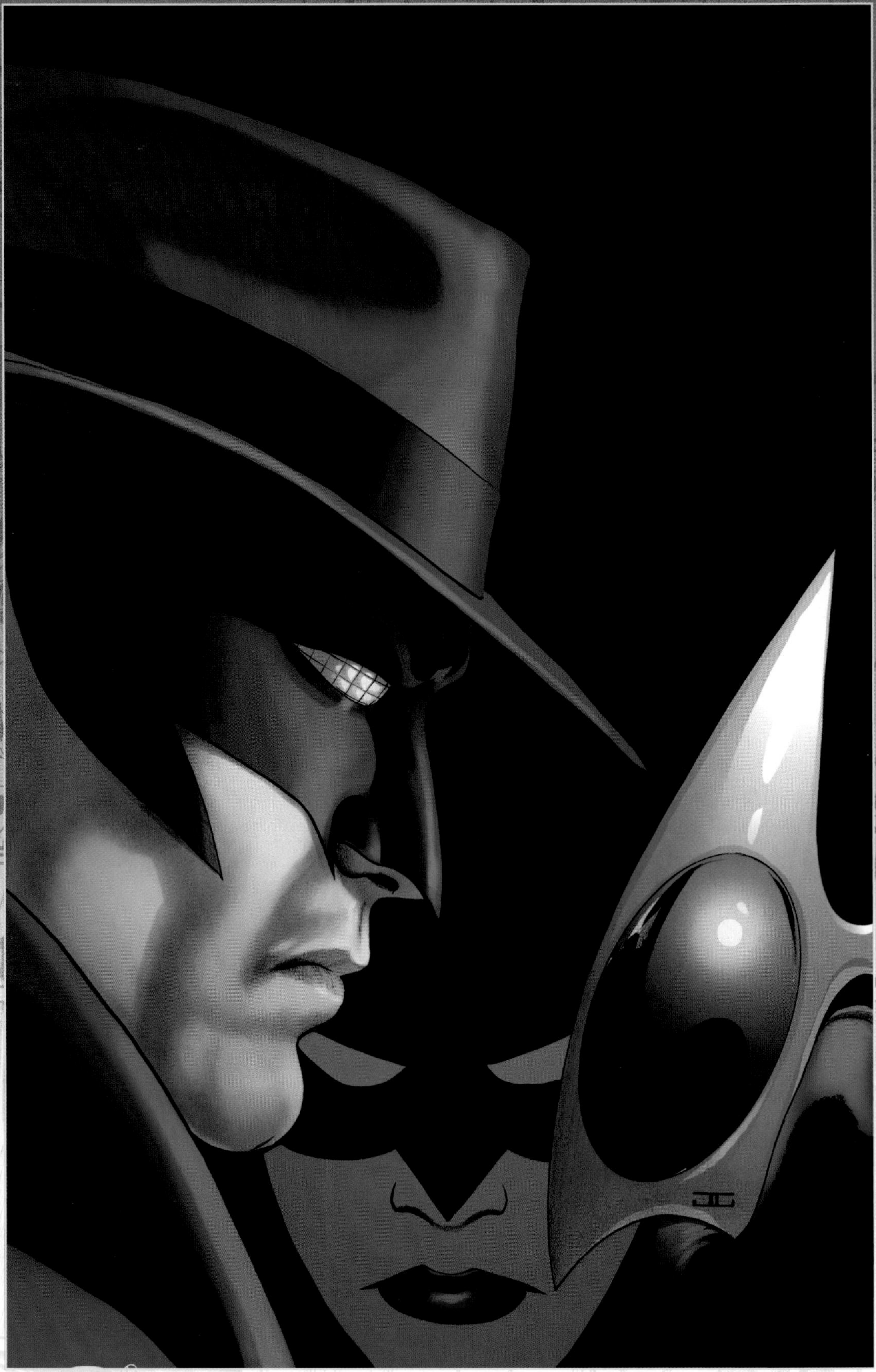

Cover to issue #5 by JOHN CASSADAY

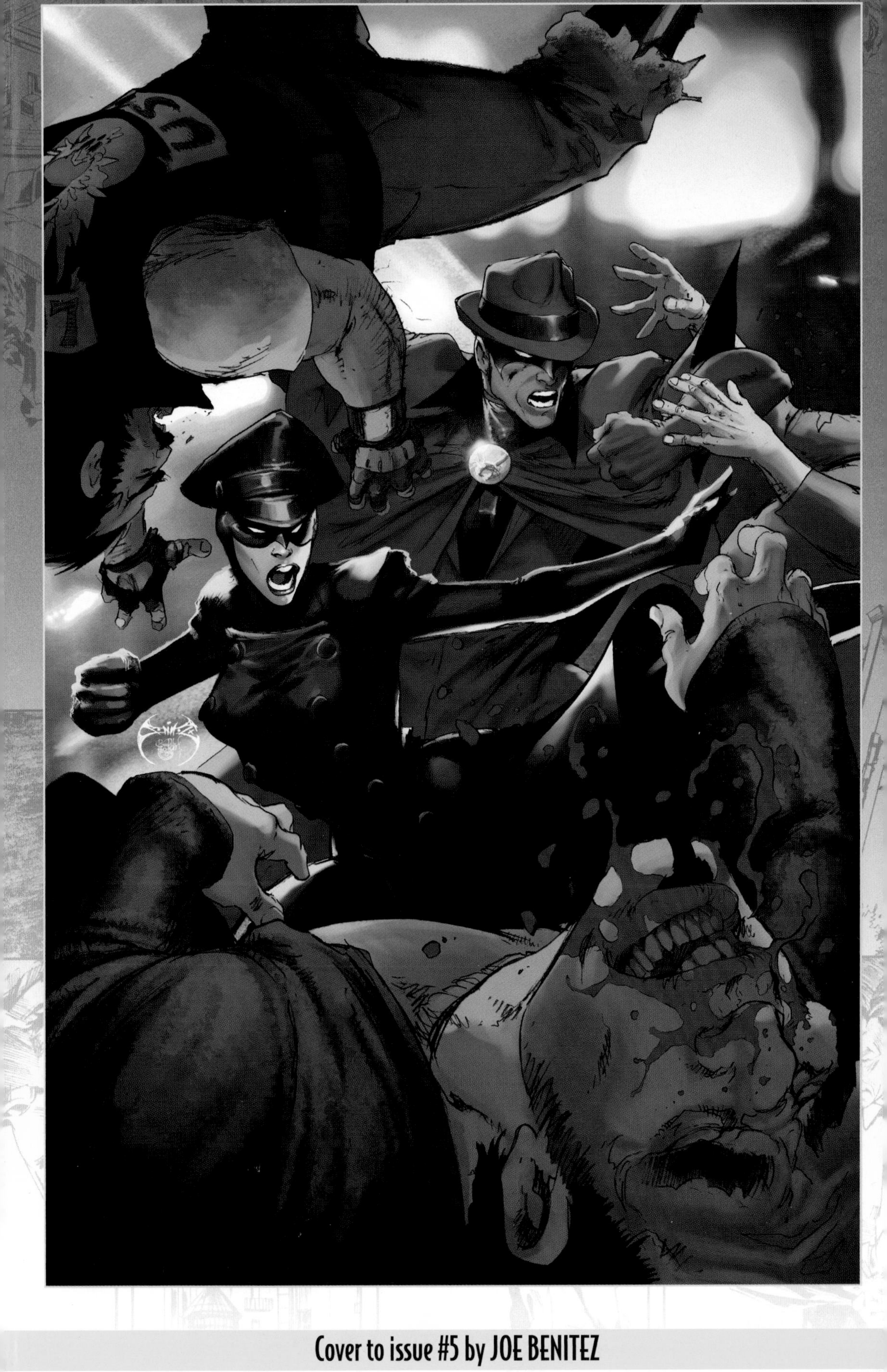

Cover to issue #5 by JOE BENITEZ

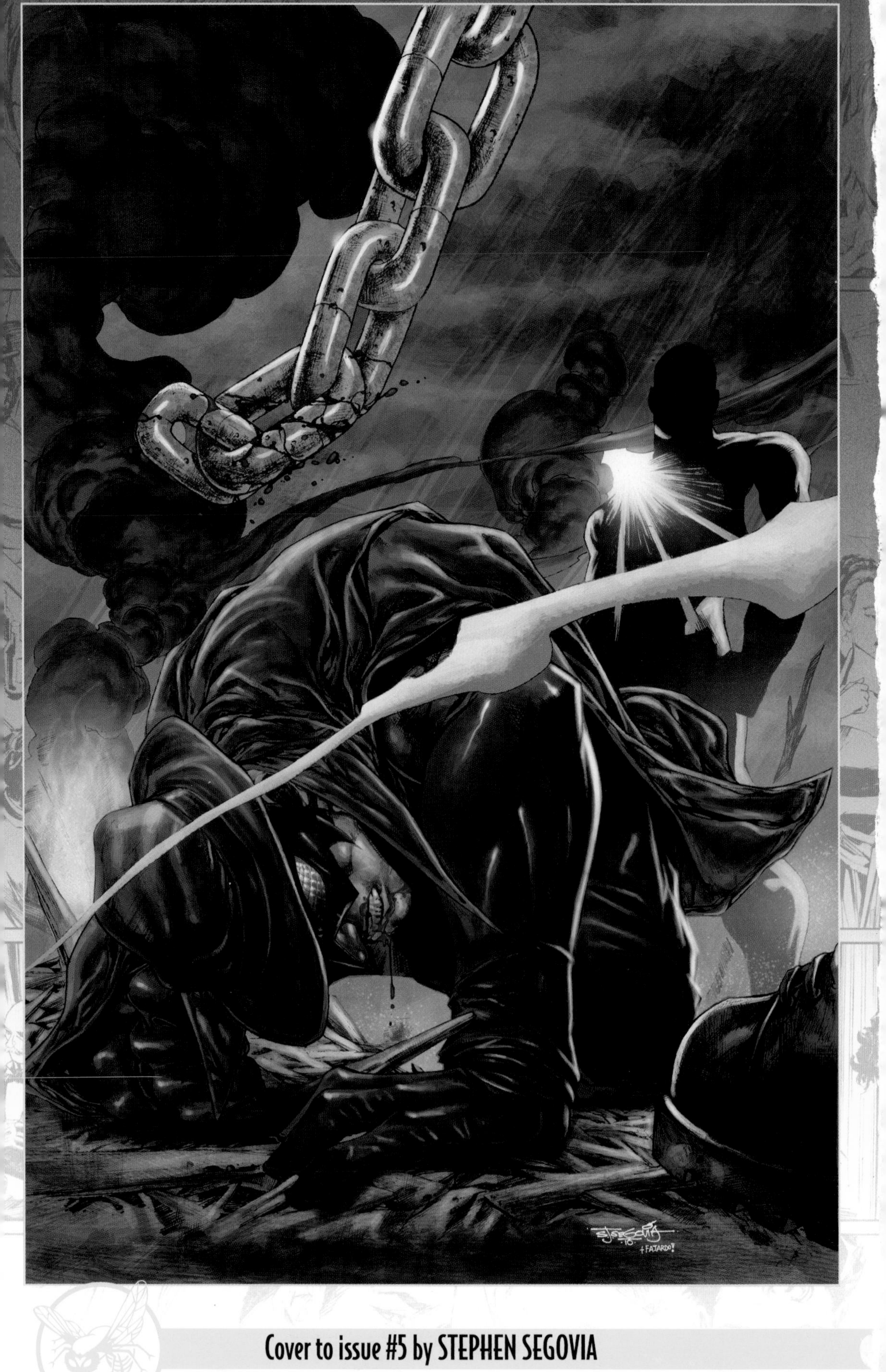

Cover to issue #5 by STEPHEN SEGOVIA

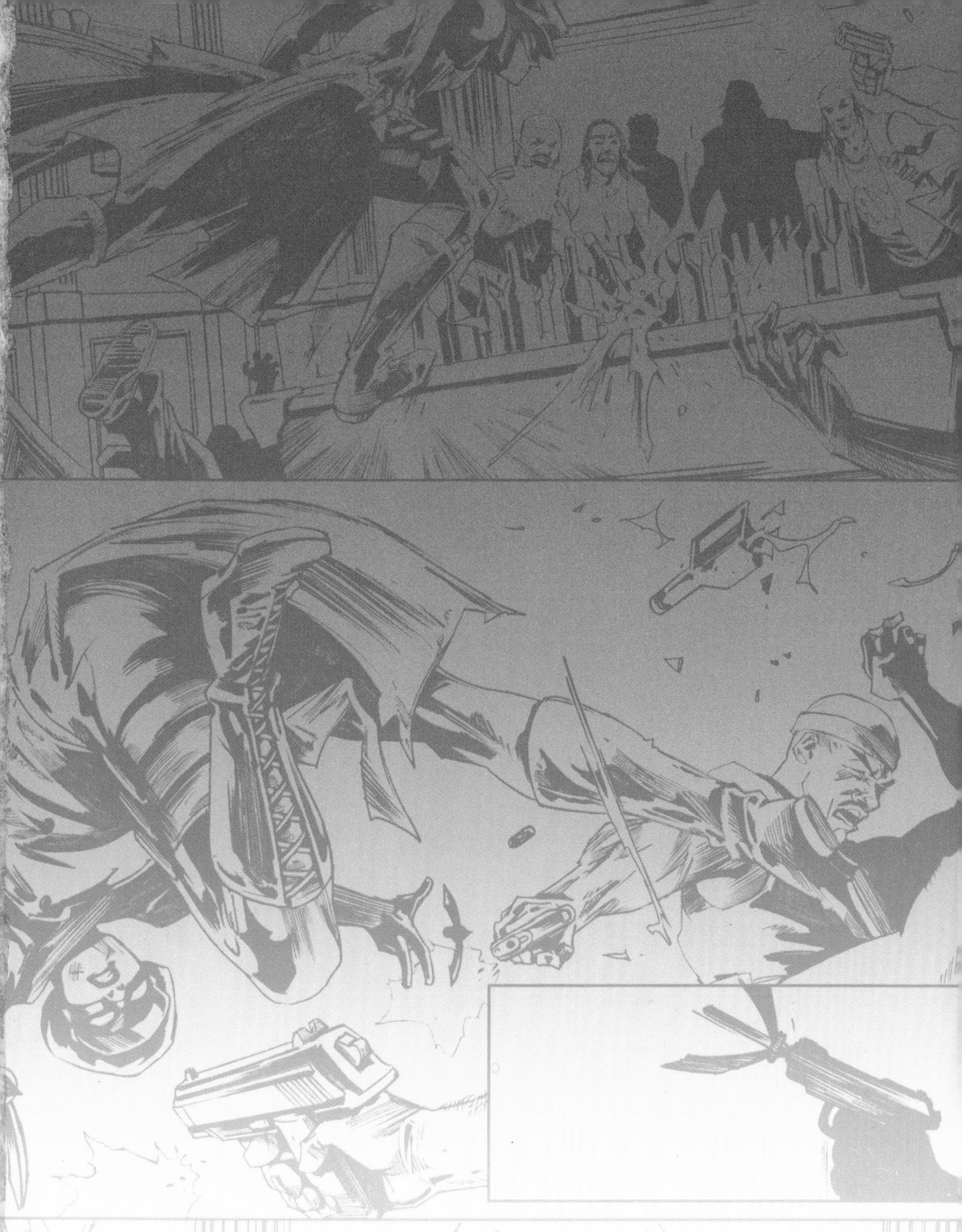

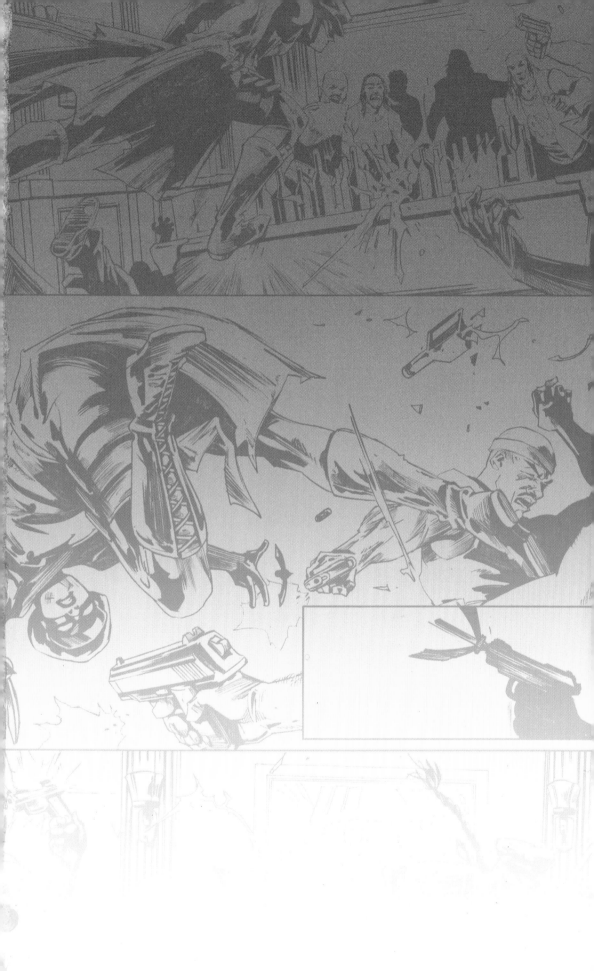

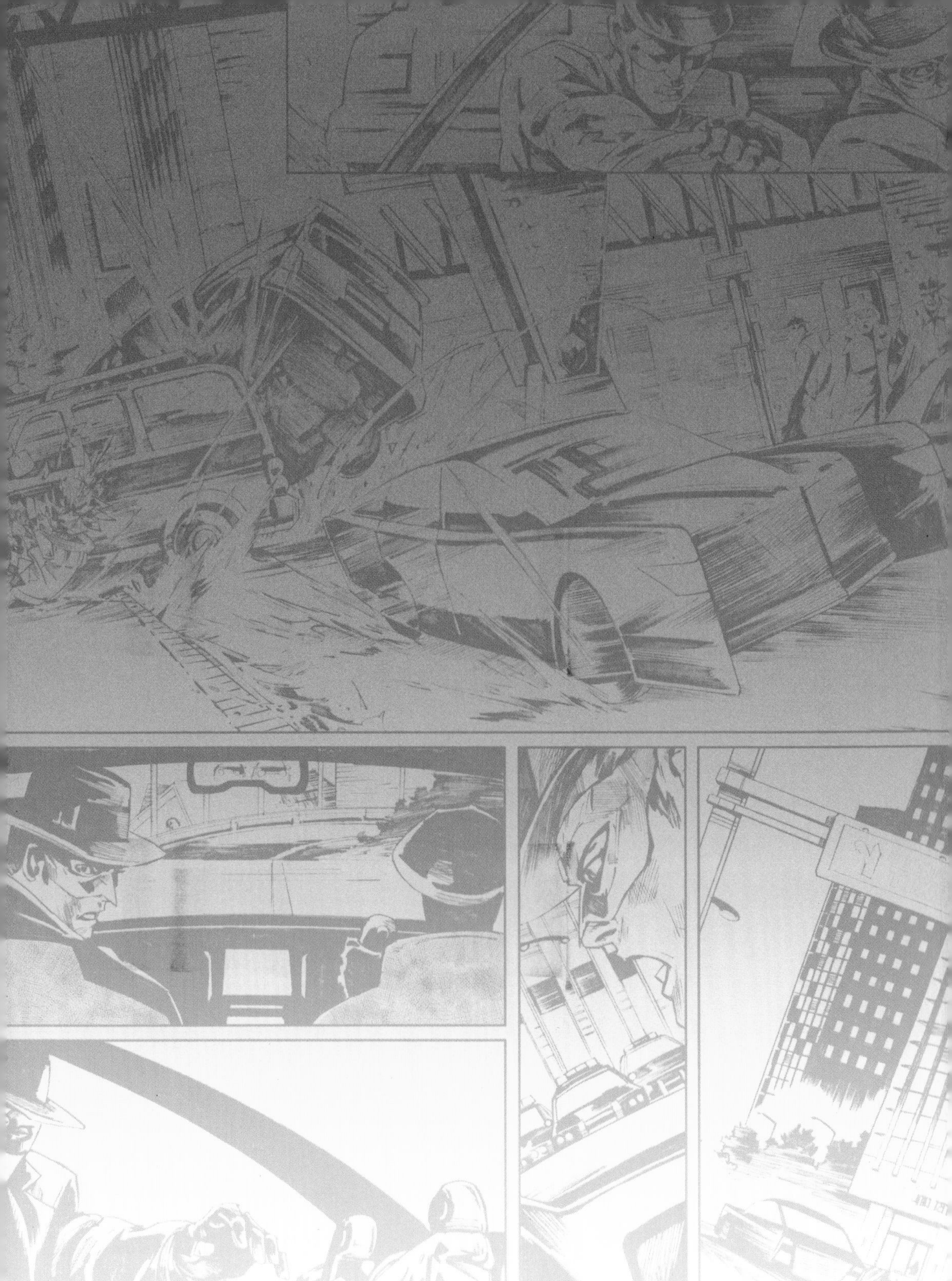